JUSTICE
DENIED

DATE DUE

MAR 4 2006

JUSTICE
DENIED

Clemency Appeals in Death Penalty Cases

CATHLEEN BURNETT

NORTHEASTERN UNIVERSITY PRESS
Boston

Northeastern University Press

Copyright 2002 by Cathleen Burnett

Library of Congress Cataloging-in-Publication Data

Burnett, Cathleen.
    Justice denied : clemency appeals in death penalty cases / Cathleen Burnett.
        p. cm.
Includes bibliographical references and index.
    ISBN 1-55553-520-8 (pbk. : alk. paper) —
    ISBN 1-55553-521-6 (hardback : alk. paper)
  1. Capital punishment—Missouri—History.
  2. Clemency—Missouri—History.   I. Title.
    KFM8365.C2 B87   2002
    345.778'0773—dc21   2002004922

Designed by Janis Owens

Composed in Stone Serif by Coghill Composition Company in Richmond, Virginia. Printed and bound by The Maple Press in York, Pennsylvania. The paper is Sebago Antique, an acid-free sheet.

MANUFACTURED IN THE UNITED STATES OF AMERICA
06 05 04 03 02   5 4 3 2 1

To
Jeff Sloan, CP#55,
whose execution gave me the passion and authenticity to oppose
state-sponsored killing,
and to the members of the
Western Missouri Coalition to Abolish the Death Penalty,
whose friendship makes it possible to persevere for the long haul.

CONTENTS

TABLES

PREFACE

Supreme Court Justice Thurgood Marshall, six months before he died, said: "Democracy cannot flourish among fear. Liberty cannot bloom among hate. Justice cannot take root amid rage. . . . We must dissent from the indifference. . . . We must dissent from the poverty of vision and an absence of leadership."

QUOTATION FROM BRIGHT (1996: 1096)

When I witnessed Jeff Sloan's execution, I knew in the core of my being that his execution was a profound wrong. By the time his post-conviction lawyer got involved in the case, it was too late to reverse the inevitable. Despite the lawyer writing a complete and thorough brief on the miscarriages of justice in Jeff's case, the courts wouldn't review the substance of his claims. He had killed his family ten years ago when he was in the midst of abusive pressures and psychological turmoil. Since then, he had matured. He was not the same person. He had a good job at the prison; the staff and other prisoners liked him. He said he could do life without parole. But it was not to be.

I had been writing to Jeff for a year and a half and I liked him. He asked me to be his "next of kin," and so as his last month unfolded, I was caught in a surrealistic drama of trying to save his life while arranging for his burial. I, too, was condemned by the rules; after driving five and a half hours to visit at the maximum security prison, I was turned away because, having been authorized as a special visitor not a regular visitor, I had had my special visit three weeks earlier. The staff made it clear that no exceptions would be made. Enforcing the rules had nothing to do with the humanity of the situation, nor with security needs. I was frustrated, just as all families of prisoners are at the mercy of seemingly irrational and unknown prison rules.

The next time I saw Jeff was the day of his midnight execution. Again, staff treated me as an enemy, as if I could stop the execution being held in the bowels of that concrete institution. I kept thinking of a science fiction story in which the hero doesn't know she has the power to stop the evil creatures and must learn the hard way how to use and control her power. I wished I knew what power to use.

That was Ash Wednesday, February 26, 1996. It was a different kind of death than I had ever encountered. The state celebrated its success in killing for revenge while I mourned alone, my friend's death a mistaken solution for the protection of society. His death certificate named the cause of death "legal homicide."

Three years and almost twenty Missouri executions later, Roy Roberts, CP#44, was executed in March of 1999. My frustration mounted as I read the Roberts clemency petition. I was astounded that the case had not been stopped somewhere along the line. Was the state so bent on executions that it would kill innocent persons? Apparently, yes. I kept thinking that if only the public knew about the case, they would not let this travesty of justice happen. I was convinced that it was the hiddenness of the death process that allowed the execution machinery to go on. Few know that executions are happening, and fewer still know what they are about. I became obsessed with the death penalty and it was interfering with my job. My anger turned into action. I began a search for all the Missouri death penalty clemency petitions. There were thirty-nine when I began. I decided to write this book including all fifty clemency petitions through the end of the year 2000.

As a sociologist teaching criminal justice to idealistic and naïve students, I was greatly troubled that what was supposed to be happening according to the law was clearly different from the reality. The fine ideals of our legal system were in many cases empty promises, especially when the crime and punishment were the most extreme. The courts were dodging the legal issues and relying on technicalities to deny justice to appellants. It appeared that the checks and balances within the legal system were broken. The abstract legal issues came to the governor as individual requests seeking compassion and searching for justice. Perhaps because he was a political officeholder, the governor rarely stopped an execution and rarely explained his decisions to the public.[1] Of course, the public was not clamoring for any explanations. They do not have access to the complex process through which we carry out the death penalty in our state. The public assumes that all is as it should be because they know little about the realities of the legal processes involved. I hope the public wants to know.

RESEARCH FOCUS

This book focuses on the final appeals to the governor in death penalty cases. The major question concerns the legal process and procedures that have developed around the implementation of the death penalty, with special emphasis on questions raised in clemency petitions. These questions involve whether juries consider all the relevant evidence in reaching a decision, whether innocent persons are convicted or sentenced to death (or both), whether official misconduct taints the due process of law, whether effective assistance of counsel is available to defendants, whether appeal courts consider substantive justice issues in correcting errors, whether political considerations interfere with judicial decision making, and whether the governor acts as a fail safe in the execution process. These questions concerning the justice of the death penalty come together at the very last stage of the death penalty process: the clemency request to the governor. "Clemency is the only mechanism that allows the condemned to tell his or her story fully" (Kobil, 1998: 540). The clemency documents are written to simplify and clarify the myriad legal issues in these death penalty cases into their essential stories. Typically the petition is written by an attorney for postconviction appeals.[2]

Clemency petitions from the state of Missouri illustrate the major problems that frustrate the justice system in death penalty cases. The Missouri focus is of critical importance to the manuscript. Missouri ranks third in the country in the number of executions conducted since reinstatement of the death penalty in the 1970s. As one of the states most actively engaged in executions, Missouri provides a range of representative issues from which to draw conclusions. In many ways Missouri's situation reflects much of what is at stake nationwide and is typical of the majority of states that permit the governor to make the clemency decision. Missouri's system of delivering the death penalty is similar to the processes in other states. The process is one of several layers of review to ensure that the proper person is receiving the appropriate punishment.

Another advantage of focusing on one state is that the legal environment defining the procedures by which the governor abides is somewhat controlled. An alternative approach that would draw clemency petitions from a variety of states would raise questions concerning possible sampling bias and would complicate the analysis of the material, since states and federal courts have different procedural rules and court opinions guiding their decision making. Therefore, the overall benefit in studying one state is greater reliability in the quality of the data. Because I have been able to collect *all* the clemency petitions for the fifty individuals who faced the death penalty in Missouri during this time period, examination of *all* the clemency cases will avoid any criticism of sample bias. Such comprehensiveness adds an important dimension to the decision-making process and strengthens the capacity of this research project to assess the role of the governor as a fail safe.

In all cases, the clemency petitions are used not to evaluate the defense claims, but rather to frame the issues, illuminating a side of the case that is typically missing from public discussion. Usual media coverage tends to focus on the crime and present only the prosecution's side of the matter (Haney, 1998: 354). The prisoners' claims found in the clemency petitions often present new issues not tested previously by jury or court; some claims are procedural questions that have blocked deliberation of the merits (substance) of the case, and other claims demonstrate reasonable doubt. In addition, the clemency petitions often portray the social background of the death row prisoner, to remind the governor that it is human life that is in the balance.

I obtained some of the clemency petitions from the attorneys, some from the governor's office, some from the Internet, and some from abolitionists. The average length of a clemency petition is eighteen double-spaced pages. In this book I provide both an overview of all fifty clemency petitions and a selection of lengthy excerpts to represent and preserve as many of the issues as possible for the reader. My task has been to edit these petitions for readability and to condense them, keeping details to a minimum so that there is space for a sufficient variety of cases to illustrate the various themes. Surprisingly, there are few legal citations in the clemency briefs. Clearly, these clemency petitions are not typical legal briefs, in the normative sense that every sentence should have a footnote. Although the average number of legal citations in the petitions is eight, the most common number of legal citations is just one. I have retained relevant citations in the notes section of this book and have offered a glossary to explain legal jargon.

Some readers may protest that I am telling only one side of the story. However, the evidence presented in the clemency petitions is factually verifiable and as such raises serious questions concerning the implementation of the death penalty in Missouri. In addition, the veracity of the evidence is supported not only by the reputations of those who have written the clemency petitions, but also by appendices and other kinds of attachments submitted to the governor that document the claims (all of which I have omitted from this analysis). Finally, many of the clemency petitions refer to dissenting opinions in earlier stages of their appeals, which further bolster the credibility of the defense claims.

Nonetheless, readers may draw whatever conclusions they desire from the materials presented. The book is not an attempt to assess the truth of the claims made in the clemency petitions. That is the burden of others. Nor does this book attempt to examine all the legal controversies that have emerged in death penalty litigation that are well covered in law review articles and evolving court decisions. The purpose of this book is to raise the awareness of the public about the defense of death row prisoners facing execution, to recognize that their claims of error represent systemic flaws rather than unique occurrences, and to suggest policy recommendations to restore integrity in the administration of justice.

Finally, my focus on the condemned prisoners is not intended to diminish the harm committed upon the victims of these crimes. Their lives, too, deserve to be remembered, and perhaps their families are the best source for telling their stories. But justice for all is a promise made to criminals and victims alike. Unless the rule of law demands that the legal system work fairly, then one person's justice is another's injustice.

One other note. All of the clemency petitions covered in this book deal with male death row prisoners. The five women who have been sentenced to death in Missouri since reinstatement do not remain on death row for various reasons. Therefore, when writing about Missouri's population of death row prisoners, I use masculine pronouns. Likewise, because the Missouri governors have all been males, I use masculine pronouns when referring to Missouri governors. When discussing the prisoners in general or the governor's role in general, I use gender-neutral language.

ORGANIZATION OF THE BOOK

The clemency petitions usually present several issues to the governor to evaluate. I have selected cases for each chapter according to their primary issues. My intention is for the reader to recognize both the significance of the issues and the diversity of issues presented to the governor. These issues directly contrast with the ideal norms and values of the justice system.

Chapter 1 establishes the social context for this focus on the delivery of justice in capital cases. The chapter also provides an overview of the death penalty process and a brief history of executive clemency. Chapter 2 explores the expectations for police investigations and presents two cases that illustrate the way police misconduct can jeopardize the reliability of the death penalty decision. Chapter 3 presents three cases to illustrate the most common problems that arise in the office of prosecutor in death penalty litigation. Playing fairly and "by the rules" is a difficult standard to achieve when the apparent popularity of the death penalty demands convictions. Chapter 4 discusses the role of the defense attorney. Virtually all death penalty cases claim to suffer from ineffective assistance of counsel. This chapter presents four cases that highlight the problems created when the defendant's trial attorney is either inexperienced at providing or unprepared to provide (or sometimes both) a vigorous defense. Chapter 5 contrasts the prescribed role of the judge with an actual situation in which the judge overstepped the appearance of neutrality in setting the death penalty. Chapter 6 examines the court review at both the state level and the federal levels to understand what quality of review is provided by these jurisdictions. Three cases demonstrate how the higher courts are relinquishing their traditional role of protecting individual rights. Chapter 7 examines governors' decision making in the death penalty process and concludes that extralegal factors interfere with governors' ability to be a fail safe. Chapter 8 reviews the death penalty criminal justice process and identifies four areas for reform. Policy recommendations are suggested and implementation strategies are proposed.

CONCLUSION

As of this writing, Missouri has executed fifty-four persons since the reinstatement of the death penalty, and most often the public is unaware that a state-sponsored killing has occurred. This blindness exists, despite the general public clamor for the death penalty, in large part because of the peculiarities of the media focus. It is easier for the media to cover the trial and the crime than it is to cover the unfolding legal issues that bear on the appropriateness of the death sentence. Pictures from the crime scene are more gripping than the technical words found in legal briefs. Unfortunately, the obscurity of the legal arguments reinforces the perception that all is as it should be. The reader will see that time after time, the criminal justice system failed the condemned, his family, the victims, and our community.

This has been a hard book to write because of the continual accumulation of stories pointing to the betrayal of the promises of the legal system. I am convinced that we are able to kill our fellow citizens because we have dehumanized them, hidden them behind prison walls, and discounted their voices. But "doing justice" requires a healthy distrust of the system, citizen awareness, and professional commitment to the ideals that make this society great. Over thirty years ago, Supreme Court Justice Thurgood Marshall said in *Furman v. Georgia* (1972) that if the American people were fully informed about the death penalty, they would find it shocking, unjust, and unacceptable. I hope this book will expose the flaws in the legal system to public scrutiny and further a passionate discussion of policy options.

GRATITUDES

In a way, this book compelled me to write it. Yet it could not have become a reality without a great deal of support from various communities.

We know what is happening in the capital cases only because of the dedicated attorneys who work on postconviction appeals to save the lives of the death row prisoners. They do not give up. Without their efforts, this book would not have been possible. I am especially grateful to Sean O'Brien, Kent Gipson, Cheryl Rafert, Doug Laird, Marta H. Hilney, Charles Maas, Cedric Brown, Michael J. Gorla, Timothy K. Kellett, Leo Griffard, Mark A. Thornhill, Gardiner B. Davis, Louis DeFeo, Lew Kollias, John Tucci, Antonio Manansala, George Winger, Gerald A. Sims Jr., Elena Franco, Susan Hunt, and James Tierney.

Over the years I have learned a great deal from my friends in the Missouri abolition movement who work so hard to tell the stories. It is their faithfulness to the cause that keeps the public light on the execution tragedies: Debbie Reuscher, Margaret Phillips, Rita Linhardt, Jeff Stack, Ted Wilson, Sr. Theresa Maly, Reva and John Griffith, Rev. Dr. Merrill Proudfoot, Roy Schaefer, Jim and Mary Reefer, Fr. Mark Miller, Pat Bartholome, Greg Harlan, Linda Taylor, Lowell Listrom, Kathleen Kennedy, Dick Dexter, Bob Myers, Ed Martin, JoCele McEnany, Rev. Michael Poke, Rev. Ernest Jones, Caron Wells, and Evelyn Welton.

Completing this manuscript required many revisions and time to do the revisions. I am grateful to the University of Missouri for giving me time away from teaching responsibilities in order to complete this manuscript. Even more important to accomplishing this task, however, were those who offered their expertise by critically reading and commenting on drafts. These special persons are Mary Reefer, Tom Carroll, Fr. Paul Jones, Jonas Spatz, Mona Danner, Sally Pomeroy, and Margaret Vandiver.

The process of writing is hard work. Along the way, many friends and family supported me. Mom and Dad, Nancy, Susan, Wendy, Margot, and Helma deserve honorable mention. Their interest helped me clarify my thoughts and sustained my desire to complete this project. I am most especially thankful for Fr. Paul Jones, Martha Fly, Sally Firestone, and Rev. Kate McClain, who listened to me ramble, sometimes pushed, helped me laugh, and always encouraged. They kept me accountable to my goal. My gratitude.

JUSTICE DENIED

CHAPTER ONE

INTRODUCTION

The power to pardon, reprieve or commute is inherent in the sovereignty of the people of the State who have conferred the exercise of this power on the Governor by virtue of Article IV, Section 7 of the Constitution of Missouri. The power exists to serve the common good and not merely the individual under sentence. . . .

The common good requires the state, and ultimately the governor, to weigh justice, assess responsibility, and mete out punishment and rewards. Humanly speaking, we cannot achieve justice perfectly, nor assess perfectly the responsibility of each offender. We need, especially regarding capital punishment, to be careful that punishment given does not pretend to a degree of justice to which human beings cannot lay claim.

The common good would be violated if our punishment responds to something we cannot know with an appropriate degree of certainty. Death is final and absolute. In George Mercer's case, there are many things we do not know absolutely and with final certainty.

FROM THE CLEMENCY PETITION
for George Mercer, CP#2,
executed January 6, 1989[1]

In the popular movie *True Crime* (1999), Clint Eastwood plays the role of a reporter reluctantly writing about a convicted killer. As he investigates the background of the case, he discovers evidence that the condemned man is actually innocent of the murder. Tension rises as time moves closer to the midnight hour of execution. Why hasn't any member of the legal system found this evidence? Will the reporter reach the governor with the proof in time for the governor to act, to stop the execution of an innocent man? Within minutes of the execution, the reporter reaches the governor with the proof of innocence, and the execution is halted even as the poison begins flowing. In the movie, truth prevails and justice is done by sparing the life of a wrongly convicted person. In real life there is growing evidence that the governor is not always willing to act as a fail safe, and is certainly unwilling to act when doubt exists as to the guilt or appropriateness of the penalty. In the movie, the governor does the right thing. In real life, the assumption is that the governor will do the right thing. But is this assumption correct?

In this new millennium, the death penalty abolition movement is increasingly on the agenda of public discussion. Whether among legal professionals or social activists, religious leaders or victim groups, controversies about the death penalty are found throughout popular culture. Movies, television programs, magazines, international focus, and simply the accelerating pace of executions bring the issue in front of a broad cross section of society. In 1993, the book *Dead Man Walking* launched the public debate anew. In her book, written by a nun sharing the development of her awareness about the death penalty, Sr. Helen Prejean invited readers to take that same journey of meeting the human beings on death row and exploring the intricacies of death penalty work. Honesty concerning her previous blindness to the needs of victims gave credibility to her exposure of the political maneuvering within the Louisiana Board of Pardons and Parole. Since that time, Sister Helen has been on speaking tours crisscrossing the country communicating the arguments against the death penalty and lifting the level of public consciousness.

THE FIRST QUESTION

Today, two basic kinds of questions are being asked of the death penalty. One is concerned with the purpose of the punishment. The second concerns the legal process and procedures that have developed around the implementation of the death penalty.

Regarding the first question, a just punishment should serve a legitimate purpose, with an appropriate means for achieving its goal. Many purposes have been suggested for having the death penalty: deterrence (to influence a person's decision not to offend), rehabilitation (to reform the offender), restoration (to make victims whole), incapacitation (to protect society by rendering an offender incapable of offending), and retribution (to get back at the offender). Taking these purposes one at a time, we can see that only retribution and vengeance have any reality to them. First, scholars have effectively established that the death penalty has no general deterrent effect (McFarland, 1983; Hall, 1986; Peterson and Bailey, 1998; Sorensen, Wrinkle, Brewer, and Marquart, 1999). Of course, once the prisoner is executed, that specific prisoner poses no further danger to society. However, such incapacitation may not be necessary to protect society. Others have shown that death row prisoners are actually less likely than other prisoners to kill again (Marquart and Sorensen, 1989). In fact, the result of an execution may actually be the opposite of deterrence. Observing the rise in violent crime after an execution, researchers (Bowers and Pierce, 1980) theorize that rather than getting the message that killing is wrong when the state executes, persons get the message that it is acceptable to react violently when someone treats you wrongly. This result is known as brutalization (Cochran, Chamblin, and Seth, 1994; Thomson, 1997; Thomson, 1999). Second, although many offenders change and become constructive prisoners, even experiencing faith conversions, such rehabilitation has not saved persons condemned to death.[2] They are executed for their behavior at the time of the crime, not for who they are at the time of the execution. Third, no one claims that executions will restore the victims to wholeness. However, some argue that victims' families and the community need the executions to bring closure to their brokenness. Increasingly, victims' families explain that the death penalty and executions actually deny them the opportunity to come to the reconciliation and forgiveness they need to heal (Murder Victims' Families for Reconciliation). In a very real sense, the death penalty and execution process revictimizes them by keeping their pain and their anger raw. Fourth, society can be kept safe from violent criminals in alternative ways. All states now have a life without parole penalty option, or "hard fifty"— long sentences that essentially keep prisoners locked up for their lifetime. Protecting society from violent offenders can also be done in ways that are cheaper than the death penalty. Estimates of the cost differential between a lifetime prison sentence and the death penalty indicate that the death penalty costs as much as $1.5 million more than life in prison without parole (Bright, 1996). Since all the other purposes are not fulfilled, only retribution and vengeance actually describe what is accomplished when the death penalty is imposed.

THE SECOND QUESTION

A second aspect of justice involves considerations of equity and fairness, ensuring that persons in similar situations receive similar punishments. This second set of questions examines the legal process and procedures that are developing around the implementation of the death penalty. These questions are legion (Acker, Bohm, and Lanier, 1998) and give plenty of fuel to those who want to abolish the death penalty.

First, the American Bar Association (ABA) stimulated abolition efforts in February 1997 when its House of Delegates voted two to one to endorse a pause in executions until states have enacted the means to ensure that fairness and due process are maintained in its administration. The House of Delegates concluded that "fundamental due process is systematically lacking in capital cases" and "[i]t should now be apparent to all of us in the profession that the administration of the death penalty has become so seriously flawed that capital punishment should not be implemented without adherence to the various applicable ABA policies" (Harris, 1997: 2).

Spearheaded by the ABA section of Individual Rights and Responsibilities, the moratorium resolution was a response to both the legislative actions of Congress and the Supreme Court's trend of backing away from substantive review to ensure fairness and due process in capital litigation. Title I of the Antiterrorism and Effective Death Penalty Act of 1996 passed by Congress specifically narrowed the appeal process for death row inmates,

> curtail[ing] the availability of habeas. The new law establishes deadlines for filing federal habeas petitions, places limits on federal evidentiary hearings into the facts underlying federal constitutional claims, sets time-tables for federal court action, limits the availability of appellate review, establishes even more demanding restrictions on second or successive applications for federal relief, and in some instances, apparently bars the federal courts from awarding relief on the basis of federal constitutional violations where state courts have erred in concluding that no such violation occurred (Harris, 1997: 11).

Although the pressure to restrict appeals was justified in part because of numerous frivolous appeals (Rivkind and Shatz, 2001: 602), the ABA remarked that "[c]ontrary to popular belief, most habeas petitions in death penalty cases do not rest on frivolous technicalities" (Harris, 1997: 11). Despite its intention to reduce frivolous appeals to the federal courts, the change in the habeas law meant that cases with meritorious issues would be less likely to be considered by the federal courts. The ABA resolution criticized the new federal legislation as having "dramatically undermined the federal courts' capacity to adjudicate federal constitutional claims in a fair and efficient manner" (Harris, 1997: 3). Because of the deference to state decisions, the law also undercut the traditional role of the federal court to maintain national standards of justice and due process.

> [T]he habeas process [changed] from a broad opportunity for federal courts to remedy constitutional violations by state officials into an exit-less maze shielding those officials from federal scrutiny even when they had clearly violated the Constitution (Lazarus, 1998: 503).

In another action, Congress completely withdrew federal funding from the postconviction defender organizations in 1995. Such action had the result of ensuring that poor defendants would have little or no assistance of counsel, especially at the higher appeals stages where thorough reviews are critical. The ABA documented serious flaws in legal representation and recommended remedies, to no avail. States consistently underfund the defense of persons accused of capital crimes even as they bolster prosecution resources. Even in the stages of litigation where counsel can be appointed to a poor defendant, the ABA observed that the federal courts have not rectified the low standard for effective assistance of counsel (Harris, 1997: 9). Because death penalty law is quite different from other criminal law, defense attorneys require significant time and resources to mount an adequate defense. Given that a private attorney would require $100,000 to be paid before a death penalty case is taken on, most Americans would be considered "poor" if found in these circumstances. Since state funding for appointed defense attorneys has been abysmally low (Paduano and Smith, 1991), the conclusion is inescapable that poor defendants are condemned to death without benefit of the due process that is a guarantee of justice for all (Bright, 1994). This problem intensified with the Supreme Court's action in taking away many avenues to correct serious errors. The ABA identified additional obstacles that death row prisoners face when attempting to raise constitutional claims in the courts.

> Prisoners have not been entitled to a stay of execution to complete their postconviction litigation. The federal courts typically have refused to consider claims that were not properly raised in state court, even if the failure to raise them was due to the ignorance or neglect of defense counsel. And prisoners have often not been allowed to litigate more than one petition,

even if they have offered strong evidence of egregious constitutional violations that they could not have presented earlier (Harris, 1997: 10).

Fairness questions are dramatically raised through the publicity of
persons wrongly convicted and then released from prison after their
exoneration. The long-standing work by attorney Barry Scheck and
the Innocence Project he established at the Cardoso Law School discovered conviction errors mainly by utilizing new techniques of DNA
testing. More attention to wrongful convictions came primarily
through the investigative efforts of Northwestern University Law
School students and their teachers. Highlighting these efforts, a conference in November of 1998 at Northwestern University Law School
presented eighty-seven persons—all wrongfully convicted of capital
murder—who have been released from death rows since the reinstatement of the death penalty in 1976. As these numbers of wrongful convictions accumulate, increasing voices from within the system point
to the numerous flaws in the legal process. Press conferences held by
former federal U.S. attorneys (Millin, 2000) and law professors
(O'Brien, 2000) give witness to the growing support for the abolition
of the death penalty. Even in Congress, the evidence of wrongful convictions spurs proposals to correct the system. During the 106th session of Congress, federal legislation was introduced to abolish the
death penalty (S1917.IS), to create a moratorium on federal executions
(HR5236.IH; S3048.IS; HR5237.IH; S2463.IS), and to provide protection so that innocent persons will not be wrongly convicted, through
providing DNA testing, competent legal services, and compensation
for the unjustly condemned (HR3623; HR4162; HR4078).

These voices warning of serious problems in death penalty litigation
were reinforced most recently in a study conducted by James Liebman
et al. (2000). These researchers found that appeal courts reversed death
penalty cases 60 percent to 70 percent of the time, leading them to
suggest that the death penalty system is broken because of this evidence of serious errors throughout the majority of states. Nonetheless,
their research could be interpreted by death penalty supporters to
endorse the credible job the appellate courts are doing in detecting
errors. However, if it is true that the courts were once effective at
detecting errors, these assurances may no longer be appropriate as the
courts change the focus of their reviews.

At the same time that the public debate has been growing, the courts
have been increasing their reliance on technicalities to avoid dealing

with these issues of administration of justice. At every stage of the process, procedural rules (which depend on effective counsel for their implementation) have assumed dominance over the consideration of substantive matters.

At the U.S. Supreme Court level, there has been a movement away from consideration of death penalty issues. Despite the appearance of micromanaging death penalty litigation, the U.S. Supreme Court, in effect, deregulates their control by deferring to the states' imposition of the death penalty (Steiker and Steiker, 1995). This shift toward states' rights has resulted in the relinquishment of the traditional role of the federal courts to ensure constitutional protections. "What the Court set up was a series of trapdoors where any procedural wrong step, no matter how trivial, resulted in a petitioner forfeiting his claims" (Lazarus, 1998: 503). In deferring to the states, the Supreme Court justifies its relinquishment of review by relying on the executive's clemency power to correct errors, to operate as a "fail safe" (*Herrera v. Collins*, 1993), to prevent miscarriages of justice. Coupled with the changes in the habeas corpus law, the Court's relinquishment of its traditional role means that few errors will be recognized by the Court.

RESPONSES

As Congress and the Supreme Court, throughout the decade of the 1990s, took the lead in cutting back on constitutional protections, state activists mobilized to fulfill the ABA's recommendation for a moratorium on executions. Abolitionists were energized when Illinois governor George Ryan declared a moratorium on executions as of January 31, 2000. Although a supporter of the death penalty and a Republican, Governor Ryan was troubled by the statistics in Illinois indicating that thirteen wrongly convicted persons were released from Illinois' death row, while twelve persons were executed. As the person responsible for life-or-death decisions, Governor Ryan wanted certainty that the Illinois capital punishment system would correct its process and eliminate the sources of error in death penalty convictions.

The moratorium movement appeared to be growing. Every day seemed to bring forward another death penalty *supporter* in favor of a moratorium (Kane, 2000). By the end of the year 2000, twenty-seven local governments and over one thousand groups supported a moratorium of the death penalty in their jurisdictions (*Equal Justice USA*, 2000). Additionally, with the sponsorship of Sr. Helen Prejean, a Moratorium 2000 movement initiated a petition drive to be presented to the United Nations at the beginning of the new year, 2001. Thirteen state legislatures considered moratorium bills in the year 2000. The New Hampshire House of Representatives passed an abolition bill that was vetoed by the governor.

For the first time in many years, public opinion polls indicated some decline in support for the death penalty, particularly in light of the publicity surrounding those wrongly convicted. A public opinion poll of Missouri residents (CSSPPR, 1999) in November 1999 reported that although 78 percent of respondents said they were to some degree in favor of the death penalty, when presented with alternatives, support for the death penalty dropped to less than half the respondents (47 percent). The researchers found that over 80 percent of respondents said that finding out that innocent individuals had been convicted had the most effect on their opinion about the death penalty. And over half (56 percent) said they would support a three-year delay of scheduled executions to investigate the effects and sentencing practices of the death penalty. This state survey mirrored shifting sentiment across the country. The first national poll of registered voters to test public opinion on a moratorium on executions was released in August 2000. Conducted by a Democratic and a Republican pollster, the poll found that 63 percent now supported "a suspension of the death penalty until questions about its fairness can be studied" (*Equal Justice USA*, 2000).

THE DEATH PENALTY PROCESS

The earliest known execution in Missouri occurred in 1810. Capital punishment was enforced until 1917 when the legislature overwhelmingly approved its abolition. The abolition was short-lived, however. In 1919, the death penalty was reinstated in a special session of the legislature after several sensational crimes aroused public sentiment (Galliher, Ray, and Cook, 1992). After the U.S. Supreme Court condemned mandatory death sentencing as unconstitutional in 1976, the Missouri statute was declared unconstitutional by the Missouri Supreme Court in 1977 because of its provisions for mandatory death sentencing.[3] The current death penalty law was reenacted later in 1977

(Wallace and Sorensen, 1994: note 28). Since 1977, various modifica-
tions in the death penalty law and in practice have developed through
legislative changes and through the issuance of rules by the Missouri
Supreme Court.

In 1978 the state legislature authorized the purchase of a lethal
injection machine, which replaced the leaky gas chamber and effectively became the only means of execution in Missouri. The first execution under the new statute was conducted by lethal injection in the
old gas chamber of the Jefferson City Penitentiary. After that time,
"death row" was moved into the newly built Potosi Correctional Center, where an execution chamber and a holding cell were located in
the infirmary.

The Missouri death penalty process is very much like that in other
states, with some notable differences.

The first stage in a capital case is the trial and direct appeal. If the
accused is too poor to hire an attorney, a public defender may be
assigned. According to the Sixth Amendment of the Constitution, the
accused has a right to appointed counsel for this first stage, which
includes the pretrial activities of arrest, interrogation, appointment of
counsel, determination of whether to set bail, notice of intent to seek
death filed by the prosecutor, discovery, possible mental examination,
investigation, and motions filed and heard by the court.

If the prosecutor decides to go forward with a death penalty prosecution, there are two phases to the trial, usually with the same jury. First
there is a guilt phase to determine whether the accused "knowingly
cause[d] the death of another person after deliberation upon the matter" (R.S.Mo. section 565.020.1). If the jury decides to convict the
defendant of murder in the first degree, then there is a penalty phase
in which mitigating and aggravating evidence may be presented. The
jury may choose between a sentence of life imprisonment without
parole and death. In Missouri, to choose death, the jury must first find
at least one statutory aggravating circumstance beyond a reasonable
doubt and decide that the mitigating evidence does not outweigh the
aggravating evidence (R.S.Mo. section 565.030). The judge must
accept whatever sentence the jury imposes. In 1984 the trial procedure
was amended to permit the judge to impose the sentence if the jury
was unable to decide or agree on punishment. The statute requires the
judge to follow the same procedure that is required of the jury. Once
the death sentence is imposed, a date may be set for execution. How-

ever, the execution will be stayed if appeals are pending so as to ensure that only accurate and fair death sentences will be carried out.

The first appeal is an automatic review called a direct appeal and is sent to the state supreme court. At the direct appeal, the state supreme court determines the appropriateness of the death sentence and whether any errors listed in the appeal jeopardized the fairness of the trial. The state supreme court can affirm the sentence of death, reduce the sentence to life without parole, or send the case back to the trial court for resentencing (R.S.Mo. section 565.035).

After the direct appeal, the death row prisoner can appeal a negative decision to the U.S. Supreme Court by filing a petition for certiorari. There is no constitutional right to legal assistance at this point, but typically the state will appoint two attorneys if the prisoner makes a request. In the "cert" petition, the prisoner is asking the U.S. Supreme Court to examine how the state supreme court reviewed the trial. If cert is denied (and it is denied in about ninety-nine cases out of one hundred), the prisoner must go on to the next series of appeals because usually an execution date is issued. The issues are not evaluated by the U.S. Supreme Court until cert is granted. If cert is granted, then a hearing is held, but there is no guarantee that the ruling will be favorable.

The second stage of a capital case is the state habeas corpus or postconviction proceedings. This action is brought by the prisoner challenging his conviction or sentence (or both) once the direct appeal stage is completed. This action is brought in the court that sentenced the prisoner. In most states, those issues that could have been raised at trial or on direct appeal but were not, will be considered waived and therefore procedurally barred in a postconviction action. They may still be claimed, but the court will determine whether they may be considered under some exception to the waiver doctrines. Claims that could not have been raised at trial or on direct appeal, such as ineffective assistance of counsel or failure to provide exculpatory evidence, may be asserted and determined on the merits. The prisoner is trying to prove "fatal error," that is, the existence of a legal procedure during the trial that substantially injured the defendant by adversely affecting the outcome of the trial. However, observation demonstrates that a trial court is unlikely to change its mind and find something invalid that it once believed to be valid. After this first postconviction appeal, either side can appeal to the state supreme court. If unsuccessful, the death row prisoner can appeal again to the U.S. Supreme Court in another petition for certiorari.

Federal habeas corpus proceedings constitute the third stage in a capital case. In Missouri, these cases are filed in the Eighth Federal Circuit, which also has judicial jurisdiction over Arkansas, Nebraska, Iowa, South Dakota, North Dakota, and Minnesota. The prisoner can enter this third stage only when all the state proceedings are exhausted. The appellant must have obtained a certificate of probable cause (now a certificate of appealability) showing that the issues raised are "debatable among jurists of reason" before being able to proceed. The federal district court will consider only those issues that have been presented and ruled on by the state courts.[4] Unless the prisoner's attorney can show that the failure to raise an issue was for a good reason (for instance, that the argument was only possible following a recent Supreme Court decision), it cannot be raised later. After the federal district court, the prisoner appeals to the Federal Circuit Court of Appeals. The last appeal is a petition for certiorari to the U.S. Supreme Court.

The federal habeas corpus appeal process was significantly changed in the Antiterrorism and Effective Death Penalty Act of 1996 (AEDPA). The sections of the AEDPA that pertain to the death penalty were designed to reduce the number of habeas corpus appeals, shorten the time permitted for filing habeas petitions, and reduce the likelihood that habeas petitions would be granted. Although most of the cases included in this book come under the old habeas law, at least six clemency petitions were directly affected by the new law because of a unique interpretation by the Eighth Circuit. Therefore, some of the specific provisions of the new federal habeas corpus law are discussed in chapter 6.

Once the courts have made final judgment, the prisoner's only hope is to appeal to the governor for clemency. The petition for clemency is filed with the governor, who in turn sends it to the Board of Probation and Parole for their investigation and nonbinding recommendation back to the governor. When making the clemency decision, the governor is not restricted by the courts' rules of evidence. In fact, the governor has unlimited discretion in the clemency decision (Missouri Constitution, Article IV, section 7).

CLEMENCY

All of the questions concerning the justice of the legal process and procedures of the death penalty cases come together at the very last stage of the death penalty process: the clemency request to the governor. The term "clemency" refers to an act of leniency in the criminal justice system. In the death penalty system, clemency can be one of three things: a reprieve, a commutation, or a pardon (or a combination of these). A reprieve is a stay of execution, granting time in order to do something else, such as considering other issues, possibly in other jurisdictions. Many governors have a great deal of discretion in shaping what happens during the period of a stay. A commutation of sentence is a reduction of the penalty, usually to a life without parole sentence. A pardon is a complete absolution of guilt for a crime, which also releases the prisoner from the penalty for the crime. A pardon rarely occurs in death penalty situations.

"While earlier notions of clemency existed in Greece, Germany and other countries, . . . the English tradition best reflects the American notions of clemency as they relate to capital punishment in the United States" (Korengold, Noteboom, and Gurwitch, 1996: 352). Mercy was granted only when there was a ruler who had sufficient power over others who could impose his will on others. It took the development of a king in the 700s before this discretionary power was exercised to increase the power and allegiance owed to the monarch. The power to pardon was traditionally associated with the king of England (Rothman, 1976: 152).

Before the development of mitigating or special defenses (Note, 1981: 895) to soften the impact, punishments were quite brutal. "It was not until 1532 that English law recognized the excuse of self-defense and even later before accidental homicide was recognized" (Holcomb, 2000: 15). Historically, clemency from the king was the main option for obtaining relief.

> Over 200 felonies carried mandatory death sentences in England during the late 18th and 19th centuries. In compensation for such tyrannical sentencing policies, as many as seven out of every eight offenders were pardoned or saw their death sentence commuted during this era (Acker and Lanier, 2000: 211–12).

Indeed, the U.S. Supreme Court recognized that "clemency provided the principal avenue of relief for individuals convicted of criminal offenses—most of which were capital—because there was no right of appeal until 1907" (*Herrera v. Collins*, 1993).

In our own development as a nation, the English pardoning power was imported into the new legal system. As Alexander Hamilton explained in the *Federalist Papers*:

> The criminal code of every country partakes so much of necessary severity that without an easy access to exceptions in favor of unfortunate guilt, justice would wear a countenance too sanguinary and cruel (Belli, 1975: 26).

As late as 1939, clemency was the only way to challenge a conviction on the basis of innocence (*Herrera v. Collins*, 1993). Thus, reliance on clemency was a key component of the criminal justice system.

In the forming of the nation, discussion took place about whether the clemency power should reside in the chief executive or in the legislature (Kobil, 1998: 533). "The framers were aware that the pardoning power should be delegated so as to be independent of the judiciary, and therefore act as a check on the courts" (Belli, 1975: 30). But initially there was considerable suspicion of a powerful executive, since the colonies had just won their independence from a dictatorial monarch. States made various choices as they wrote their constitutions. Some changed back to give the executive responsibility, as the passage of time removed their distrust of the executive. Today, twenty-five out of thirty-eight states with the death penalty give the authority to the governor to grant clemency. In nine states, the governor must have a recommendation of clemency from a board or advisory group. In three states, the governor sits on the clemency board, which makes the determination. Three others give the authority to a board to decide, not the governor (DPIC, 2001).

Despite being situated in the executive branch of government, the clemency option is an integral part of the death penalty process. In *Herrera v. Collins* (1993), Chief Justice Rehnquist speaking for the plurality clearly relies on the governor's clemency role:

> Clemency is deeply rooted in our Anglo-American tradition of law, and it is the historic remedy for preventing a miscarriage of justice where judicial process has been exhausted. In England, the clemency power was vested in the Crown and can be traced back to the 700s. . . . Executive clemency has provided the "fail safe" in our criminal justice system. . . . It is an unalterable fact that our justice system, like the human beings who administer it, is fallible.

With the Supreme Court relying on the governor to act as a fail safe, the executive branch becomes a key step in the administration of justice as well as a check on the judicial branch of government. Some governors would reject such a role, viewing clemency powers as "interfering with the judicial process," but such a view is not credible (Belli, 1975: 38).[5] Given the severity and irrevocability of the death penalty punishment, executive clemency is a critical feature of the justice system. Chapter 7 explores what happens to clemency petitions in the governor's office.

The clemency petition is the opportunity given to death row prisoners to plead their case to the governor, asking for mercy, pleading for justice. In these petitions we find the "shortcomings of the criminal law dramatized" (Abramowitz and Paget, 1964: 188) with life-or-death consequences. As we examine the clemency petitions presented to the governors of Missouri, we will be able to understand the burden governors shoulder when the Supreme Court relies on them to be the fail safe of the death penalty system. In reality, it may not be possible for a governor to step outside of the political office and evaluate the clemency petition on the merits of its arguments.

Although discretionary, executive clemency is more than simply mercy. There is a clear emphasis in tradition on its role in correcting mistakes (Abramowitz and Paget, 1964). As death penalty cases proceed from trial through the appeals process, there are numerous opportunities for errors to occur. We begin where the legal process begins, with the police investigation, and look at what trial problems are identified in clemency petitions with regard to the police and prison guards. These problems shed doubt on the reliability of several Missouri death sentences in which the due process of law was jeopardized by a rush to judgment.

CHAPTER TWO

THE POLICE INVESTIGATION

Murder is not a matter, where the past can be forgotten and one person executed to close a file.

FROM THE CLEMENCY PETITION
for Glen Sweet, CP#60,
executed April 22, 1998[1]

The first stage in the criminal justice process is the investigation and arrest of an accused. It is primarily the police who take on the task of "solving" the crime—identifying the persons involved as well as the motive and actions that led to a murder. Until the Warren Court (1953–1969), very few legal restrictions were placed on police behavior and on the methods they used in solving crimes. As police professionalism developed, police organizations were increasingly pressured to be accountable to the public through assurances of police effectiveness. One of the primary indicators relied on by the police to communicate their effectiveness became clearance rates—the number of crimes solved by arrest as a proportion of the crimes known to police. This statistic is easily understood and gave the public a sense of the diversity of police work, as different crimes had different clearance rates. Of all serious crimes, homicides are the most likely to be cleared by an arrest because the perpetrator is usually known to the victim and police have a ready source of suspects to investigate.[2] In 1999, 69 percent of all homicides were cleared by arrest (FBI, 2001).

THE PROMISE OF EFFECTIVE POLICE INVESTIGATION

Police work involves keeping the community safe through public service, order maintenance, and finding persons responsible for crimes. This chapter focuses on crime-solving activities as the first step in responding to murder cases. As mentioned earlier, the Warren Court era had a significant impact on the way police did their work by interpreting the Bill of Rights to protect "the innocent against the massive power of the state in criminal proceedings" (Schmalleger, 2001: 22). The classic Supreme Court cases of *Mapp v. Ohio* (1961) and *Miranda v. Arizona* (1966) guided police investigations by giving substance to the protections named in the Fourth Amendment with regard to search and seizure matters, and in the Fifth Amendment, which addresses issues of self-incrimination. As a result of these and other court decisions, police redefined their traditional protocols in crime solving to reflect these new rules of law. These cases put procedural controls on the previously unrestricted intrusive techniques the police use to solve criminal cases.

Crime solving involves investigation, the search and seizure of evidence, interrogating and eliciting confessions, and developing witnesses. All of this work should be done with an eye toward the reliability of the evidence so as to protect against wrongful convictions and to ensure that it is the guilty who are punished. In many jurisdictions, the first officers on the scene of a crime are followed by other police investigators whose job is to verify the completeness and accuracy of the preliminary investigation (Dantzker, 2000: 107). The circumstances of obtaining evidence influence how believable the evidence is and even whether it will be used in court. It is only when the evidence is reliable that guilt can be established beyond a reasonable doubt and the resulting conviction believed to be legitimate.

The work of the police in our society balances two goals: crime control and due process (Packer, 1968). The goal of crime control is to protect innocent people from crime by preventing or repressing criminal conduct. The emphasis in achieving this goal is on speed and efficiency in dealing with suspects, with less concern for legal technicalities that might slow down the investigation. The goal of due process, on the other hand, is focused on the protection of the accused from the power of the state. This goal is achieved by recognizing that suspects are presumed innocent until proven guilty and must be treated with the minimum standards of due process that all persons should expect. The Police Code of Ethics incorporates these two goals into the ideal for police behavior:

> As a law enforcement Officer my fundamental duty is to serve mankind [*sic*]; to safeguard lives and property; to protect the innocent against deception, the weak against oppression or intimidation, and the peaceful

against violence or disorder; and to respect the Constitutional rights of all men to liberty, equality, and justice (Crank and Caldero, 2000: 12).

From the Code of Ethics, it is inferred that how the police get the evidence is as important as what evidence they get. Ultimately, the concern for the method of obtaining evidence is based on a concern for the reliability of the result. For example, coerced confessions are not acceptable because they are believed to be untrustworthy. Developing dependable evidence is difficult when the police do not witness the crime taking place. It is well known that "[t]he classic problem of detection is to discover reliable information that will permit the identification and arrest of a perpetrator" (Senna and Siegel, 1998: 175). When a life is at stake we expect that greater care will be taken to be sure that the right person is accused and convicted of the crime.

When dealing with homicides, public pressure to solve the crime is often very strong. Sensitive to the public pressure, the police organization adds its own pressure to solve the crime quickly, both to reassure the public about its safety and to remove doubts about police ineffectiveness. With the police commitment to "getting the bad guys off the street," the police may be tempted to cut corners to make an arrest. This "corruption" of the process is justified in part by the police tendency to assume guilt as a working premise (Crank and Caldero, 2000: 43). Their assumption is reinforced by the media, which portray criminals as evil characters who must be apprehended and removed from society (Merlo and Benekos, 2000: 32). However, if the wrong person is arrested and convicted, public safety is not improved. A wrongful conviction may provide closure for the police, but it creates an illusion of public safety, which can actually jeopardize real safety. This illusion is functional, however, as it maintains the legitimacy of the police in contemporary society by giving the appearance of effectiveness in their work.

THE REALITY OF POLICE INVESTIGATION

Many advocates of capital punishment contend that, with the substantial safeguards available for defendants, mistakes will rarely be made. Yet this logic does not account for the noble cause, the tendency of the police to presume guilt, and vengeful sympathies for the victims, and the evidence suggests otherwise. . . . It may be that, because of their emotionally charged atmosphere and police-prosecutorial presumptions of defendant's guilt, death penalty cases are the most likely, rather than the least likely, to result in mistakes (Crank and Caldero, 2000: 46).

The "noble cause" of making the world a safer place is indeed a worthy goal for the police. However, it is the nature of bureaucratic organizations to focus on the means to achieve the goals and, in so doing, lose sight of the goals (Blumberg, 1979). For example, when the police are able to "close the books" on crimes, they appear to be effective in their crime-solving efforts. The normal practice of bargaining with an offender when she is willing to take responsibility for other unsolved crimes is an efficient way to improve clearance statistics (Sudnow, 1965). Especially when crime control values dominate, improving clearance rates may become the goal, rather than serving as a means to achieve the goal of community safety. Police may be tempted to give the person in custody details of a crime so that he can confess or give testimony against another in exchange for a lesser charge. In homicide cases, the extraordinary pressures to solve the case may provoke police to take shortcuts that (if known) would jeopardize the confidence in the evidence gathered. If questionable behavior is used to solve a crime, it is likely that such actions will be undetected, since covering up questionable behavior is another bureaucratic adaptation to protect the department from outside criticism. Consequently, errors may be injected into the death penalty investigation with only the best of motives to blame. Unfortunately, these errors are likely to happen when the police lose sight of their ethical responsibility to the suspect in their passion to solve the crime.

In Missouri clemency cases, eleven of the fifty clemency petitions (22 percent) raise issues concerning police misconduct during the investigation (see table 2.1). In each of these eleven cases, the police actions began a course of events that the accused were not able to overcome. The most common complaint concerning the police was the coercion of an unreliable confession, mentioned in four of the eleven cases. In three clemency petitions, false testimony by police or prison guards was claimed. In four of the clemency petitions, police gave some sort of reward to witnesses to give testimony against the accused. These are serious charges of police misconduct and may be responsible for wrongful convictions and death sentences. Nine (82 percent) of these eleven petitioners claim that they were actually innocent of the crime, while two claim they were only guilty of second degree murder.

TABLE 2.1
Claims of Police Misconduct

Misconduct	Frequency	Cases
Coercion of confession	4	Thomas Battle, Walter Blair, Donald Reese, Jessie Wise
False testimony by police or prison guards	3	A. J. Bannister, Frank Guinan, Lloyd Schlup
Reward to witness	4	Walter Blair, Maurice Byrd, Larry Griffin, Donald Reese
Suggestive photo identification	1	Larry Griffin
Denial of attorney during interrogation	3	A. J. Bannister, Darrell Mease, Glen Sweet

We know that the police are instrumental in shaping cases through their investigations. Radelet, Bedau, and Putnam (1992) highlight wrongful capital convictions in which the rush to identify a suspect leads to overlooking evidence that points to another suspect. In the press to make an arrest, since certainty can be manufactured, errors are less important than closure. The two selections presented in this chapter portray police practices that may have focused too soon on "making the case," such that the resulting convictions and death sentences are cast in doubt when later investigation is conducted. The case studies presented here are examples of two common problems of police investigations identified in the clemency petitions: unreliable confessions and reliance on false testimony. The cases also foreshadow our later discussions with the inclusion of other defects in the legal system that contribute to the unreliability of the result. We will see that what begins as a flawed investigation is ratified throughout the legal process.

CASE STUDY:
UNRELIABLE CONFESSIONS

Donald Reese, CP#65

Mr. Reese was found guilty of killing Chris Griffith and James Watson at a rifle range in 1988. His conviction and sentence were based on a coerced inculpatory statement that was written by a sheriff for Mr. Reese to sign. No fingerprints or other unique physical evidence connected him to the crimes. Many leads were developed during the investigation that should have led law enforcement to other suspects.

▼▲▼

Application for a Reprieve from, or Commutation of, a Sentence of Death[3]

This petition is presented on behalf of Donald E. Reese, who is scheduled to die by lethal injection on August 13, 1997 at 12:01 A.M. Mr. Reese is presently being held in the administrative segregation unit at the Potosi Correctional Center under warrant of death issued by the Missouri Supreme Court.

Mr. Reese respectfully requests that Governor Carnahan issue an indefinite stay of execution in order for Mr. Reese to present facts and evidence in support of this application. His conviction for murder and sentence of death were based on a coerced inculpatory [incriminating] statement that was written by a sheriff for Mr. Reese to sign. Counsel has accumulated substantial information that should have been presented at trial that Mr. Reese was clinically depressed and probably suicidal at the time of the involuntary statement. In addition, there were no fingerprints or other unique physical evidence connecting him to the crimes, and many leads were developed during the investigation that should have led law enforcement to other suspects.

Evidence to be presented will show that Mr. Reese received inadequate representation by counsel at trial. The procedural restrictions placed upon the federal courts prevented meaningful review of his constitutional claims. Evidence was available prior to trial that at the time of the offenses, Mr. Reese, a victim of child abuse, and a passive, dependent personality with an IQ in the low 80's, suffered severe emotional problems related to estrangement from his wife. This information will show that Mr. Reese's convictions were tainted by the coerced statement, and that he is not an appropriate candidate for the death penalty. Mr. Reese is seeking a new trial. If, however, the facts presented are not sufficient to set aside his conviction, then he is requesting a commutation of his sentence of death to life in prison.

While it has abdicated its responsibility to provide meaningful federal review of constitutional claims in death cases (Palacios, 1996), the United States Supreme Court has determined that the Office of the Governor has the obligation to be a "fail safe" in our criminal justice system (*Herrera v. Collins*, 1993). As Judge Lay of the United States Court of Appeals for the Eighth Circuit so eloquently stated:

> What separates the unlawful killing by man and the lawful killing by the state are the legal barriers that exist to preserve the individual's constitutional rights and protect against the unlawful execution of a death sentence. If the law is not given strict adherence, then we as a society are just as guilty of a heinous crime as the condemned felon. It should thus be readily apparent that the legal process in a civilized society must not rush to judgment and thereafter rush to execute a person found guilty of taking the life of another (*Mercer v. Armontrout*, 8th Cir. 1988 at 1431).

If given the opportunity, counsel will present evidence that Mr. Reese's conviction and death sentence arose from an inadequate legal process which does not contain sufficient procedural safeguards to correct its defects. Mr. Reese would not be viewed as a threat to society and is not a reasonable candidate for execution.

The Crime and the Investigation

. . . The murder of four men at the Marshall Junction Wildlife Area shooting range on September 9, 1986, initiated the largest investigation known to that area of Missouri. The blood-covered bodies of two victims were found in the back seat of a car on the parking lot. Another body was behind the car, and the fourth victim was found many yards away in the underbrush. All had been shot several times.

The Marshall Junction Wildlife Area was known by residents to be a drug sale location. Two victims had possessed fifteen hundred dollars in one hundred dollar bills. They had claimed to be going to Marshall Junction Wildlife Area to test a repaired rifle, but they could have used a rifle range within blocks of the place where the rifle had been repaired.

The rural major case squad investigation was headed by the elected sheriff of Lafayette County. There was tremendous public pressure to make an arrest. At the scene, investigators seized hundreds of spent shell casings from various caliber weapons, an unopened pack of Marlboro cigarettes, a Pepsi hat, a 30.06 caliber rifle and a .22 pump action shotgun.

Investigators discovered that five people had purchased .30 caliber ammunition in Marshall, Missouri within the previous two years. Mr. Reese's purchase was two years before the murders; the other four purchases were all more recent. One of the other purchasers, an unemployed man, purchased jewelry with a $100.00 bill on the day of the murders. He smoked Marlboro cigarettes and owned a .30 caliber weapon. A bank teller made change for one-hundred dollar bills for two men the day after the murders: neither man was Donald Reese. A victim's gas credit card was used at a gas station in another town. The user was not Donald Reese.

Investigators went to Mr. Reese's home on September 14, 1986 to ask him about the ammunition purchase. Later that day, investigators returned with the chief investigator and another sheriff. They searched Mr. Reese's house and car, and discovered Marlboro cigarettes in hard and soft packs, a small box of .30 carbine magazines, and a red baseball cap. A spent .30 caliber shell casing was found in the cowling of Mr. Reese's car. He was very cooperative and even talked to the investigators about his marital problems: his wife Kathy, upon whom he was emotionally dependent, had recently taken the two children and left him.

Donald Reese was arrested without a warrant and taken to the head-quarters of the rural major case squad on September 15, 1986. He was advised of his *Miranda* rights and signed a waiver. He was questioned by two investigators. Mr. Reese denied any involvement in the murders, and asked whether the investigators thought he needed a lawyer. He was interrogated again later that day and continued to deny any involvement in the crimes.

At 10:15 at night on September 15, Mr. Reese was escorted through a hostile crowd to his arraignment in the Saline County Courthouse. He was charged with four counts of first degree murder, four counts of armed criminal action and three counts of first degree robbery.

Mr. Reese was again interrogated the next morning. He denied any involvement in the crimes. During this interrogation, he filled out an application for public defender services, checking the box marked "YES" when answering the question whether he wanted public defender representation. A lawyer was not provided for him at this time.

The chief investigator took over the interrogation in the afternoon, and the questioning went on for six hours. During that time, the investigator brought in Mr. Reese's estranged wife, who harangued him about money during two separate meetings. She had been told that she would receive a reward if she helped extract a confession from her husband. Later, she received $500.00. Immediately after the second meeting with Kathy, the chief investigator wrote out a five page statement which Mr. Reese signed. That night, he took members of the major case squad to the location of his gun and the billfolds of three of the victims.

No evidence at trial connected Mr. Reese to the crimes except for the statement written by the chief investigator. Mr. Reese's fingerprints were not on any shell casings; were not on the victims found in the car, nor on their car, even though the victims were allegedly dragged across the gravel and lifted into the car; were not on a box of shells located on top of those victims; were not on the Marlboro box found at the scene. None of his clothes had any trace of blood on them. His car did not have any trace of blood. This, even though one of the victims had a ruptured aorta. Mr. Reese's fingerprints were not on the victims' billfolds. No ballistics evidence was introduced at trial to connect any gun owned by Mr. Reese, nor any particular shell, nor to any wound of any victim. His knowledge of the location of the gun and billfolds is consistent with his having witnessed the murders.

The statement contains claims which are inconsistent with facts developed during the investigation. The statement says that Mr. Reese picked up all the shell casings he could find and threw them away along the road. The investigation reports state that shell casings were found all over the parking lot and shooting range, however, none were found along the road, although investigators searched a wide area. The statement says that Mr. Reese took a particular route to drive out of the area. However, a witness on the road stated that the vehicle he saw did not take that route. The statement claims that Mr. Reese chased Mr. Griffith across a grassy area and shot him. However, blood was found on the gravel but not on the grass. The statement says that Mr. Reese stole $50.00 bills from the victims, but the money hidden at the creek bed was in $100.00 denominations.

One reason why erroneous convictions occur in capital murder cases is that investigators are under a heightened level of pressure to close the case where a heinous crime is committed. Studies suggest that the extent to which a killing is brutal and horrifying and attracts public attention actually magnifies the danger of mistakes or misconduct (Gross, 1996). In Mr. Reese's case, the investigation stopped when he was arrested. But nothing connected him to the murders with any greater weight than could be applied to the other people who had been investigated. In addition, Mr. Reese was a member of the community with a home and family and a job. Police coercion and manipulation of a man in severe emotional distress resulted in a signed statement that should have had no evidentiary weight.

The Trial and the Lawyer

Coerced statements are inherently unreliable. . . . Police error was compounded by trial counsel's failure to actively raise the conflicting facts at

Mr. Reese's suppression hearing, and to raise Mr. Reese's clinical depression and susceptibility to suggestion. The pre-trial hearing on his motion to suppress the involuntary statement should have been used to show the court Mr. Reese's background, education, experience, and physical, mental and emotional health in order to evaluate his capacity to resist pressure in the police dominated atmosphere of custodial interrogation.

Counsel in Mr. Reese's federal habeas corpus case obtained a psychological evaluation through Dr. Richard Wetzel. Dr. Wetzel, a licensed psychologist, conducted several interviews and tests of Mr. Reese. He concluded that Mr. Reese was suffering from severe clinical depression at the time of the custodial interrogations, and that when his estranged wife told him at the jail that reconciliation was impossible, he was unable to consider his own best interests. Mr. Reese stated to Dr. Wetzel that at the time of his wife's final attack, he didn't care what happened to him: he told Dr. Wetzel that he hadn't committed the offenses, but since his marriage was over, he didn't care what happened to him. Had trial counsel presented this expert opinion at the suppression hearing, the statement could not have been used as evidence against Mr. Reese. Since there was no other direct incriminating evidence connecting Mr. Reese to the murders, the state would have had insufficient evidence to convict him.

The Constitution guarantees each citizen charged with a criminal offense the right to effective assistance of counsel (*Strickland v. Washington*, 1984). . . . Counsel's duty to make reasonable investigation goes so far as to include having sufficient information to make decisions as to which areas of trial strategy should be pursued and expanded upon and which should be disregarded.

Capital murder cases are bifurcated trials. First, the jury hears the guilt phase (whether this defendant committed the offenses charged) and then hears a new proceeding to consider punishment. Counsel's duty to investigate and make informed decisions about strategy extends to the penalty phase of the trial.

Trial counsel's strategy at trial was to raise reasonable doubt in the minds of the jurors that Mr. Reese was the perpetrator of the murders. Under this circumstance, it was obvious that the case would go to the penalty phase. However, trial counsel paid scant attention to the necessity to develop mitigating circumstances for the penalty phase. Although he had Mr. Reese examined cursorily by three mental health professionals, not one of them interviewed Mr. Reese's children, or his sisters, or his mother, or even his ex-wife. Not one of them had access to Mr. Reese's school and military records. The only interviewee was Mr. Reese himself, whom Dr. Modlin described as: "inept in conversation and communication. He seems a simply organized person without much capacity for thought, reflection, or imagination."

Dr. Wilcox administered the Inwald test. This is used to determine a person's suitability for employment in law enforcement and is utterly unsuitable in formulating or developing a criminal defense strategy or presenting mitigating evidence to a jury.

Dr. Daniel evaluated Mr. Reese the day before trial to determine whether at the time of the murders, Mr. Reese had suffered a paradoxical rage reaction to the prescription medication Librium. All Dr. Daniel could say is that Mr. Reese had a prescription for the medication.

The futility of the work of these mental health professionals is apparent by virtue of the fact that none testified during the guilt or penalty phases of the trial. Counsel in Mr. Reese's federal habeas corpus proceeding obtained Dr. Wetzel's to conduct an evaluation. All of the information Dr. Wetzel used in his evaluation was available to trial counsel. He visited Mr. Reese on four occasions totaling twenty hours, and had direct and indirect contact with family members and long-time friends. He would have testified, had he been permitted to, that Mr. Reese had a background of psychological impairment arising from his childhood victimization by a brutal father; a dismal childhood of abject poverty, and low intelligence. His findings include:

1. The killing of the four men is foreign to the character and personality of Mr. Reese.

2. Mr. Reese had severe clinical depression on the day of the shooting.

3. Mr. Reese has a chronic personality disorder with dependent and avoidant features.

4. Mr. Reese continued to be in a state of severe clinical depression and was unable to consider or care about his own best interests at the time . . . he confessed.

The penalty phase of a capital murder trial is frequently, as here, the only opportunity to present the defendant to the jury. The purpose of the penalty phase is to give the jury facts on which to consider any mitigating circumstances in favor of the defendant. Trial counsel hired a penalty phase lawyer to assist him only ten days before trial. The new lawyer interviewed family members for the first time *during the trial*. During the penalty phase, she asked five family members the same eight questions. No question was designed to elicit a response which would personalize Mr. Reese for the jury. Counsel should have given the jury facts to support:

1. Mr. Reese was under the influence of extreme mental or emotional disturbance at the time of the murders due to his marital problems and possible reaction to his prescription medication;

2. Mr. Reese had no significant criminal history. (The prosecution asked witnesses whether they knew of two twenty-three year old misdemeanors, but no conviction was ever placed in evidence.)

3. Mr. Reese is the father of two children and a member of a family who will deeply feel his loss if he is sentenced to death.

In a death penalty case, an individualized determination on the basis of the character of the individual and the circumstances of the crime is essential in the penalty selection stage (*Lockett v. Ohio,* [1978]). Certainly, the jury was entitled to know that "killing is foreign to the character and personality of Mr. Reese" before it made its penalty selection.

Trial counsel failed to present a scintilla of mitigating psychological evidence. It has been argued that the quality of legal representation is often the deciding factor in whether a defendant receives the death penalty (Bright, 1994). Courts of appeal base their decisions on the record below. Since there was no record below, Mr. Reese has been denied the right to present this mitigating evidence at any stage of the judicial process. Mr. Reese's trial was not "fair" as required by *Strickland,* because trial counsel abdicated his responsibility. Mr. Reese's case is, therefore, worthy of intervention.

▼▲▼ _____

Donald Reese's case generated considerable public attention focusing on the crime, which no doubt pressured the police to resolve the case quickly. The police tactics to obtain his confession were questionable: the denial of an attorney at the interrogation and psychologically coercive questioning. Giving a reward to Mr. Reese's ex-wife for her role in obtaining a confession gave the appearance of undue pressure, particularly when other suspects were not pursued. The police appeared to narrow their focus to one suspect and then create evidence to support their conclusion. Unfortunately for Mr. Reese, his defense attorney did not present any mitigating evidence at the trial. In death penalty cases, the bifurcation of the trial provides the opportunity to inform the jury about reasons to let the defendant live, rather than to impose the death penalty. Then, when new information was developed by a later attorney, it was denied a hearing in any court. Donald Reese was executed on August 13, 1997.

CASE STUDY:
FALSE TESTIMONY

Larry Griffin, CP#10

Larry Griffin was sentenced to death for the June 26, 1980, drive-by shooting of Quintin Moss, a known drug dealer. The alleged motive for the crime was revenge for Mr. Moss killing Mr. Griffin's brother several months earlier. The prosecution's only direct evidence of Mr. Griffin's guilt was presented through the eyewitness testimony of Robert Fitzgerald, a career criminal and federally protected witness, whose car allegedly had broken down on the corner shortly before the crime occurred.

Thirteen years later in a federal prison, Mr. Fitzgerald admitted committing perjury when he positively identified Mr. Griffin in court as the person he saw shoot Mr. Moss. Mr. Fitzgerald also testified that the police suggested to him that he pick out Mr. Griffin's photo before he did so. Also in 1993 another witness came forward with testimony supporting Mr. Griffin's innocence. Kerry Caldwell was a hit man for a drug gang that operated in St. Louis in the 1980s. In 1990 he also joined the federal witness protection program and became a prosecution witness in another case. He subsequently testified before a federal judge that he was the lookout man when three men—other than Mr. Griffin—killed Mr. Moss.

▼▲▼

Application for Executive Clemency and/or Commutation of a Sentence of Death[4]

The Crime and Police Investigation

Quintin Moss died of numerous gunshot wounds which he received at approximately 3:30 P.M. on June 26, 1980. Mr. Moss was gunned down on the corner of Sarah and Olive in St. Louis, Missouri, on that date in front of numerous witnesses.

Once the police arrived at the scene of the shooting, the police had difficulty finding anyone who would admit seeing anything. This is not uncommon in inner-city criminal investigations. Since the details of the crime were sketchy and because of the lack of cooperative witnesses, the police immediately focused on Larry Griffin and other members of his family as suspects. The police knew that Quintin Moss had been a suspect in the murder of Dennis Griffin, Larry Griffin's brother, which had occurred on or about January 1, 1980.

At the scene, the police encountered a white male who was later identified as Robert John Fitzgerald. At that time, Mr. Fitzgerald was living under an alias provided by the government as a federally protected witness. Mr. Fitzgerald was taken to the police station and shown a group of five photos of various suspects. Mr. Fitzgerald positively identified a photograph of Larry Griffin as being one of the three perpetrators of the drive-by shooting.

Later that same day, the St. Louis Police Department located the vehicle, a late model Chevrolet, used in the drive-by shooting of Quintin Moss. The police learned that the car was owned by an individual named Ronnie Thomas. Inside the trunk of the vehicle the murder weapons were found, as well as a red baseball cap and other items of physical evidence. The car and the various items were dusted for fingerprints, none of which were identified as belonging to Larry Griffin or any other suspect in the case.

The police investigation uncovered another witness, a St. Louis police officer named Andre Jones. Mr. Jones stated that on the afternoon of the murder, he saw three individuals coming out of a house in the City of St. Louis not too far from where the murder occurred, one of whom was carrying what appeared to be shotguns. One of the men was wearing a red baseball cap. Officer Jones later testified that one of the men was known to him to be Larry Griffin. However, Officer Jones described the man he identified as Larry Griffin as having facial hair, whereas eyewitness Robert Fitzgerald testified that the man he identified as Larry Griffin was clean shaven.

The police were also aware of the fact that a similar drive-by shooting had occurred at the same location, in which Quintin Moss was present, about six weeks prior to June 26, 1980. A couple of hours after this earlier shooting, the police chased and apprehended Larry Griffin and his nephew Reginald Griffin in a car which they believed matched the general description of the one used in the earlier drive-by shooting. No weapons were found on either of the Griffins and no charges were ever filed in connection with this incident. However, evidence of this previous incident was presented at trial.

Based upon Mr. Fitzgerald's photo identification and other circumstantial evidence, Larry Griffin was charged with the offense of capital murder for the shooting of Quintin Moss. He was arrested and jailed a few weeks later. Mr. Griffin's family retained a young attorney named Frederick Steiger to represent him at trial.

Inexperienced and Unprepared Trial Counsel

Mr. Steiger had been out of law school approximately two years and was engaged in a general criminal law practice at the time he was retained. Mr. Griffin's case was the first murder trial Mr. Steiger had defended in his career. Prior to that time, he had tried a few criminal cases involving less serious offenses. Mr. Steiger had never before been involved in the litigation of a death penalty trial.

In preparing for trial, Mr. Steiger took the deposition of Robert Fitzgerald. From the deposition Mr. Steiger learned of Mr. Fitzgerald's numerous criminal convictions, the fact that he had pending felony credit card fraud charges against him, and the fact that he was a federally protected witness. However, Mr. Steiger failed to conduct further inquiries or investigations into the reasons Mr. Fitzgerald was placed in the Federal Witness Protection Program. In addition, Mr. Fitzgerald steadfastly denied to the court that he had been offered any promises of leniency or other favorable plea bargains on his pending charges in exchange for his testimony against Mr. Griffin. [T]he jury returned with a guilty verdict for the offense of capital murder. Frederick Steiger has indicated that he was devastated and totally caught off guard by the jury's guilt phase verdict. As a result, he presented absolutely no evidence and very little argument during the penalty phase. The jury returned a death verdict after penalty phase deliberation. . . .

New Information

Recently Boston investigator Terrence McDonough was retained to locate and investigate the background of Mr. Fitzgerald. Mr. McDonough found through available court records and other information in the Boston area the reason that Mr. Fitzgerald was placed in the witness protection program. Mr. Fitzgerald was involved in the 1974 murder of a police officer in the Boston, Massachusetts area. He agreed to snitch on his codefendants, most notably a man named Myles Connor, who later stood trial for that offense. Had Mr. Griffin's jury heard that Mr. Fitzgerald was a federally protected witness because he was involved in the murder of a police officer, it would have severely damaged his credibility in the eyes of that jury.

. . . After a nearly six month search, Mr. McDonough located Robert John Fitzgerald in a Florida prison. While incarcerated in Florida, Mr. Fitzgerald told Mr. McDonough that he had committed perjury when he positively identified Larry Griffin in court as the person he saw shoot Quintin Moss. Mr. Fitzgerald further stated that, although he still stands by his photo identification, the police told him that Larry Griffin was involved before showing him the photo that he picked out at the police station. Mr. Fitzgerald later testified regarding these facts under oath in the evidentiary hearing before Judge Filippine on October 6, 1993.

Regarding the photo identification procedures, Mr. Fitzgerald testified that he was taken down to the police station shortly after the murder occurred. One of the police officers then threw a photograph which later turned out to be that of Larry Griffin in front of Mr. Fitzgerald and told him "we know that this man is involved." Thereafter, the same police officer showed him a photo array with five photographs, one of which was the previously mentioned photo of Larry Griffin. Not surprisingly, Mr. Fitzgerald picked out Larry Griffin's photo and at that time made a positive photo identification of Larry Griffin as being one of the men he observed shooting Quintin Moss.

Had the jury heard the circumstances surrounding the photo identification procedure, Mr. Griffin believes that the credibility of Mr. Fitzgerald's identification would have been severely undermined and could have very well led to his acquittal. The suggestive circumstances surrounding this photo ID could have given trial counsel additional ammunition in which to attack Mr. Fitzgerald's credibility and the reliability of his out-of-court identification of Larry Griffin.

More importantly, Mr. Fitzgerald completely recanted his positive in-court identification of Mr. Griffin during the trial. Mr. Fitzgerald has testified under oath that he could not identify Larry Griffin in-court as one of the persons he saw shoot Quintin Moss. Nevertheless, he identified him anyway. This testimony by Mr. Fitzgerald at Mr. Griffin's trial can only be described as plain and simple perjury.

Mr. Fitzgerald's recent revelations would have totally destroyed his credibility in the eyes of the jury. In fact, if he had told the truth before and during Mr. Griffin's trial, Mr. Griffin would have very likely been entitled to a directed verdict of acquittal or would not have been charged at all due to insufficient evidence. In any event, Mr. Griffin believes that no jury would have convicted him if Mr. Fitzgerald would have testified truthfully regarding his out-of-court and in-court identifications in this case. . . .

The Federal Courts

There has been a disturbing trend in recent federal habeas corpus jurisprudence. In numerous cases, the federal courts have turned a deaf ear to inmates' compelling claims of actual innocence. The difficult decision of whether a prisoner with a valid claim of actual innocence should die is left to the chief executives of the states involved. The United States Supreme Court in *Herrera v. Collins* (1993) held that federal courts cannot intervene to grant a death row inmate a new trial on the basis of a free-standing claim of actual innocence. [There must be some other constitutional claim raised beside a claim of actual innocence before the Supreme Court would consider the case.] In reaching this conclusion, the Supreme Court noted that the executive clemency, which is available in every state which has a death penalty, is the only available forum for inmates to assert their claims of innocence prior to execution.

Larry Griffin's claim of actual innocence has been repeatedly turned aside by the federal courts because under *Herrera*, it is practically impossible for a death row inmate to receive relief from the federal courts on a free-standing claim of actual innocence. Larry Griffin did not have any underlying constitutional violations which were not reviewed under the actual innocence exception. Under *Herrera*, Larry Griffin's claim that he is actually innocent without the presence of any accompanying constitutional violations could not be reviewed by the federal court.

Two years later, in *Schlup v. Delo* (1995), the Supreme Court noted the distinction between free-standing *Herrera* claims and the "gateway innocence" claims presented in Mr. Schlup's case. The court noted that for a petitioner to prevail on a *Herrera* claim, he must meet an extraordinarily high burden, that for all practical purposes would be all but impossible for a habeas petitioner to meet.

Therefore, Larry Griffin was placed in a tremendous legal bind as a result of the Supreme Court opinions in *Herrera* and *Schlup*. Because he had no independent constitutional violation flowing from his claim of actual innocence, he could not avail himself of the more lenient *Schlup* standard, where actual innocence can act as a gateway to review otherwise barred constitutional claims. Since his actual innocence claim was a free-standing one like *Herrera's*, the standard of review was so rigid that no habeas petitioner, including Larry Griffin, could possibly meet it. Therefore, Larry Griffin's actual innocence claim has been turned away by the federal courts.

The opinions in *Herrera* and *Schlup*, read in conjunction with each other, appear to create a classic "catch-22" situation which was recognized by former Justice Harry Blackmun:

> Having adopted an "actual innocence" requirement for review of abusive, successive, or defaulted claims, however, the majority would now take the position that "the claim of actual innocence" is not itself a constitutional

claim, but instead a gateway through which a habeas petitioner must pass to have his otherwise barred constitutional claim considered on the merits. In other words, having held that a prisoner who is incarcerated in violation of the constitution must show he is actually innocent to obtain relief, the majority would now hold that a prisoner who is actually innocent must show a constitutional violation to obtain relief. The only principle that would appear to reconcile these two positions is the principle that habeas relief should be denied whenever possible (*Herrera*, 113 S.Ct. at 880–881).

The judicial review of Larry Griffin's case embodies the fears of Justice Blackmun's dissent in which he warned against apparent "result oriented" jurisprudence emerging in capital habeas corpus litigation. An examination of the federal court's treatment of Larry Griffin's actual innocence claims gives a name and a face to Justice Blackmun's chilling warning about the hollowness of current federal habeas review of convictions and death sentences.

In federal district court, petitioner [Larry Griffin] presented the testimony of Robert John Fitzgerald, Kerry Caldwell, Terrence McDonough, and Frederick Steiger in the October 6, 1993 evidentiary hearing on the issue of actual innocence. In that hearing, Mr. Fitzgerald reiterated that he perjured himself when he positively identified Larry Griffin in court and Mr. Caldwell provided direct exonerating testimony based upon his eyewitness account of the shooting of Quintin Moss. [Mr. Caldwell did witness and take part in the June 26, 1980 drive-by shooting in which Quintin Moss was killed. Mr. Caldwell has testified under oath that he observed Mr. Moss on the corner of Sarah and Olive that afternoon dealing drugs. Mr. Caldwell immediately paged Daryl Smith. A few minutes thereafter, Daryl Smith, along with Humphrey Scott, and Ronnie Parker drove to Sarah and Olive in a car owned by Ronnie Thomas-Bey and shot Quintin Moss to death.] Nevertheless, Judge Filippine entered an order denying habeas relief, finding that neither Mr. Fitzgerald's nor Mr. Caldwell's testimony was sufficiently credible to justify habeas corpus relief.

Larry Griffin has attempted to point out the absurdity of this finding in both the Eighth Circuit and in the United States Supreme Court. Both of these courts, however, have turned a deaf ear to these claims. In fact, the Eighth Circuit did not even permit Larry Griffin, through counsel, to brief and argue the merits of his actual innocence claim before summarily rubber-stamping Judge Filippine's findings.

If given a full and fair opportunity in the courts, counsel would have pointed out the fallacy in Judge Filippine's findings which are ludicrous as a matter of common sense. In regard to Robert Fitzgerald, it is clear he had much to gain by falsely identifying Larry Griffin during his trial. Mr. Fitzgerald was incarcerated at the time he testified against Larry Griffin on several felony credit card charges. As soon as Larry Griffin was convicted, the St. Louis prosecutors marched him into court, agreed to let him be sentenced to time served and he was released from jail. Obviously, Mr. Fitzgerald had much to gain by falsely identifying Larry Griffin to the satisfaction of the prosecutors, namely his release from jail.

In contrast, Robert Fitzgerald had absolutely nothing to gain by coming forward some twelve years later and admitting he committed perjury in Larry Griffin's 1981 trial. The critical question becomes which statement is more credible: the 1981 trial testimony in which Mr. Fitzgerald felt pressured to identify Mr. Griffin to get his deal to be released from jail; or his 1993 recantation in which he exposed himself to potential perjury charges by recanting his in-court identification. The answer is obvious. The 1993 recantation, under any objective view of the totality of the circumstances, is the statement of Mr. Fitzgerald that has the most credibility. By analogy, under common law and most state hearsay rules, statements against penal interest are viewed to have enhanced credibility rather than diminished credibility as Judge Filippine apparently found under these circumstances. Therefore, petitioner believes that Judge Filippine's finding that Mr. Fitzgerald's 1993 statements lack credibility is totally without foundation and should be ignored by the Governor in reviewing this application.

Similarly, Judge Filippine found that Kerry Caldwell's testimony exonerating Larry Griffin lacked credibility. [One of the primary factors relied on by Judge Filippine in finding that Mr. Caldwell lacked credibility was the fact that Daryl Smith and Humphrey Scott are dead, and Ronnie Parker's whereabouts were unknown. It is now known that Mr. Parker is alive and serving a life sentence in Potosi for another murder.] This is also an extremely ironic and perverse conclusion in light of the fact that Mr. Caldwell had previously testified in the very same court for the federal government in the prosecution of the Moorish Temple defendants.[5] The court's treatment of the Caldwell credibility issue is a striking example of a perverse double standard that appears to exist in criminal cases. If a convicted felon gives testimony that helps the prosecution or the government, he is credible; however, if his testimony helps exonerate a criminal defendant, his testimony is unworthy of belief. Most experienced criminal practitioners are aware of this unspoken rule, which sadly pervades the criminal justice system and reeks of corruption and promotes injustice whenever it is followed. . . .

Because of the failure of the federal courts to intervene to prevent the unjust execution of an innocent man, this decision now falls to the Honorable Governor Carnahan as Chief Executive of the State of Missouri. Larry Griffin strongly believes a full review of the record in his case shows that his claim of innocence is real and substantial. In his case, the only eyewitness has stated under oath that his positive in-court identification of Larry Griffin was false and that his out-of-court photo identification was tainted by suggestive police misconduct. . . .

Ineffective Assistance of Counsel

Larry Griffin has alleged in his federal habeas litigation that his trial attorney, Frederick Steiger, was constitutionally ineffective in numerous respects. Mr. Griffin has noted earlier that Mr. Steiger was a young attorney, fresh out of law school, who had never tried a murder case at the time he proceeded to represent Larry Griffin in a trial for his life. To his credit, Mr. Steiger now candidly admits that he was overmatched by the experienced prosecutor. Mr. Steiger also candidly admits that he made numerous mistakes during Larry Griffin's trial. Finally, Mr. Steiger admits that he suffered from a common delusion among inexperienced attorneys who are handling their first capital trial, an irrational belief that the defendant would certainly be acquitted in the guilt stage, thus any preparation for the penalty phase would be unnecessary.

. . . The most glaring example of ineffective assistance of counsel was trial counsel's decision to put on an alibi defense without fully investigating the alibi for independent evidence that would either corroborate it or entirely destroy its credibility. Mr. Steiger put on an alibi defense through the testimony of Gilbert Greenlee, Larry Griffin's sister's boyfriend, that Larry Griffin was with him on the afternoon of the murder selling a boat to an unidentified man who had responded to an ad in *Trading Times* magazine.

Mr. Steiger's fundamental blunder, which is inexcusable behavior for any reasonably experienced attorney, was his failure to attempt to corroborate the alibi through records or live testimony from the representatives of *Trading Times* magazine. If Mr. Steiger had done his homework, he would have discovered the same evidence that the prosecution effectively used to rebut the alibi; that is, the records from *Trading Times* magazine, which strongly suggest that since the ad was canceled during working hours on the day of the murder, the actual sale of the boat probably took place the day before the murder. Had Mr. Steiger learned of this information before trial, he would have undoubtedly exercised his judgment not to put on this alibi defense and instead rely on the more reasonable theory of focusing his attack on the sufficiency and credibility of the prosecution's evidence. If this had been done, Larry Griffin is confident that he would have been acquitted of the murder in this case.

. . . Other glaring errors by counsel which deserve brief mention include the fact that counsel failed to put into evidence that Larry Griffin is left-handed to contradict Mr. Fitzgerald's previous testimony that the assailant he identified as Larry Griffin shot the victim with his right hand. Trial counsel also failed to call an available witness, Robert Campbell, who could have totally debunked the prosecution's contention that Larry Griffin was somehow involved in the previous drive-by shooting which occurred in May of 1980. Finally, Mr. Steiger completely failed to conduct any investigation or prepare in any fashion for the penalty phase of trial. . . .

Prosecution Misconduct

Larry Griffin also presented evidence to the federal courts that the prosecution failed to reveal exculpatory evidence to him which would have aided his defense at trial. First, the prosecution failed to reveal that Robert Fitzgerald was arrested a few months before the murder for false impersonation of a law enforcement officer and assault. Second, the prosecution failed to inform counsel of their knowledge of the reason Mr. Fitzgerald was placed in the witness protection program. Mr. Griffin also believes there were some serious improprieties involving the plea bargain given to Mr. Fitzgerald on his pending credit card fraud charges in exchange for his testimony against Mr. Griffin. The prosecution and Mr. Fitzgerald both denied any favorable plea bargain was given to Mr. Fitzgerald in exchange for his testimony. Yet, on the very day Larry Griffin was convicted of capital murder, prosecutors appeared with Mr. Fitzgerald in court, permitted him to be sentenced to time served, and he was immediately released from jail. These facts belie the impression given by the prosecutor and Mr. Fitzgerald that he had not received any favorable treatment in exchange for testimony against Mr. Griffin. If the jury had been made aware that Mr. Fitzgerald would immediately secure his release from jail after testifying, this fact could have seriously undermined his credibility. . . .

A complete examination of the record reveals that this case is not appropriate for the death penalty, and Mr. Griffin and his current counsel are at a loss to understand why it was viewed as a death penalty case at the time which it was tried. From this counsel's experience as a criminal defense attorney, he is unaware of any other Missouri case involving a drug related drive-by shooting in which the death penalty was either sought or obtained. In fact, during this counsel's career as an assistant public defender in the 1980's (the same period in which this case falls) when drug related drive-by shootings sadly became commonplace, such crimes were almost always charged as second-degree murder. It was extremely rare for such a case to even justify a first-degree murder charge, and in those cases the death penalty was always waived. Thus, even if the evidence of Mr. Griffin's guilt was overwhelming, this would not be an appropriate case for which this state should dole out the ultimate punishment. Coupled with the fact that there are serious questions as to whether Mr. Griffin is guilty and whether he received a fair trial, his execution for this crime would be unconscionable. . . .

In a capital case it would offend fundamental notions of justice and fairness to permit an execution to go forward if there is any doubt whatsoever regarding the guilt of the condemned. Larry Griffin's case is riddled with doubt. To permit his execution under these circumstances would forever stain the integrity of Missouri's system of justice. Governor Carnahan should therefore act, under the powers vested in him by the constitution and laws of the State of Missouri, to prevent this travesty of justice from occurring.

▼▲▼

In Larry Griffin's case, the police prematurely focused on one suspect and ignored other clues, then tainted the process of the eyewitness identification. As a result, the key witness gave false testimony and a false identification. False testimony is a very critical problem in jury trials, because jurors give a tremendous amount of credit to eyewitnesses. In this case, the jury received an inaccurate accounting of the evidence. In addition, the prosecutors made a deal with their "star" witness and withheld evidence about him, giving them an unfair advantage over the defense. In essence, the jury did not have complete or accurate information when they made their decision. These defects were worsened by the inexperience of Mr. Griffin's defense counsel. Finally, the federal courts were deaf to these significant issues, including much new information developed by the post-conviction attorney. Mr. Griffin was executed on June 21, 1995.

CONCLUSIONS

In this chapter, we have seen allegations of serious police misconduct that were compounded by ineffective assistance of counsel and procedural barriers in the courts. The objective of the clemency petitions is to build the most favorable case possible to persuade the governor to grant a reprieve of the death sentence. The petitions offer new evidence not considered by the jury but which is both verifiable and reliable. While clemency petitions are admittedly partisan, the issues they raise are troubling.

We have seen that both cases in this chapter suffered from poor lawyering and were unsuccessful in persuading the federal courts to review the substance of their issues. In each of these cases, it is possible that an experienced and well-funded trial lawyer could have overcome the initial problems created by the police.

These applications for clemency bring serious allegations before the governor. Although located in individual petitions, these complaints are more than allegations concerning individual bad actors. Rather, the commendable police motivation to keep the community safe likely leads to an overeagerness to make arrests in homicide cases as an "end" in itself (Crank and Caldero, 2000: 8). These clemency petitions point to serious systemic flaws in the investigative function of police.

Although the topic of this chapter is police misconduct, in both of these cases there are multiple problems created by the criminal justice system that commingle to jeopardize the effective administration of justice. In the United States, the police and the prosecutors are closely aligned. If the police make errors, we expect the prosecutors to make adjustments to reach the correct outcome. We turn next to a closer look at the role of prosecutors to assess their ability to do justice in these death penalty cases.

CHAPTER THREE

THE PROSECUTOR'S MISCONDUCT

In addition, the state withheld evidence and misled the jury on a critical issue that could have affected the credibility of Ernest Jones' testimony. At the time he testified against Mr. Blair, Jones was facing pending felony charges in Jackson County for the offenses of assault, burglary and drug possession. Mr. Jones testified under oath that he had not been offered any deals or promises of leniency by the Prosecutor's Office on these pending charges in exchange for his testimony against Mr. Blair. Ironically, less than a month after Mr. Blair's trial had ended, Mr. Jones appeared in court and received probation on these pending charges. The prosecutor's own statements to the court at the Ernest Jones' sentencing hearing indicate that Mr. Jones perjured himself at trial with the assent and knowledge of the prosecutor:

I had several discussions with Mr. Jones and his attorney prior to his testifying [against Walter Blair], telling him that I thought for tactical reasons it would be better not to discuss the specifics of a plea bargain in this case, but that I would make sure and recommend a lenient disposition of this case in exchange for his probation—or words to that effect—or in exchange for his cooperation. Mr. Jones' attorney, Mr. Peter Sterling, also testified under oath that he had reached a tacit agreement with Mr. Bell that Mr. Jones would not have to go to the penitentiary on any of his pending charges if he testified for the state against Walter Blair.

Moreover, Prosecutor Bell was caught using perjured testimony of a similar nature in another Jackson County capital murder case, State v. Dale Patterson (1981). In that case, the Missouri Supreme Court reversed Patterson's capital murder conviction due to the fact that Bell had not disclosed to the defense that he had agreed to dismiss pending charges against the state's star witness. The fact that both state and federal courts have not granted Mr. Blair any relief on the basis of the prosecutor's use of perjured testimony should not prevent Governor Carnahan from exercising his discretion to commute Mr. Blair's sentence. It would offend basic notions of fairness and justice to permit the use of perjured testimony to be used by the state to execute Walter Blair while Dale Patterson is permitted to live.

FROM THE CLEMENCY PETITION
for Walter Blair, CP#8,
executed July 21, 1993[1]

We have seen in the previous chapter that prosecutors rely on the police to develop the initial details of a murder case. It is the responsibility of the police to identify the suspect and the responsibility of the prosecutor to get a conviction. Both share responsibility in developing the evidence to "make the case."

THE PROMISE OF THE
PROSECUTOR'S ROLE

Like the police, prosecutors operate under ethical rules that guide their actions and limit the abuse of powers. These ethical rules can be found in the American Bar Association's *Lawyers' Manual on Professional Conduct* (1997). These model rules make clear that the role of the prosecutor is that of a "minister of justice" and it is not simply an advocate. The prosecutor is to "seek justice, not merely to convict" (Pizzi, 1999: 137). This expectation to seek justice can be at odds with the more concrete and publicly pressing need to "win" a conviction at trial. And yet the obligation to uphold justice goes to the heart of the legal system. Thus, the ideal prosecutor should search actively for "facts and law that would clear the innocent as well as for evidence to charge and convict the guilty" (Holten and Lamar, 1991: 120). This dual role is difficult to maintain when the political pressures of the job demand responsiveness to public fears. The public wants the "bad guys" convicted and lacks understanding of the prosecutor's responsibility to protect the innocent. The media shape these public views when giving most attention to the crime and to arrests, but to little else. The inference is drawn that an arrest is the same as guilt, and if the system is effective, a conviction is inevitable. This public focus on conviction is exacerbated by the fact that, in many jurisdictions, the prosecutor is an elected position, and just as the police look to clearance rates to evaluate their effectiveness, prosecutors use rates of conviction as the primary evidence of their job performance. Not having personal access to the daily reality of the prosecutor's office, the public sees only outcomes (that is, convictions or acquittals), not *how* those outcomes were obtained. Additionally, measuring and communicating indicators of process to outsiders is very difficult. As a result, accountability issues will lead to an emphasis on convictions to the exclusion of process, which is not unlike the police reliance on arrests.

And yet, the importance of fair play in the adversarial process is clear in the Model Rules presented in *Lawyers' Manual on Professional Conduct* (ABA 61: 607):

> The prosecutor's job isn't just to win, but to win fairly, staying well within the rules. As a "minister of justice" the prosecutor is required by the ethical standards "to see that the defendant is accorded procedural justice and that guilt is decided on the basis of sufficient evidence."

Elements of fairness include not withholding evidence that could help the defense (ABA 61: 601) and not alluding to evidence that is not otherwise admissible (ABA 61: 725). Stated positively, the prosecutor is obligated to turn over to the trial attorney any information that could, in any way, assist the defendant. This fairness requirement is the basis of a constitutional decision (*Brady v. Maryland* [1967]). In *Brady v. Maryland*, the Supreme Court held that no matter what the motivation,

> the suppression by the prosecutor of evidence favorable to an accused upon request violates due process where the evidence is material either to guilt or to punishment, irrespective of the good faith or the bad faith of the prosecutor.

Model Rule 3.8(d) makes this expectation very broad, requiring "disclosure of exculpatory evidence without regard to its significance and without any defense request" (ABA 61: 601).

The National District Attorneys Association also promulgates standards for the behavior of prosecutors. For example, Standard 17.17 states that closing arguments at trial should be "characterized by fairness, accuracy, rationality and a reliance upon the evidence" (Healy, 1977: 278). In this standard we see the professional obligation to uphold the process of doing justice in the course of attempting to prove the defendant guilty beyond a reasonable doubt. No doubt these professional guidelines are needed as explicit reminders of duty to counterbalance the tendency to focus exclusively on convictions. The rules themselves state that their purpose is to secure fair competition in the adversary system (ABA 61: 701) and also to preserve public confidence in the office of the prosecutor (ABA 61: 616). A related consequence is the preservation of the overall integrity of the system.

THE REALITY

> In real life of course, prosecutors must win and hold onto office if they are to put into effect their ideals of justice. On the other hand, it is well to keep in mind that a prosecutor who values a political career to the detriment of doing what he or she senses to be justice is unworthy of the office (Holten and Lamar, 1991: 194).

Often the prosecutor will campaign on the platform of being tough on crime, tougher than the opponent, and point to a record of convictions to persuade the public that he or she is the best candidate for the position. The focus on these outcomes blurs the equally valued, but more difficult to measure, quality of process. Consequently *doing justice* comes to mean only punishing the guilty without worrying much about *how* persons are found to be guilty. Similar to the pressures in police work, the focus on conviction rates can result in shortchanging the important values of due process and fairness, with a related possibility that increasingly persons who are not guilty will be convicted.

With respect to the prosecutor's role, there are many sources for error to enter into the trial outcome. Huff, Rattner, and Sagarin (2000) report that wrongful convictions can result from plea bargaining, community pressure for a conviction, false accusations, knowledge of a criminal record, errors by medical examiners and forensic science experts, errors in criminal record keeping and computerized information systems, and voluntary or deliberate false confessions, among other factors. Some of these factors show up in Missouri clemency petitions.

In twenty-two of the fifty Missouri clemency petitions (44 percent), strong claims were made that the prosecutors overstepped the line of legitimate advocacy in their desire to obtain convictions (see table 3.1). The various types of excess are not inconsequential. "When courts and commentators talk about prosecutorial misconduct, they usually are referring to the prosecutor's argument to the jury" (ABA 61: 616). This conclusion is supported by the Missouri experience with the most common complaint about prosecutorial misconduct referring to excessive statements made to the jury. In twelve (55 percent) of these twenty-two cases, the prosecutor's argument to the jury was overzealous and inappropriate in some way that could rise to constitutional significance. The death row petitioners argue that this type of excessiveness is not just "harmless" error. This type of argumentation by the prosecutor should be considered unconstitutional because whatever was said would unfairly influence jurors in their decision making.

In research that discloses over four hundred Americans wrongly convicted of crimes punishable by death, Michael Radelet, Hugo Bedau, and Constance Putnam (1992) underscore the role of prosecutors in creating wrongful convictions by withholding exculpatory evidence from the defense. As we have seen, whatever their motives, such

TABLE 3.1
Claims of Prosecutorial Misconduct

Misconduct	Frequency	Cases
Argument to jury	12	Walter Blair, William Ted Boliek, Ralph Davis, Emmitt Foster, Larry Griffin, David Leisure, Kelvin Malone, Sam McDonald, Roy Ramsey, James Rodden, Robert Walls, Jessie Wise
Withholding exculpatory evidence	9	Walter Blair, Emmitt Foster, Larry Griffin, Robert Murray, Robert O'Neal, Glen Sweet, Robert Walls, Doyle Williams, Jessie Wise
Deal with witness	5	Larry Griffin, Bruce Kilgore, Robert Murray, Doyle Williams, Jessie Wise
Peremptory jury strikes	2	Maurice Byrd, Milton Griffin El
Timely notice/surprise witness	2	Bruce Kilgore, Winford Stokes

actions clearly violate ethical and constitutional expectations. With-holding exculpatory evidence from the defense shows up in Missouri clemency petitions as an issue in nine (18 percent) of the fifty clemency petitions (or 41 percent of the cases with prosecutor issues). In five of the clemency petitions (10 percent), witnesses who falsely (according to the petition) identified the condemned as the killer were rewarded by the prosecution for their testimony. This type of deal making leads to unreliability in the murder conviction as well as in the death sentence. Since the juries were not aware of these problems with the evidence, their deliberations were based on incomplete or even false information.

Normally, prosecutors have a self-interest in sustaining convictions to demonstrate their success. So when prosecutors support the clemency application, governors traditionally have used the prosecutor's support as a standard to grant clemency (Abramowitz and Paget, 1964). Such action by prosecutors clearly embodies their role as "minister of justice." In two of the Missouri clemency cases (4 percent), the prosecutor became a witness before the governor on behalf of the condemned. Unfortunately, their supplications did not prevail and the death row prisoner was executed.

The three cases presented next were chosen to reflect the major issues that are mentioned in the clemency petitions concerning the prosecutor's role in capital cases. They highlight the prosecutor's role in potentially contaminating the jury's decision-making ability. Death sentences that are obtained when the prosecutor withholds exculpatory evidence from the defense or excludes all African-American members of the jury pool or makes unconstitutional arguments to the jury are flawed decisions. Either the jury does not have complete information or the fundamental fairness of the jury itself is at issue. These selected petitions illustrate how these significant questions were not addressed in the courts and as a result come to the governor's desk for resolution. Although these cases were chosen for their focus on the prosecutor's behavior, they all include other themes as well. The interaction of the several issues makes it difficult to separate them and should strengthen their appeal to the governor.

CASE STUDY:
WITHHOLDING EXCULPATORY EVIDENCE
AND ARGUMENTS TO THE JURY

Emmitt Foster, CP#29

Codefendant Michael Phillips received a life sentence plus two thirty-year sentences for the 1983 killing of Travis Walker and the related assault of Deann Keys in North St. Louis. Emmitt Foster was sentenced to death although there was evidence to support his claim of innocence. The prosecution withheld exculpatory evidence in the investigation report, and there was no physical evidence to link Mr. Foster to the scene of the crime. The prosecutor made improper racial comments during the closing arguments.

▼▲▼
Application for a Reprieve from,
or Commutation of, a Sentence of Death[2]

Factual Background

Travis Walker and Deann Keys shared a one bedroom apartment at the Northland Village Apartments, 7425 Park Town South, Apt. 202. Travis Walker died as a result of gunshot wounds he sustained in the early hours of November 20, 1983. Ms. Keys received four gunshot wounds to the head. However, she lived and was the star witness for the prosecution and testified as to the events that took place the morning of November 20, 1983. There was no physical evidence to link Emmitt Foster to the murder of Travis Walker or to the assault on Ms. Keys.

At trial, Ms. Keys testified to the following: she was awakened by the ringing of her telephone at 2:00 A.M. on November 20, 1983. Ms. Keys recognized the caller's voice as that of Michael Phillips, a friend of Travis Walker's and also a teammate on the same softball team. Ms. Keys testified that Mr. Walker spoke to the caller and hung up in an angry mood saying that Mr. Phillips had called seeking help with a flat tire. Mr. Walker left the apartment and Ms. Keys remained in bed. She next heard Mr. Walker and two other men. Although she could not see the men from the bedroom, Ms. Keys recognized one of the voices as that of Michael Phillips. Ms. Keys testified that Mr. Phillips then asked Mr. Walker permission to use the telephone and for a towel to dry off from the rain. Ms. Keys testified that Mr. Phillips entered the bedroom, pointing the gun at her. He ordered her to rise and go into the living room. She then testified that she was ordered by Mr. Phillips to lie down on the floor next to Mr. Walker, who was already lying on the floor. Ms. Keys testified it was at this time she saw the second assailant who she knew to be John Lee. Ms. Keys testified Mr. Phillips ransacked the apartment looking for jewelry. She heard a shot, felt a shot and lost consciousness. When Ms. Keys awoke, she was bleeding from her mouth. She testified she left the apartment to get help and she was seen outside her apartment by Tyrone Mitchell who testified Ms. Keys "was bleeding out of the mouth and everything." Ms. Keys returned to the apartment and wrote the names "John Lee" and "Michael Phillips" on an envelope. The police were summoned and at that time, Ms. Keys was back in her apartment. St. Louis Police Officer, Scott Johnston, arrived on the scene within minutes. Accompanying him was Officer Michael Busalaki. They found Travis Walker lying face down in the living room area of the apartment with "a large pool of blood around his head and no apparent signs of life." They heard moaning from the bedroom and found Ms. Keys lying on the bed face down "and she was bleeding extremely a large amount of blood dripping from her mouth and her facial area." According to Officer Johnston "every time she opened her mouth, blood would come out." Because there was no physical evidence such as fingerprints, footprints, hair samples or any other evidence that Emmitt Foster had been to the apartment the night of November 20, 1983, the state's case relied on the testimony of Deann Keys. Ms. Keys testified she heard Travis Walker enter the apartment with two individuals. She recognized the voice of Michael Phillips, although she did not recognize the voice of the second individual who was with Phillips. Ms. Keys was asked:

Q: Could you see them when they came in from where you were?
A: No.
Q: From the bedroom you cannot see into the hallway?
A: No.

In order for her to see and identify the second assailant, she would have had to have left the bedroom in order to identify the person whose voice she did not know.

Exculpatory Evidence Withheld from the Defense

The state, knowing that the case hinged on the testimony of Deann Keys, withheld exculpatory evidence; that being the investigation report signed by Sydney R. Anderson, Investigator, and approved by Raymond Harris and George Gantnep, M.D., chief medical examiner, St. Louis County, Missouri. The report of Sydney R. Anderson entitled, *Evidence in the Matter of Travis Walker, Deceased,* details the observations he made of the crime scene, his observations of the victim's body and objects in the room specifically in the area where Mr. Walker's body was found. Investigator Anderson also makes the following observation in his report: "Ms. Keys was unable to talk due to damage from her wound, but from evidence at the apartment, it appears that she was in bed when she was shot." This was crucial information. Not only did it directly point to evidence which showed Ms. Keys was shot in the bedroom, it also corroborates a report that was taken at Normany Osteopathic Hospital which states "Ms. Keys was shot while in bed." Neither of these two pieces of information was presented to the jury. This information directly contradicts the testimony of the key witness and raises reasonable doubt to the events as reported by Ms. Keys. This exculpatory information, the report of Sydney Anderson, was not presented to the defense. Lead defense attorney, William Alyward, presented an affidavit on Emmitt's behalf which states in pertinent part at paragraph 4:

> This report was never turned over to me as defense counsel for Mr. Foster. I make this statement with certainty because Mr. Anderson states in his report that he believed Deann Keys to have been shot while in bed. This evidence would have been critical to Mr. Foster's defense and would have been used to prove Mr. Foster was actually innocent of the crime as well as to impeach and discredit the testimony of Ms. Keys.

The prosecution's case was shaky at best. There was no physical evidence to link Emmitt to the scene of the crime. The only eyewitness had sustained four gunshot wounds to the back of the head prior to the identification of her assailants, and from all indications was shot in an area of the apartment which would have precluded her from seeing the second assailant. In order for the state to make its case, they had to ensure that this evidence, which would have presented reasonable doubt as to the guilt of Emmitt Foster, did not come before the jury. They succeeded in doing so and in the process, violated Mr. Foster's constitutional rights under United States Supreme Court precedent, *U.S. v. Bagley* (1985) and *Brady v. Maryland* (1963). These cases hold that undisclosed evidence becomes "material" if there is a reasonable probability that the outcome of the trial would have been different had the evidence been disclosed. All of the physical evidence in the apartment points to the fact that Mr. Walker was shot in the living room and Ms. Keys was shot in the bedroom. Police investigative reports go into detail in the contents of the living room of the apartment, making note of "a green colored plastic woman's hair curler was observed about 1 foot above (south of) the victim's head." However, there is no mention in the report of blood on the floor in the position where Ms. Keys states she was shot. There was, however, a large pool of blood that was mentioned under the head of Mr. Walker, and the report of Mr. Anderson as well as the police report make mention of the blood in the bed where Ms. Keys was found. All of this information points to the fact that Ms. Keys was shot in the bedroom and did not have the opportunity to see the second assailant. No jury has been presented with this evidence. The evidence would have been critical to a fair trial and Mr. Foster has been denied his constitutional rights to due process and equal protection under the law due to the prosecution's withholding of exculpatory evidence and the state stands poised to execute an individual who is innocent of the murder for which he is sentenced to die. . . .

Improper Closing Argument by the Prosecution

The prosecution injected passion and prejudice into the mitigation phase of the trial in an attempt to assure the sentence of death. Mr. Foster presented as mitigation evidence parishioners of an African Methodist Episcopal Church to which he belonged. These individuals testified to his participation in various church projects, church activities and attending morning services. During cross-examination of one of these witnesses, the prosecution displayed a picture of an individual wearing a Muslim fez and sitting between an American flag and a Muslim flag and asked the individual if they knew that Emmitt Foster was a Muslim. The picture was never disclosed to the defense prior to trial and it has never been substantiated that this is a picture of Emmitt Foster nor is it known when the picture was taken. The use of the picture clearly violated Mr. Foster's constitutional rights and was used to inflame the passions and prejudices of the jury. In closing argument, the prosecution went on to fan the flames of prejudice by making improper personal references to Emmitt Foster. The prosecutor made the following statements:

> A friend, a friend for a few bucks, some pieces of jewelry, that's the manner of man they will have us believe we shouldn't do this. Let him go among the prison population, a prison population where every day other people are locked up for lesser crimes. Guards have to come to work unarmed. You have no right to do that with this man. I submit to you that that's what we mean by deterring him. They too, the people who have to go to the penitentiary for other crimes which they have committed have lesser but certain rights and they have a right not to be exposed to *that* and the guards while they do an unbelievably courageous job have a right to some protection. They have a right to *that* (indicating Mr. Foster) not being there and that's what we call deterring him.

The prosecution went on to say in its closing argument:

> They [referring to the victim's family] have the right to have their son and grandson and brother for the rest of his natural life until somebody superior to us deemed it time for him to die and not *that* (indicating Mr. Foster).

The prosecution then argued, using reference to the Muslim religion by stating:

> It is right that he should be executed. There has been some religious discussion here. The Christians have the Golden Rule "do unto others what you would have them do unto you." Muslim's [*sic*] reverse this process and the Koran says "do not do unto others what you would have him to do unto you." And Confucius says "man should do that which is right not for hope of reward or for fear of punishment. Man should do what is right because that is what it means to be a man." That is what is the essence of man and *that* (indicating Mr. Foster) is no man.

The prosecution had one intention and that was to de-humanize Emmitt Foster to make him less than a person in order to make it easier for the jury to come back with a sentence of death. This was clearly improper. To compound that, the prosecution relied on passion and prejudice based on race and religion and improperly presented impeachment evidence from the cross-examination to bring in the question of race and religion. The prosecutor clearly understood bringing up the Muslim religion in front of an all white jury would play upon any racial animus the jury might harbor and subject Mr. Foster to the prejudice and narrowmindedness of those who would be inclined to feel differently about people of other races and religions. This clearly inappropriate argument went without objection or the judge's admonishment of the prosecutor of his improper closing argument. All of this to the prejudice of Emmitt Foster and done by the prosecutor in order to assure the penalty of death. This was clearly unreasonable, unconstitutional and should be addressed at this time by the only recourse Emmitt Foster has left to him, that of executive clemency.

Ineffective Assistance of Counsel

. . . Emmitt Foster was denied effective assistance of counsel in violation of *Strickland v. Washington* (1984) due to his attorney's failure to inform him of his right to testify at the penalty phase of his trial. Mr. Foster presented an ineffective assistance of counsel claim in the state courts of Missouri and again to the federal district court. In both his state appeal and at the district court, his claim was denied. On appeal to the Eighth Circuit, a three judge panel unanimously found that Mr. Foster's right to effective assistance of counsel had been denied based upon his trial counsel's failure to inform him of his right to testify in the penalty phase of his trial. At Mr. Foster's 27.26 hearing in the Circuit Court of St. Louis County,[3] Peter Dunn, lead counsel in the penalty phase of the trial, admitted he did not discuss with Mr. Foster whether or not he should take the stand during the penalty phase. Mr. Dunn stated "As I recall it, the subject came up principally about testifying in the guilt phase of the trial. I cannot presume discussing his testifying in the penalty phase of the trial." Mr. Dunn went on to state during cross-examination:

> **Q:** Did you tell [Mr. Foster] he could testify in the penalty phase if he chose to do so?
> **A:** I don't recall discussing the penalty of him testifying at the penalty phase.
> **Q:** Didn't it occur to you that his testimony in the penalty phase would allow the jury to have more insight into the man Emmitt Foster was?
> **A:** I guess the answer to that is no.

Q: So you didn't think that could be helpful in terms of it leading to some mitigating evidence?

The panel unanimously found this to be ineffective assistance of counsel. In order to establish harm, the petitioner must show that "there is a reasonable probability that but for counsel's unprofessional errors, the result of the proceedings would have been different." The *Strickland* inquiry asked whether "the result of the proceedings was fundamentally unfair or unreliable." . . . The unanimous panel of the Eighth Circuit was overturned by the court *en banc* which focused entirely on the harm question of the *Strickland v. Washington* test for ineffective assistance of counsel. The court *en banc* failed to look at the totality of the circumstances regarding the failure of counsel to inform Mr. Foster of his right to testify. The harm clearly follows when a criminal is not informed of his constitutional right to testify. . . . The three judges in dissent of the opinion of the court *en banc* looked at the entire testimony of the penalty phase of the trial. Mr. Foster presented testimony of his involvement with the African Methodist Episcopal Church, his involvement in church projects working with children on Saturday afternoons and being a friend to fellow parishioners. These three judges are of the opinion that Mr. Foster needed to testify to give the jury a point of reference and to show that he deserved to live. The three judges found: "in this case prejudice [harm] is apparent from the record." The judges in dissent found prejudice [harm] in the closing argument presented by Mr. Dunn [lead defense counsel],

> As I stand here before you in this court, I must confess to you that I am afraid, I am afraid for myself, I am afraid for Emmitt, that I don't have the ability to speak for him, that I won't be able to find the words that must be said now and most of all I am afraid that even if I did, you wouldn't be swayed.

The United States Supreme Court finds a criminal defendant's right to testify most important. The court states:

> None of these modern innovations [in criminal procedures] lessen the need for the defendant personally to have the opportunity to present to the court his plea in mitigation. The most persuasive counsel may not be able to speak for a defendant as the defendant might with halting eloquence speaking for himself [before the imposition of a sentence] *Green v. United States* (1961: 304).

Conclusion

. . . The constitution and statutes of the State of Missouri vest in the Governor the power to grant clemency and pardons and this is a case that cries out for the use of such power. Mr. Foster asks that you take your responsibility to act as "fail-safe." Mr. Foster has presented evidence which has not been previously presented to a jury which raises more than reasonable doubt as to his innocence of this crime. He has no other recourse or forum in which to present this information. Without your intervention Emmitt Foster will be executed on May 3, 1995 at 12:01 A.M. CDT for a crime he did not commit.

For the above reasons a stay of execution should be granted so that a full consideration of this application for commutation of sentence can be reviewed and given the necessary consideration and so that the life of an innocent man can be spared.

▼▲▼ ───────

Emmitt Foster was not able to prove his innocence of the murder, in part because the prosecutor withheld critical evidence that would have contradicted the eyewitness's testimony. In addition, the prosecutor made extreme statements to the jury during closing arguments that were intended to dehumanize Mr. Foster. Drawing on racial stereotypes and prejudices, the prosecutor took unfair advantage of the defense attorney's failures to present the strongest case possible for Emmitt. Unfortunately for Mr. Foster, the Eighth Circuit Court en banc did not agree with the three-judge panel and denied his claim of ineffective assistance of counsel. Emmitt Foster was executed May 3, 1995.

───────

CASE STUDY:
WITHHOLDING EXCULPATORY EVIDENCE
AND UNRELIABLE WITNESSES

Robert O'Neal, CP#35

Robert O'Neal was convicted of killing fellow inmate Arthur Dade in the Missouri State Penitentiary in 1984. The prosecution failed to disclose that one of its lead witnesses, Officer John Maylee, had a prior criminal record. Disclosure of that information certainly would have substantially reduced, if not destroyed, Officer Maylee's credibility at trial.

───────

▼▲▼
Application for Commutation
of Sentence of Death[4]

Barring relief in the federal courts, the final decision on whether Robert O'Neal lives or dies rests with the Governor of Missouri. The sole question remaining in Mr. O'Neal's legal appeals is whether he was deprived of a fundamentally fair trial by the State's failure to disclose favorable and material evidence in clear violation of his due process rights. We believe the record shows that to be the case. But even if Robert O'Neal is denied relief by the courts on this basis, a more fundamental issue remains: whether the State should be permitted to put to death a prisoner whose conviction was obtained in some undetermined part because of the State's clear violation of its obligation to disclose material information? . . .

Robert O'Neal Did Not Receive a Fair Trial

Robert O'Neal and Arthur Dade were inmates at the Missouri State Penitentiary when, in February 1984, an altercation erupted, during which Mr. O'Neal stabbed Mr. Dade. Mr. Dade died shortly thereafter, and Mr. O'Neal was charged with capital murder.

Prior to his trial on the murder charge, Mr. O'Neal filed a discovery request specifically asking the State to disclose any prior criminal convictions of any persons the State planned to call as witnesses. The State's response indicated that there were none. At trial, the State's case rested primarily on the credibility and reliability of two witnesses: Correction Officers John Maylee and Roger Flowers. Officer Maylee was the more important witness, because he claimed to have seen three men, one of whom was Mr. O'Neal, approach Mr. Dade and attack him.

Officer Maylee testified that he had seen the incident from a position on another floor of the housing unit, some forty feet from where Mr. Dade was killed. His testimony was suspect due to his admitted vision problems, his distance from the scene, and prior inconsistent statements he had made about where he was when the incident occurred. Moreover, his testimony varied in several material respects from that of Officer Flowers. For example, Officer Maylee testified that Mr. O'Neal ran toward Mr. Dade, armed with a weapon, and attacked him from the front. Officer Flowers testified that he first saw Mr. O'Neal *behind* Mr. Dade, that he did not see any weapon, and that he believed the incident to be merely a fight. Officer Flowers said he broke up the fight; Officer Maylee testified he never saw Officer Flowers at the scene.

Mr. O'Neal's defense was that he acted in self defense, and his version of events was corroborated by the testimony of other inmates who witnessed the incident from vantage points much closer than those where either Officer Maylee or Officer Flowers claimed to be. Therefore, during trial, the prosecution attacked the credibility of these inmate witnesses by eliciting and focusing on their prior criminal convictions. During the closing argument, the prosecutor essentially reduced the issue for the jury to a credibility determination between the State's witnesses and the defense witnesses. Again, he emphasized the criminal convictions of the defense witnesses, and contrasted this with the believability of Officer Maylee and Officer Flowers, whom he described as "professional career people" who respected the judicial system. The jury returned a verdict finding Robert O'Neal guilty of capital murder. After the penalty phase of the trial, the jury sentenced Mr. O'Neal to death.

It was not until November 1993, when Mr. O'Neal's habeas appeal was pending before the Eighth Circuit Court of Appeals that Mr. O'Neal learned through an article in the St. Louis Post Dispatch that John Maylee, the State's key witness against him, had three prior felony convictions. In fact, this same John Maylee, whose credibility the prosecution had repeatedly contrasted with that of Robert O'Neal's witnesses—because *they* were convicted felons—had a prior criminal record which included assault with intent to maim and rob, assault with intent to commit robbery, and felonious stealing.

Because the State essentially reduced the question of Robert O'Neal's guilt to the issue of witness credibility, its failure to disclose Officer Maylee's prior criminal record not only violated Mr. O'Neal's due process rights, but effectively deprived him of a fundamentally fair trial. Disclosure of that information certainly would have substantially reduced, if not destroyed, Officer Maylee's credibility at trial, and therefore must significantly undermine confidence in the verdict.

Arthur Dade's Psychiatric History

The unfairness of Robert O'Neal's trial and the resulting death sentence were further compounded by the failure of his trial counsel to introduce evidence regarding the psychiatric history of the victim, Arthur Dade. That record reveals that Mr. Dade, in addition to a record of violence at the penitentiary, had to be hospitalized with a diagnosis of paranoid schizophrenia; that he was actively delusional, including hearing voices; that he had an "enemies list" and wrote the Warden in 1982 that he thought people were trying to kill him; that he assaulted staff, including Roger Flowers; that he indicated to individuals both inside and outside the prison that he believed a transmitter had been planted in his body to destroy his brain and muscle tissues; and that drugs were found in his cell on multiple occasions.

Such information would have been crucial evidence corroborating the testimony of Robert O'Neal and his witnesses that Mr. O'Neal acted in self-defense when attacked by Mr. Dade. This is especially so because the evidence showed that Mr. Dade was heard to refer to Mr. O'Neal as "Banjo," the nickname of *another* inmate with whom he seemed to have confused Mr. O'Neal, and that he had threatened to kill "Banjo."

Conclusion

. . . Granting clemency to Robert O'Neal would result in a sentence of life without parole. His conviction almost unquestionably resulted in some significant part from the State's failure to honor its discovery obligations, a due process violation regardless of whether the State's omission was intentional or inadvertent. Mr. O'Neal's counsel failed to adduce evidence about Mr. Dade's mental condition that would have provided considerable support for the assertion of Mr. O'Neal and his witnesses that Mr. Dade was the one who attacked, and that Mr. O'Neal responded in self defense. . . . It does the State no credit to execute an individual—any individual—who has not received a fundamentally fair trial. It deprives Mr. O'Neal of his life without the due process to which he is entitled. Granting clemency to Robert O'Neal is the only fair, just and decent course.

▼▲▼ _____

Robert O'Neal was in prison when the killing of Mr. Dade occurred. Mr. O'Neal claimed his action was in self-defense, which would have made it justifiable homicide. However, his defense was handicapped by the prosecution's withholding of evidence that had been explicitly requested. Consequently, the jury did not have complete information by which to evaluate the strength of the case, either for or against Mr. O'Neal. Combined with the lack of investigation by his defense attorney, the prosecutor's actions created an outcome that in retrospect is questionable. Mr. O'Neal was executed December 6, 1995.

_____

CASE STUDY: UNRELIABLE WITNESSES AND QUESTIONABLE JURY SELECTION

Maurice Byrd, CP#21

Maurice Byrd was sentenced to death for the murders of James Wood, Carolyn Turner, Edna Ince, and Judy Cazaco in Pope's Cafeteria in Des

Peres in 1980. Robbery had also been part of the crime. The prosecution had no eyewitnesses, but relied on pretrial statements (later recanted) made by Mr. Byrd's wife that he told her he had killed three people in Missouri. The prosecution otherwise relied on the self-interested testimony of jail cell mates who were in a position to gain advantage in their own cases by testifying against Mr. Byrd. This case also had a serious issue of racial bias in that Mr. Byrd was an African-American and the victims in the case were Caucasians. He was tried and convicted by an all-Caucasian jury after the state prosecution used its peremptory strikes to exclude the African-American veniremen.

▼▲▼

Supplemental Application for Grant of Reprieve or Commutation of Sentence[5]

A Reprieve Should Be Granted Pending Investigation of the Alleged New Evidence

Subsequent information has come to public knowledge raising the question as to whether or not Maurice Byrd committed the crime for which he is to be punished. The present question is not whether or not the new information is true. The question at this time, especially in the face of the irreversibility of death, is—Is it in the public welfare to investigate the allegations of fact prior to execution?

The integrity and credibility of the judicial system is the value that must be preciously guarded. Irreparable harm would flow if citizens lacked faith in the role of the jurisprudence system to mete out justice. The pardon power exists for the promotion of the public welfare, including the preservation of the integrity and credibility of the jurisprudence system. This power should be exercised even in the face of the objections of the offender because it is the good of society that is primarily to be served and not the wishes of the offender.

Significant exculpatory evidence substantiating petitioner's claim of innocence was not discovered until four years after his trial. The jury which convicted and sentenced him was unaware of this evidence.

Put into the context of the trial, the new facts are as follows:

Four employees of Pope's Cafeteria in the West County Mall in St. Louis were fatally shot in an inner office at the Cafeteria on October 23, 1980. Their bodies were discovered when two other employees arrived at about 7:40 that morning and several thousand dollars were missing from a safe there. For months afterwards, St. Louis County Police received numerous and conflicting leads from people, including arrestees in other crimes, claiming to identify the persons responsible. A large reward, reported at $50,000, was offered for information solving the crime.

Maurice Byrd was ultimately arrested, convicted and sentenced to death on four counts in a trial conducted in 1982. Mr. Byrd testified at trial, denying the accusation and explaining that the morning of the crimes he went to his job for an insect control company, arriving at his employer's offices at 7:50 A.M. The company serviced businesses at the West County Mall, including Pope's Cafeteria, but he did not go to any such facilities that day.

Four years after Mr. Byrd's trial, an eyewitness came forward who was in the parking lot outside Pope's Cafeteria the early morning that the crime occurred. The witness contacted the attorney representing Mr. Byrd at that time and informed him that she saw two black men leaving the Mall entrance by Pope's Cafeteria carrying a large bag. They were zipping up white coveralls as they walked toward her. She asked them if the mall was open already, and one man offered to take her inside. The other man (who was carrying the bag) protested, "No, we don't have any time" and was in a hurry to leave. The men got into a "white-washed" van with no license plates and left. The witness left the Mall parking lot and returned later that morning to find that the Mall had been closed by the police. The witness learned of the murders at Pope's Cafeteria the following day. She became alarmed when she later saw Mr. Byrd's picture in media reports alleging his complicity in the crime because he was not one of the men she saw at the scene the morning the crime occurred. She recognized Mr. Byrd's picture as someone she had seen working at the mall and had even spoken to him, although she did not know his name. Yet she maintains that he was not one of the men she saw leaving the mall with the large bag.

The exculpatory testimony the new witness had to offer was not available to the jury which convicted Mr. Byrd. The witness did not come forward at the time of his trial due to the fears she and her husband felt of retaliation by the men she saw leaving the crime scene. She continued to remain silent until late 1986 when she contacted Mr. Byrd's attorney at that time, David Hemingway.

The evidence this witness had to give would have warranted the jury's doubt in Mr. Byrd's guilt and continues to raise the grave possibility that Missouri will execute Mr. Byrd for a crime he did not commit. The state produced no eyewitness testimony to the crime. Had Mr. Byrd been one of the men involved in the crime, this witness would have recognized and identified him as such. Her testimony, unavailable at trial, that Mr. Byrd was not one of the men she saw leaving the crime scene strongly bolsters Mr. Byrd's continuing claim of innocence.

The prosecution presented no eyewitness testimony putting Mr. Byrd at the crime scene, but relied instead on pre-trial statements (later recanted) made by Mr. Byrd's purported wife, Sandra Byrd, alleging that Maurice told her he had killed three people in Missouri to join her and their infant son in Savannah, Georgia. She made this statement knowing that a $50,000 reward had been offered and after police told her that they would take care of her. When subpoenaed to testify at the trial in 1982, she testified under oath that Maurice did *not* make the statements she alleged to the police.

The prosecution otherwise relied on the self-interested testimony of jail cell mates, who had access to police reports about the Pope's Cafeteria case, who claimed that Mr. Byrd had admitted killing people in Missouri. These inmates were in a position to gain advantage in their own cases by testifying against Mr. Byrd.

In sharp contrast to the self-serving motivation of the prosecution witnesses to make false accusations against Mr. Byrd, the witness who came forward in 1988 had no self-interest to fabricate evidence in Mr. Byrd's favor. To the contrary, her ultimate decision to come forward is strongly against her interest in the risk of retaliation she faces by the men she saw leaving the scene.

The sworn affidavit which, if true, negates clearly the commission of capital murder. We do not know whether the affidavit is true or false. That is not the question. The question is whether it is in the public interest to prudently and seriously investigate the statements made in the affidavit prior to implementing the death penalty.

Although the attorneys handling Mr. Byrd's appeals have persistently sought a new trial based on the new witness' testimony, Missouri law does not provide any remedy by which to present new exculpatory evidence discovered after the direct appeal from a defendant's conviction. The legal procedures available after the direct appeal specifically exclude claims of such newly discovered evidence from recognition. Such claims cannot be raised in the state post-conviction motion under the Missouri Supreme Court's rules, nor in a state court petition for habeas corpus. Neither can a defendant raise the matter by seeking habeas corpus in federal court. Mr. Byrd's direct appeal was completed in 1984, two years before the new witness came forward. The state courts, therefore, refused to consider

Maurice's pleas for a hearing and new trial on the new evidence which was unknown at the time of his trial. . . .

Racial Bias Question

Court documents indicate serious facts which demand consideration. Maurice O. Byrd is black. All the victims in this case were white. He was tried and convicted by an all white jury after the state prosecution used its peremptory strikes to exclude the black potential jurors.

In selecting the jury, the prosecutor used peremptory jury strikes to remove all of the potential jurors who shared Mr. Byrd's race. The trial court judge made a clear record of this. The jury chosen to decide the case consisted of twelve white jurors and two alternate jurors.

The answers given by the four Black jurors which the prosecutor removed to obtain an all-white jury reveal no basis other than race to explain their exclusion from the jury:

A. R.D., worked as a grade-school teacher in St. Louis County and had degrees from the Hampton Institute and Rutgers. Ms. D. stated unequivocally that she could consider both the death penalty and life imprisonment when asked by the prosecutor. Her husband worked as a divisional manager in a business. She unequivocally confirmed that she could be a fair and impartial juror, even though she had heard about the offense on trial. She also indicated that she had been the victim of theft from her purse where she worked, a factor which prosecutors generally consider as favorable as making them more sympathetic to the prosecution.

B. Y.B., a Southwestern Bell repair supervisor, also told the prosecutor unequivocally that she could consider a sentence of death as well as a life sentence. Ms. B. had served for eighteen months on a grand jury in the mid-1970s and heard many criminal cases. She stated that she perceived no difficulty in serving on the jury in Mr. Byrd's case.

C. M.L. indicated that she had heard about the Pope's Cafeteria case, but did not recall the details. Ms. L. had lived in St. Louis for twenty-five years and worked as a maid to families in the area. She also unequivocally stated that she could be a fair juror. She stated that she would base her decision on the evidence appearing in court.

D. M.G. also testified that she could consider the death penalty. She reaffirmed that fact under defense questioning, stating that once proven guilty, she "could go for the death penalty." She indicated that she had heard nothing about the case. Ms. G. unequivocally stated she could be a fair and impartial juror. Ms. G. expressed some concern about viewing pictures of the victims, a factor which prosecutors normally view as favorable to their side in obtaining the juror's sympathy. She maintained that she could follow the law and make a fair and impartial decision based on the evidence.

In February, 1990, the U.S. General Accounting Office filed a report to the Senate and House Committees on the Judiciary entitled, *Death Penalty Sentencing: Research Indicates Pattern of Racial Disparities.* The Office researchers found a pattern indicating racial disparities in the charging, sentencing, and imposition of the death penalty. In eighty-two percent of the empirical studies examined, the race of the victim was found to influence the likelihood of being charged with capital murder or receiving the death penalty, that is, those who murdered whites were found to be more likely to be sentenced to death than those who murdered blacks. The studies found that the "race of victim influence" was found at all stages of the criminal justice process. Three-fourths of the studies examined found that black defendants were more likely to receive the death penalty than white defendants.

Affidavits of attorneys practicing in Missouri also support the fact that blacks have been systematically excluded from juries in similar cases.

Racial Discrimination Not Heard by Courts

Court documents submitted throughout Mr. Byrd's appeals indicate that there has never been a hearing in any Court, state or federal, on this issue. Both testimony and statistical evidence can be offered on behalf of the discrimination which occurred in Mr. Byrd's trial. However, the Courts have said that they do not have the power to grant relief on this issue and the Courts say they are powerless to grant relief. Therefore, it is appropriate to appeal to the Chief Executive Officer, the Governor, on behalf of clemency. If Mr. Byrd is executed, the allegations of racial discrimination will stand unanswered.

In 1986, the United States Supreme Court changed the law to enable defendants to challenge a prosecutor's exclusion of all members of his race by peremptory jury challenges (*Batson v. Kentucky*). However, the courts have refused to extend the reach of this change to cases like Mr. Byrd's where the direct appeal had been decided prior to the May 1986 decision in *Batson*. The only remaining corrective procedure is through the pardon power. . . .

The judicial system is inadequate in Mr. Byrd's case to ensure the reliability of his conviction and sentence because it fails to provide a forum in which the witness' testimony and credibility can be aired and assessed.

Clemency is the only safeguard available to ensure that Mr. Byrd is not wrongfully executed. . . . We request that Maurice Byrd be provided at least a commutation of sentence to life and no parole. Given the racial composition of the defendant, the victims, and the jury, there is occasion for prejudice of facts and process against him such that it would be extremely difficult if not impossible to determine guilt or sentence in an impartial manner.

▼▲▼ _____

Maurice Byrd claimed he was innocent of the crime. As is often the case, exonerating evidence is not discovered until years after the trial. In Mr. Byrd's case, the new information was too late to be considered by any court according to their own rules. In this case, the witness was afraid to come forward any earlier. It is not likely that the trial attorney could have done anything about such a delay. However, had the testimony been available at trial, it would have reduced the weight given to prosecution's witnesses who apparently had something to gain by cooperating with the prosecution. In addition, the appearance of racial bias in jury selection probably would have been reversed if the trial had taken place after the *Batson* decision. Because the judicial system was not responsive to Mr. Byrd's appeals, refusing to evaluate the new information, the clemency petition was the only opportunity Mr. Byrd had to present this information. Mr. Byrd was executed on August 23, 1991.

_____

CONCLUSIONS

The clemency petitions presented in this chapter have documented alleged unethical and unconstitutional behavior by the prosecution. Each case raises the possibility that the death penalty is inappropriate. How could a wrong result happen? Prosecutors have withheld exculpatory evidence from the defense. Prosecutors used prejudicial and inflammatory language when speaking to the jury. Prosecutors excluded all African-Americans from a jury without cause. Prosecutors gave incentives to witnesses in exchange for their testimony against the accused. This questionable behavior should have been checked by the appellate courts.[6]

These clemency petitions provide a window on a pattern of problems that originate in the prosecutor's office. As professionals, prosecutors must balance their passion for convicting the guilty with their responsibility for upholding the integrity of the system. Excesses can result in wrongful convictions and execution.

These prosecutors are not simply individual "bad apples." When their behavior is ignored, if not condoned, by the rest of the criminal justice system, they represent institutional failures. "Commentators generally agree that disciplinary proceedings against prosecutors are relatively rare" (ABA 61: 620). These are not just idiosyncratic problems. Their prevalence is reflective of a flawed system that demands convictions without careful attention to process.

In both stages of the capital murder cases considered so far (the police investigation and the prosecution), the trial attorney has been a contributing factor in not exposing the system's errors in a timely fashion. No doubt well-trained prosecutors took unfair advantage of ill-prepared defense attorneys. The philosophy of our adversary system of justice emphasizes our dependence upon having equally matched opponents so that in their clashing, truth will emerge. In death penalty cases, having the best defense is a matter of life or death. We turn next to focus on unmasking some of the problems with defense attorneys at the trial stage.

CHAPTER FOUR

THE DEFENSE ATTORNEY

Four significant factors form the basis for Mr. Powell's clemency plea: the hung jury on sentencing; the improper relationship and sexual conduct between Mr. Powell and his lawyer; Mr. Powell's mental retardation; and his lawyer's errors of law and judgment that were never reviewed on their merits in the courts.

The 34-year-old public defender trying her first death penalty case was unstable, mentally ill and ill-prepared to represent him; she fell in love with him and had sexual relations with him during his trial. The object of her desire and her client, Mr. Powell, was a border-line mentally retarded, 18 year-old youth with a family background so horrendous that it is virtually unimaginable. In addition, his lawyer made grievous errors of law and judgment, some of which were never reviewed in the course of his appeals, because they were found to be procedurally barred. Finally, despite his lawyer's emotional involvement with Mr. Powell and her lapses and failings in the course of her representation of him, his jury was unconvinced of the appropriateness of a death sentence. Because a jury of his peers could not agree on a death sentence, the trial judge alone made the sentencing decision.

FROM THE CLEMENCY PETITION
for Reginald Powell, CP#64,
executed February 25, 1998[1]

THE PROMISE OF ASSISTANCE
OF COUNSEL

The Sixth Amendment of the Bill of Rights promises each accused the assistance of counsel for defense at trial so that fairness will be guaranteed for all persons accused of crime. This constitutional protection is considered one of our fundamental rights. It is a guarantee that is now taken for granted by the general public, although providing lawyers for poor misdemeanor defendants who might be sentenced to jail was only decided in 1972 in *Argersinger v. Hamlin.* However, it was in 1932, in *Powell v. Alabama,* that the U.S. Supreme Court stated that due process of law required states to provide court-appointed counsel for indigent defendants in death penalty cases. Because the language of the Sixth Amendment is specific to trials, there are disputes about what stages beyond the trial in death penalty litigation legal representation should be provided (McGill, 1990; Steiker and Steiker, 1995; Mello, 1997b). In this chapter, however, the primary focus is on the trial level, for which there is no debate concerning the constitutional necessity for legal representation.

Over the years, court cases have clarified what is essential if the Sixth Amendment protection is to be meaningful. In *McMann v. Richardson* (1970), the U.S. Supreme Court held that the right to assistance of counsel is the right to *effective* assistance of counsel. What is effective assistance of counsel, however, is debated. The Supreme Court's standard for effectiveness is explained in *Strickland v. Washington* (1964) by its negative: Ineffectiveness would be determined by examining (1) whether the attorney's action (or inaction) was deficient by reasonable standards and (2) whether the attorney's errors were so serious as to deprive the defendant of a fair trial, a trial whose result is reliable.

This two-pronged test in *Strickland* rests heavily on the norms of professional conduct. For example, an important element of fairness explicitly mentioned in *Strickland* is the professional duty to avoid conflicts of interest. One place to find these "reasonable standards" is the American Bar Association, which has published *Guidelines for the Appointment and Performance of Counsel in Death Penalty Cases* (1989). The goal of these guidelines is to ensure quality representation for all stages of the case. The *Guidelines* are fairly specific about the minimum requirements for eligibility to be appointed to a death penalty case (Guideline 5.1). The attorney should have five years' experience with litigation in criminal defense; should have participated in at least nine criminal jury trials, three of which as lead counsel in a murder or aggravated murder case; and should have been involved in at least one death penalty case. The attorney should be knowledgeable about expert witnesses and evidence, be familiar with jurisdictional procedures and practices, have participated in continuing education specific to death penalty litigation, and have a zealous commitment to the representation of capital cases.

Other guidelines discuss the need for reasonable compensation that "reflects the extraordinary responsibilities inherent in death penalty litigation" (Guideline 10.1). The defense work itself should include adequate time and resources for preparation (Guideline 11.2); and counsel should conduct independent investigations relating to both phases of the trial (Guideline 11.4). These guidelines are specific to death penalty litigation, although they resonate with the experience of criminal law practitioners generally. The ABA's Model Rules of Professional Conduct (Meserve, 1998) mandate in Rule 1.1 that a lawyer provide competent representation to a client: "Competent representation requires the legal knowledge, skill, thoroughness and preparation necessary for the representation." Unfortunately, these ideals have not been implemented in reality.

THE REALITY

Many horror stories can be told regarding the lack of competency of defense attorneys in death penalty cases (Finer, 1973; Bright, 1994; Acker and Lanier, 1999). It has been said that the quality of capital representation generally is very poor, as evidenced by the greater suspension, disbarment, or discipline rate than that for attorneys in general (Coyle, Strasser, and Lavelle, 1990).

> For example, defense lawyers have appeared at capital trials intoxicated. They have slept through portions of trials. . . . They have admitted to having never read the statute governing capital trial proceedings, to being unaware that a separate penalty trial followed on the heels of a capital conviction, . . . to being incapable of naming more than a single criminal case ever decided by the Supreme Court. . . . They have made reference before juries to their clients in racially offensive terms . . . and have filed one-page appellate briefs, among other things (Acker and Lanier, 1999: 434–36).

Commentators attribute the generally deficient actions of trial defense counsel to the very inadequate funding provided by states (Klein, 1986; O'Brien, 1990; Paduano and Smith, 1991; Bright, 1994, 1996; Vick, 1995; Gross, 1996; Moore, 1996; Mello, 1997b). Court-appointed attorneys have been compensated at rates well below prevailing market rates, not even covering office expenses. This means that lawyers lose money for each hour they devote to the death penalty case. Some states have caps on the amount of money available per death penalty case, which are so low that the hourly rates could actually be in the range of two to three dollars per hour. Douglas Vick (1995: 338) describes this resource deprivation as a "state-created systemic defect tainting most death sentences."

Thus, poor legal representation of death penalty defendants is more likely due to institutionally based factors of lack of time, resources, and expertise rather than to personal issues of irresponsibility or disreputable motivation. Competent attorneys do not have the time or financial means to accept these cases, leaving less effective attorneys to do the necessary work with insufficient effort. Unfortunately, the *Strickland* standard has not been useful in correcting these deficiencies (Vick, 1995). The courts are not providing death-sentenced prisoners with relief when their attorneys fail them. When the prisoner claims ineffective assistance of counsel, the courts apply a strong presumption of competency as a burden that must be overcome. The courts interpret the *Strickland* language restrictively, ignore errors of omission, and attribute both actions and inactions to the lawyer's strategic decisions, which are not to be second-guessed. This approach virtually eliminates any possibility of recognizing serious errors. Supreme Court Justice Blackmun in his dissent in *McFarland v. Scott* (1994: 1259) speaks of the *Strickland* standard as being impotent:

> Practical experience establishes that the *Strickland* test, in application, has failed to protect a defendant's right to be represented by something more than "a person who happens to be a lawyer."

If clemency petitions are a reliable source of information, the quality of defense in Missouri death penalty cases has been grossly inadequate. Forty-three of the fifty clemency cases (86 percent) in this study were initiated before the first execution in 1989. All of these death row prisoners were "defended by counsel appointed during a period when Missouri's system of providing legal services to indigent defendants was among the worst funded (49th among the states) in the nation" (O'Brien, 1990: 520). Attorney errors began to be mentioned in clemency petitions almost from the beginning, in 1990. Overall, in thirty-seven of the fifty cases (74 percent), attorney issues were raised (see table 4.1). In twelve petitions out of fifty (24 percent), the defendant's trial lawyer had *no* trial experience with death penalty litigation. The most frequent attorney issue raised was the failure to investigate (in twenty-nine of the fifty cases, or 58 percent). In four cases, trial attorneys called *no* defense witnesses. Several petitions indicated that their trial attorneys did not understand the bifurcation of the capital trial, were surprised by the determination of guilt, and were unprepared for the sentencing phase. In six cases, a conflict of interest interfering with both the defense at trial and the raising of appeals was alleged.

It is well known that in death penalty cases, mitigation evidence is

TABLE 4.1
Lawyer Ineffectiveness

Misconduct	Frequency	Cases
Failure to investigate	29	A. J. Bannister, Thomas Battle, Martsay Bolder, William Ted Boliek, James Chambers, Ralph Davis, Larry Griffin, Ricky Grubbs, Frank Guinan, George Harris, Anthony LaRette, Frederick Lashley, Leonard Laws, David Leisure, Samuel McDonald, Robert O'Neal, Richard Oxford, Reginald Powell, Donald Reese, James Rodden, Gary Roll, Lloyd Schlup, Bobby Shaw, Andrew Six, Jeff Sloan, Glen Sweet, Robert Walls, Jessie Wise, Richard Zeitvogel
Lack of trial experience in capital litigation	12	Martsay Bolder, Larry Griffin, Anthony LaRette, Frederick Lashley, David Leisure, Sam McDonald, Emmett Nave, Reginald Powell, Lloyd Schlup, Andrew Six, Jeff Sloan, Robert Walls
Conflict of interest	6	David Leisure, Reginald Powell, Gary Roll, Glen Sweet, Jessie Wise, Richard Zeitvogel
Disbarred	2	William Ted Boliek, Jeff Sloan
No witnesses called	4	James Chambers, Ricky Grubbs, Kelvin Malone, Gary Roll
Trial and appellate mistakes	7	Ralph Davis, Bruce Kilgore, Darrell Mease, Roy Ramsey, Roy Roberts, Gary Roll, Jessie Wise

the key to humanizing the defendant and critical in saving the defendant's life from the executioner (Haney, 1998). Juries are less likely to recommend a death sentence if they can empathize with the defendant. However, according to the clemency petitions, only eleven (22 percent) Missouri death penalty cases had any mitigation evidence raised during their trials. Mitigating factors such as the age of the defendant, mental defects, and family testimony were raised in only two cases each. The failure to raise mitigating factors is clearly related to the experience level of the defense attorney.

The omission of mitigating evidence at trial is in sharp contrast to forty-one cases (82 percent) raising mitigating factors in the clemency petition to the governor. One characteristic of the defendants that might provide some sympathy is that they had made some positive contribution to the community prior to the crime. Clearly in this situation are six Vietnam veterans (12 percent of the total). Other mitigating factors mentioned were having a job, church involvement, volunteer work, or no prior criminal record. In twenty-seven (54 percent) of the cases, there was some sort of psychological condition that was raised to the governor as a mitigating circumstance. These psychological conditions challenge the ability of the condemned to premeditate the crime and go directly to the issue of one's guilt of first degree murder. In five of the fifty cases (10 percent), there are significant issues concerning competency to be executed.[2]

Of the thirty-seven petitions that raise attorney issues, all raise multiple problems. These clemency petitions raise significant concerns about the quality of defense provided to death penalty defendants and about the effectiveness of the *Strickland* standard to protect the Sixth Amendment guarantee of a right to counsel in criminal trials.

It has been difficult to select cases to highlight when so many clemency petitions point to egregious attorney problems. For example, Ralph Davis's charges were upgraded to capital murder by the prosecutor because his trial attorney requested and was granted a continuance.[3] Mr. Davis was not told this would happen, nor was he consulted by his attorney in the matter, although the attorney was well aware of the prosecutor's intentions. The attorney hired to represent Mr. Davis in his postconviction appeals process did not file the routine Missouri Supreme Court Rule 29.15 motion to set aside the sentence. A third lawyer filed the motion, but it was not signed by Mr. Davis. The result of this error was the dismissal of the motion, and Mr. Davis's claims of constitutional error were procedurally defaulted in federal court.

Or consider that Gary Roll's trial lawyer required him to sign a "Statement of Defendant on Eve of Trial," which was intended to protect the lawyer from any criticism.[4] Some of the paragraphs stated that Mr. Roll was totally sane (in direct conflict with potential defenses or mitigation evidence), that Mr. Roll was entirely satisfied with his counsel's performance but wanted him to withdraw at the conclusion of the case and seek to have a public defender appointed, that Mr. Roll irrevocably assigned all of his assets to counsel, and that he permitted his attorney to make the entire statement public, thereby waiving the attorney-client privilege. The irony of this statement is dramatic, as the lawyer clearly was not ready for trial. He did not ask questions on voir dire, did not make an opening statement, and did not cross-examine the state's first witness.

But these are not the cases on which we focus. Instead, we turn to four cases that crystallize the predominant issues being raised against trial defense attorneys. Each of these cases present trial errors that go uncorrected.

CASE STUDY:
INEXPERIENCE AND LACK OF TRAINING
IN DEATH PENALTY LITIGATION

Martsay Bolder, CP#5

Early in 1979, Theron King was assigned as Mr. Bolder's cell mate in prison. Mr. King was twenty years older than Mr. Bolder, and he used his age and experience to taunt Mr. Bolder. Eventually the harassment became too much for Mr. Bolder. Mr. Bolder stabbed Theron King. Evidence obtained after the trial indicated that Mr. King died of an infection caused by hospital staff six weeks after the stabbing when they removed fluid from Mr. King's chest by passing a hypodermic needle through the location of his abdominal wound. Mr. Bolder requested that the governor convene a hearing to determine whether using the wound area for this procedure constituted medical malpractice.

▼▲▼
Application for a Reprieve from,
or Commutation of, a Sentence of Death[5]

Background Facts

Martsay Bolder entered the Missouri State Penitentiary at age seventeen. Despite his youth, Mr. Bolder had been certified as an adult and convicted on a second degree murder charge. The Missouri State Penitentiary is a difficult place for any inmate but it presented special dangers for young Mr. Bolder. The principal source of this danger was inmate Theron King.

A. The Stabbing and Subsequent Death of Mr. King
Early in 1979, Theron King was assigned as Mr. Bolder's cellmate. Mr. King was twenty years older than Mr. Bolder and he used his age and experience to taunt and harass Mr. Bolder. For example, Mr. King told Mr.

Bolder that he knew, but refused to disclose, the circumstances of the murder of Mr. Bolder's older brother. Mr. King also spread gossip that Mr. Bolder was engaged in homosexuality. Mr. King's harassment continued after he was removed from Mr. Bolder's cell. Eventually, the harassment became too much for Mr. Bolder. In April 1979, Mr. King saw Mr. Bolder in the jail yard and started to call him names, including "pussy assed nigger." Mr. Bolder confronted Mr. King and, when Mr. King refused to retract his epithets, Mr. Bolder stabbed Mr. King.

Mr. King incurred a wound to the abdomen that was not attended to promptly. No surgeon was available for 45 minutes and, by that time, Mr. King had lost a great deal of blood. An emergency surgery was performed without the benefit of sterile conditions. Mr. King died six weeks later. The autopsy report identified the cause of Mr. King's death as "generalized infection resulting from a stab wound."

If, indeed, the stab wound caused the infection that befell Mr. King, Mr. Bolder would be legally responsible for Mr. King's death. The autopsy conclusion, however, seems suspect due to the passage of time before the infection had its ultimate effect. Evidence recently obtained indicates that the autopsy conclusion was only half correct. Mr. King did die of an infection but the infection was not caused by the stab wound. Rather, the infection was caused by hospital staff when, weeks after the stabbing, they removed fluid from Mr. King's chest by passing a hypodermic needle through the location of Mr. King's abdominal wound. Mr. Bolder believes that using the wound area for this procedure was malpractice. The hospital's use of the wound area also may explain why Mr. King's infection-related death occurred six weeks after the stabbing.

The new evidence has not been fully investigated. Its source, however, appears reliable. The significance of the evidence cannot be overstated. If Mr. King really died of malpractice, rather than a stab wound, Mr. Bolder could have been convicted of no more than aggravated assault and he would not have been eligible for the death penalty.

B. Mr. Bolder's Trial

The newly discovered evidence regarding Mr. King's death was not available at the time of Mr. Bolder's trial. The evidence regarding the provocation leading to the stabbing and evidence regarding Mr. Bolder's background, however, was available. Unfortunately for Mr. Bolder, the evidence was ignored by his lawyer.

Mr. Bolder's trial was assigned to a young Jefferson City lawyer who practiced criminal law part-time and who had no experience in capital murders. The lawyer's preparation consisted of speaking with his father, a doctor, regarding the medical cause of Mr. King's death and meeting with Mr. Bolder on five occasions. Mr. Bolder's trial lasted only one day and virtually all of that time was devoted to the prosecution's case. Mr. Bolder's lawyer introduced no evidence and limited his closing remarks to a short speech regarding the difficult burden the jury would face in its sentencing decision.

Missouri capital punishment trials occur in two phases. In the first phase, the jury determines the defendant's guilt or innocence. If the jury finds the defendant guilty of capital murder, the second phase commences. In this penalty phase, the jury may be presented with evidence demonstrating why the death penalty should not be invoked. Mr. Bolder's lawyer failed to produce important evidence in both phases.

In the guilt phase, Mr. Bolder's lawyer failed to present any of the evidence regarding the despicable conduct of Mr. King and the anger it caused to well up in Mr. Bolder. Although such evidence certainly would not have excused Mr. Bolder's decision to stab Mr. King, it would have supported a jury verdict of either first or second degree murder for which the death penalty, as a matter of law, could not be imposed. Moreover, if this evidence has been argued in the penalty phase, the jury would likely have issued a life sentence.

Perhaps more importantly, Mr. Bolder's lawyer failed to make any investigation for witnesses who could testify at the penalty phase of Mr. Bolder's trial. Missouri's capital punishment statute allowed penalty phase evidence on any topic that could influence the jury's decision on life or death. Mr. Bolder's lawyer, however, did not read the capital murder statute carefully. Consequently, the lawyer was not aware that he could present mitigation evidence at the penalty phase and he conducted no investigation for mitigation witnesses.

If Mr. Bolder's lawyer had read the statute and looked for mitigation witnesses, he would have been armed with valuable penalty phase testimony. Mr. Bolder's current lawyers, upon their appointment to represent Mr. Bolder in his federal habeas corpus action, promptly located neighbors, acquaintances and a counselor to Mr. Bolder who recounted facts of Mr. Bolder's childhood and adolescence. In sum, these witnesses explained that Mr. Bolder grew up in a destructive climate of poverty, violence and mental disease. Mr. Bolder's father was present in the home only to vent his wrath during drunken binges and little maternal care was provided. Notwithstanding these remarkable burdens, Mr. Bolder was thoughtful and considerate to his neighbors and friends and responded admirably when able to escape the ghetto with his counselor.

Without the benefit of any evidence demonstrating the provocation which caused the stabbing or Mr. Bolder's very difficult background, it is little wonder that the jury returned a death verdict. If the jury had heard the available evidence, however, their verdict most probably would have been a life sentence. The federal habeas corpus judge, who heard the evidence believed it "inescapable" that the jury would have returned with a life in prison verdict had Mr. Bolder's lawyer presented the full facts.

Reasons Why a Reprieve or Commutation Should Be Granted

Mr. Bolder should be granted a reprieve until his pending habeas corpus petition is decided on the merits. Alternatively, Mr. Bolder's sentence should be commuted. Commutation is appropriate because Mr. Bolder's sentence is disproportionate to his crime and because his sentence is the result of attorney negligence.

The reasons on which Mr. Bolder seeks relief are valid. They should not be discounted simply because all but the medical malpractice issue previously have been presented to the courts. The number of Mr. Bolder's prior court proceedings does not equate to a reasonable opportunity to present the important facts of his case. Indeed, all but one of Mr. Bolder's court appearances have been notable for their avoidance of the facts, either due to attorney error or due to procedural technicalities relied on by the courts to ignore the merits. The exception was the federal habeas corpus case in which the judge found Mr. Bolder's death sentence to be illegal. Thus, a reprieve or a commutation by the Governor would not "overrule" any valid fact finding of a court or jury. Rather, an order granting a reprieve would acknowledge that important issues regarding Mr. Bolder's guilt remain unresolved and an order granting a commutation would be entirely consistent with the outcome of Mr. Bolder's only untainted court proceeding. Below, Mr. Bolder explains the three basic reasons that a reprieve or commutation should be ordered.

A. Mr. Bolder Should Be Granted a Reprieve of His Death Sentence While the Federal Court Considers His Newly Discovered Evidence

The evidence regarding the medical malpractice cause of Mr. King's death was discovered by Mr. Bolder only a few weeks ago. As soon as an affidavit was obtained supporting the evidence, Mr. Bolder's lawyers filed a federal habeas corpus petition. If the medical malpractice issue is determined in Mr. Bolder's favor, his death penalty will be void as a matter of law. A ruling that Mr. King died of medical malpractice would mean that Mr. Bolder's crime was no more serious than felonious assault.

A reprieve of Mr. Bolder's sentence is necessary until the habeas corpus petition can be ruled on the merits. If a reprieve is not granted, Mr. Bolder may be executed while the issue of his guilt of capital murder remains unresolved. In order to avoid the possibility of executing an innocent man, a reprieve should be issued. . . .

B. Alternatively, Mr. Bolder's Death Sentence Should Be Commuted Because It Is Due to the Neglect of His Attorney

. . . Under the Sixth and Fourteenth Amendments to the United States Constitution, all states are required to provide a lawyer to their indigent criminal defendants. The lawyer is required to perform in a reasonably competent, or "effective" manner. If an appointed lawyer performs incompetently or "ineffectively," the defendant is denied a constitutional right and a sentence tainted by the lawyer's ineffectiveness cannot stand.

The constitutional right to an effective lawyer provides critical protection to fairness in criminal sentencing. Jurors, no doubt, attempt an honest assessment of the case but they can be guided only by what is presented to them by the case lawyers. If the lawyer appointed by the state to defend the case does a shoddy job, the jury may be deprived of the most important facts upon which its life or death decision should be made. In that circumstance, the jury may order death although it would have ordered a life sentence if the critical facts had been presented. Thus, consistent enforcement of the right to effective counsel can avoid death sentences that reflect the defense lawyer's lack of effort and attention, rather than the nature of the crime.

In his federal habeas corpus hearing, Mr. Bolder demonstrated that his state-appointed trial lawyer had provided ineffective assistance, including his failure to understand the law and to contact mitigation witnesses, which was inexcusable. The habeas corpus judge ruled "counsel's conduct so undermined the proper functioning of the adversarial process that the sentencing hearing cannot be relied on as having produced a just result."[6] Due to his finding, the judge ruled that the state must offer a new penalty phase hearing to Mr. Bolder.

The state appealed the habeas corpus judge's hearing to a panel of the Eighth Circuit Court of Appeals and obtained a reversal. It is important to note that the appellate panel did not disagree with the habeas corpus judge's finding that trial counsel's failures were the root cause of Mr. Bolder's death sentence. Rather, the appellate panel found that a technical rule allowed them to re-instate the death sentence.

The appellate panel's technical ruling itself presents a situation of bitter irony. The panel concluded that the habeas corpus judge should not have considered the issue of the trial lawyer's ineffectiveness on the merits because the issue had not first been presented to the state courts. However, the issue was not presented to the state courts because the lawyer appointed by the state to represent Mr. Bolder in his state post-conviction hearing, duplicated the error of Mr. Bolder's trial lawyer. The state post-conviction lawyer has admitted that he did not locate and present testimony from the mitigation witnesses because "it didn't occur to me." Thus, Mr. Bolder has twice been the victim of poor lawyering and procedural rules prohibit any other court from issuing an appropriate ruling on the merits of his claim.

The appellate panel's decision to reverse the habeas corpus judge, while avoiding the merits of Mr. Bolder's ineffective assistance claim, has been controversial. One member of the three-judge appellate panel wrote a dissenting opinion that harshly criticized the action of his two brethren. The dissenting judge argued that the merits of Mr. Bolder's claim ought to be considered and that, on the merits, Mr. Bolder would prevail. Later, the panel majority's decision was submitted to all active judges in the Eighth Circuit for their consideration of whether the full court should review Mr. Bolder's tainted sentence. Consideration by the full court may occur only upon the vote of a majority of the judges. In Mr. Bolder's case, the judges split five to five and, consequently, the full court did not consider the panel's decision. Given that consideration by the full court occurs rarely, the split indicates significant concern by the judges. Moreover, in connection with the full court's action, two judges wrote a special opinion in which they stated that executing Mr. Bolder would be a "miscarriage of justice."[7]

. . . The inappropriateness of Mr. Bolder's sentence has been recognized and written about by judges in every judicial forum where his case has been heard. In the Missouri Supreme Court Judge Seiler and Judge Bardget described Mr. Bolder's death sentence as "excessive and disproportionate."[8] In the federal courts, the district judge who heard Mr. Bolder's previous habeas corpus petition and judges of the Eighth Circuit Court of Appeals have concluded that Mr. Bolder's death sentence is the direct result of inadequate lawyering and that a life sentence would have been issued if Mr. Bolder's trial lawyer had performed adequately.[9]

Despite the repeated judicial concern over Mr. Bolder's sentence, he has not been able to obtain relief in the courts. The federal district court, on habeas corpus review, determined that Mr. Bolder's sentence was unfair and granted habeas corpus relief. However, the district court's order was reversed by the Eighth Circuit Court of Appeals on a technical issue of procedural law. The Circuit Court did not disagree with the district court's conclusion that, on the merits, Mr. Bolder's sentence was unjust, but sent him back to death row.

. . . Mr. Bolder was denied his constitutional right to competent legal representation at his trial. The judge who fully considered the issue found that Mr. Bolder's trial lawyer overlooked mitigating evidence so powerful that, had the jury heard the evidence, it almost certainly would have returned a life sentence. To allow Mr. Bolder's execution would, therefore, disregard the constitution's mandate that all criminal defendants be given a fair opportunity to present relevant facts regarding their case to the jury and it would end the life of a man who deserves to live.

▼▲▼ _____

In Martsay Bolder's case, the defense attorney had no experience in capital murder cases and failed to conduct a thorough investigation or introduce any evidence at trial. The jury had no information to consider in mitigation of the crime. His defense was in name only. Martsay Bolder was executed January 27, 1993.

CASE STUDY:
NO INVESTIGATION

Leonard Laws, CP#20

Leonard Laws was given the death sentence for the 1980 murders of Charles and Lottie Williams of Glenco. The undisputed evidence from the trial transcript was that Mr. Laws provided the lookout and was outside the building while two others actually committed the murders. One of the other codefendants received a fifteen-year sentence in exchange for testimony. The other codefendant was executed in 1990.

▼▲▼
Application for Grant of Reprieve or
Commutation of Sentence[10]

Mr. Laws has maintained that he does not want to continue his appeals. A next of friend brief, filed in federal courts on behalf of Leonard Laws by his father contesting his competency to terminate his appeals process, has been denied by the U.S. Supreme Court and a new date, May 17, 1990 was set by the Missouri Supreme Court.

This application is significant because his defense attorneys indicate that he has good grounds for successor habeas proceedings but Mr. Laws refuses to continue his appeals. The undersigned believe that, because of serious facts and questions in Leonard Laws' case, there is cause for mercy and the public interest would be best served by commutation. . . .

First, Leonard Laws was convicted in St. Louis Circuit Court on September 17, 1982 of two counts of capital murder on the basis of accomplice liability. The undisputed evidence was that Mr. Laws provided the lookout and was outside the building while two others actually committed the murders. He is not completely innocent, and did admit to participating in a burglary of the building, but did not participate in the actual killings. While the two murders were horrible, Mr. Laws did not kill the victims so we believe there is basis for mercy, "a change of punishment from greater to less." This is an issue of proportion.

Second, while Leonard Laws was outside the building, two other persons did in fact do the killing. One of those received only a 15 year sentence in exchange for his testimony. Certainly, a sense of fairness and balance says that Mr. Laws is entitled to at least have the death penalty reduced to life without parole.

Third, after Leonard Laws was convicted, no mitigating evidence was presented to the jury for consideration before they gave him the death penalty. Mitigating reasons are circumstances of the situation or defendant which suggest the need for mercy, that the sentence should be lightened, or that it not be as severe as it could be. No such evidence was submitted by his attorney, although such was available. Therefore, we make this plea for mercy.

Fourth, Leonard Laws was a decorated veteran of the Vietnam conflict in the Army from June 26, 1970, was wounded in combat and received an honorable discharge. Trial counsel did not interview his family and relatives. However, they stated in subsequent affidavits that prior to his entry into the Army at 17 years of age, he was a "church-going, helpful young man" who frequently took care of his sister's young children. They said that after his service he was changed, alone, nervous and withdrawn.

There is evidence suggesting that Leonard Laws was and is suffering from Post Traumatic Stress Disorder, a mental problem which is recognized by the American Psychiatric Association's DSM III Manual. This disorder is accompanied by extreme mental or emotional disturbance or duress, which are mitigating in Missouri law and are certainly grounds for clemency. They were not raised as mitigating evidence, however, in the original trial court. On appeal, courts have not been willing to consider this evidence, saying it should have been raised in the original trial court. We are raising it here as an issue for clemency.

Leonard Laws had psychiatric examinations in Whitfield State Hospital in 1974 and 1975, Whitfield, Mississippi. This was while serving time in Mississippi on an aggravated assault charge. Evaluations resulting from these examinations indicate personality changes after returning from Vietnam. In fact, they indicate a drastic personality change. He was changed from a young man who never had any trouble with the law to one who was constantly in trouble and in prison.

Leonard Laws saw combat in Vietnam and he was wounded. Study after study has shown significant and very high relationships between the extent of combat experience and the presence of post traumatic stress disorder.[11] All of Mr. Laws' behavior points to the presence of this disorder.

Key symptoms associated with post traumatic stress disorder are: isolation; rage reactions; avoidance of feelings; alienation; anxiety reactions; sleep disturbance; hyper-vigilance; and dissociative/"flashback" episodes; depression; and suicide tendencies. All of these have been documented as present in Leonard Laws' background and life up to this time.

Lastly, circumstances of Laws' immediate life suggest that mercy, life in prison, would be merited. Two volunteers, a St. Louis businessman and a vowed religious nun, have been regular visitors of Leonard Laws over the past eight years. They said that he has "changed progressively over the years—a complete attitude change from belligerence to resignation, tender-hearted, artistic, loving, gentle and spiritual." Leonard Laws frequently indicated remorse for the other offenses he admitted to having committed. Before being placed on death row, he was in the general population at the Missouri State Penitentiary and he frequently told them he wished he could go back there to "work, help other people, use his mind, and study." He took numerous Bible Study Courses.

This request is that his sentence be commuted to life without parole so that he could live a secure but humane life, helping others, and serving as an example to society, to the extent prison life would permit.

▼▲▼

Leonard Laws received a disproportionate sentence of death because one of the killers struck a deal with the prosecution. In this case, the death penalty was not given for the most heinous actions. Instead, giving testimony against Mr. Laws resulted in just a fifteen-year sentence for the codefendant. Mr. Laws's attorney offered no mitigation evidence (which was available) to give the jury reasons to spare his life.[12] Leonard Laws was executed May 17, 1990.

CASE STUDY:
CONFLICT OF INTEREST

Richard Zeitvogel, CP#36

Richard Zeitvogel was sentenced to death for the killing of fellow inmate Gary Dew in a Jefferson City prison in 1983. Mr. Zeitvogel was a witness to an attempted murder in the basement of the prison chapel. He helped prison officials solve the crime by identifying Mr. Dew as one of the attackers. Mr. Dew's attorney, Julian Ossman, told Mr. Dew who had identified him. While awaiting sentencing, despite Mr. Dew's threats of retaliation against Mr. Zeitvogel for "snitching" on him, Mr. Dew and Mr. Zeitvogel were placed in the same cell. After Mr. Dew's death when Mr. Zeitvogel was charged with capital murder, Julian Ossman, the same attorney who represented Mr. Dew, was appointed to represent Mr. Zeitvogel. Mr. Ossman failed to adequately present evidence of self-defense to the jury or evidence that the chapel incident led to Mr. Dew's death.

▼▲▼
Petition for Executive Clemency[13]

Comes now Richard S. Zeitvogel, a prisoner condemned to die by the State of Missouri, and respectfully requests that the Governor commute his sentence of death, or stay his execution, now scheduled for 12:01 A.M. December 11, 1996. In support of his request, Mr. Zeitvogel states that he is innocent of the crime of murder; he has always maintained that he acted in self defense when he killed Gary Dew. Furthermore, Mr. Zeitvogel has not had a fair opportunity to present his case to any court or jury; he was denied that right by the incompetence of attorneys who represented him at critical points in his appeal. The particulars of these assertions follow.

1. The Evidence That Mr. Zeitvogel Acted in Self Defense Is Overwhelming

Richard Zeitvogel is condemned to die because he helped prison officials solve the attempted murder of Charles Robinson. This seems an unlikely proposition to begin a plea for clemency, but the facts bear us out. On May 15, 1983, Charles Robinson, an inmate at Missouri State Penitentiary, was savagely attacked in the basement of the prison chapel by three other inmates later identified as Gary Dew, John Methfessel and Chester Bettis.

Mr. Robinson was discovered tied to a chair bleeding profusely from severe head wounds and immediately hospitalized. That night, investigators from the Cole County Sheriff's Department were dispatched to the penitentiary to investigate the attack. Deputy Sheriff Spicer prepared the initial offense report. Mr. Robinson told prison authorities that while he was working at the chapel that night, John Methfessel and two other inmates demanded to use a room for homosexual activities. When Mr. Robinson refused them access, the inmates tied him to a chair and beat him over the head with the blade portion of a paper cutter. The assault ended only after Mr. Robinson pretended he was dead.

Deputy Spicer and other law enforcement authorities interviewed several other inmates that night. One of the inmates interviewed was Richard Zeitvogel. Mr. Zeitvogel told authorities he had been outside the chapel earlier in the evening and had seen three white males sitting on the back steps. Mr. Zeitvogel identified the inmates by their "yard names"— "Roundhead," "Kong" and "Crazy." "Roundhead" was John Methfessel, "Kong" was Chester Bettis, and "Crazy" was Gary Dew. The Cole County Sheriff's Department Offense Report prepared by Deputy Spicer that night listed Gary Dew as the number 1 suspect in the Robinson attack.

On July 1, 1983, Gary Dew, Chester Bettis and John Methfessel were all charged in a two-count complaint filed in the Cole County Circuit Court. Count I of the complaint charged defendants with the class B felony of burglary for unlawfully entering the basement of the penitentiary chapel for the purpose of stealing. Count II charged defendants with the class A felony of assault in the first degree for attempting to kill or to cause serious physical injury to inmate Charles Robinson.

The public defender's office was appointed to represent Mr. Dew and Mr. Methfessel. After a preliminary hearing, Mr. Dew and Mr. Methfessel were bound over for trial on both counts. An information was filed in Cole County Circuit Court charging Mr. Dew and Mr. Methfessel with burglary and assault. Mr. Dew was also charged with being a prior and persistent offender because he had been previously found guilty of two or more felonies.

Prior to trial, Julian Ossman was assigned to represent Mr. Dew. Mr. Ossman filed Applications for Writs of *Habeas Corpus Ad Testificandum* requesting the trial appearance of Chester Bettis, Charles Robinson and one Mitchell Gadberry. Mr. Dew was tried and convicted on both counts. The court ordered a pre-sentence investigation report which was subsequently filed. A copy was mailed to Julian Ossman.

While awaiting sentencing, despite Mr. Dew's threats of retaliation against Mr. Zeitvogel for "snitching" on him, Mr. Dew and Mr. Zeitvogel were placed in the same cell. At approximately 4:30 P.M. on March 25, 1984, Corrections Officer James Clemons was conducting a routine count of Housing Unit 5C in the Missouri State Penitentiary. When Officer Clemons entered Group 2 he heard Mr. Zeitvogel yell "I killed my cellie." Mr. Dew was in fact dead inside the cell he and Mr. Zeitvogel were forced to share. Mr. Zeitvogel was immediately removed from the cell and questioned by correctional officers and the Cole County Deputy Sheriff. A Department of Corrections Report prepared that night recites the following information obtained from Mr. Zeitvogel: . . . he and Dew had argued earlier about Zeitvogel telling prison authorities about Dew and another inmate being involved in the unrelated assault at the prison chapel. According to Zeitvogel, Dew hit him in the face, the two struggled and fought for several minutes, and Zeitvogel choked Dew with a strip of sheet. Mr. Zeitvogel stated he tried to revive Dew and then tried to get the guard's attention by flashing an emergency light. An attempt was made to record the interview, but the tape recorder malfunctioned. Mr. Zeitvogel later voluntarily gave Deputy Spicer fingernail scrapings and a blood sample.

. . . After Mr. Dew's death, the Cole County Prosecutor's Office filed a Memorandum of Nolle Prosequi and Mr. Dew's case became a closed file. Mr. Zeitvogel was charged with capital murder. Julian Ossman, the same attorney who represented Mr. Dew, was appointed to represent Mr. Zeitvogel.

Mr. Zeitvogel has consistently and vehemently stated he acted in self defense. From the first interview with prison authorities Mr. Zeitvogel told of Mr. Dew's animosity toward him and the reason for it.

Julian Ossman had personal knowledge that Mr. Zeitvogel had made the statements against Mr. Dew since he was the very attorney who provided Mr. Zeitvogel's statements to Mr. Dew. Despite having first hand knowledge of the reason for the animosity which existed between Mr.

Dew and Mr. Zeitvogel, Mr. Ossman failed to present even minimal credible evidence in support of self-defense. Most egregiously, Mr. Ossman failed to ever disclose his conflict of interest.

Even though Mr. Ossman was personally familiar with the chapel incident and Mr. Dew's role in that crime, the jury never heard evidence of the chapel incident. Instead, the jury only heard vague testimony from several inmates regarding existing animosity between Mr. Dew and Mr. Zeitvogel. No clarification was ever elicited or presented by Mr. Ossman throughout Mr. Zeitvogel's trial.

Mr. Ossman presented only two witnesses in support of Mr. Zeitvogel's claim of self-defense. Inmate Charles Stevenson testified having overheard conversation from Gary Dew directed to a guard:

> Man, you got to get me out of that cell, because if you don't get me out of that cell I' doing just like I did that motherfucker down there in chapel. . . . You've got to get me out of this cell before I kill him.

Despite Mr. Stevenson's testimony referring to the chapel assault and Mr. Ossman's personal intimate knowledge of the chapel crime, no further evidence was elicited from the witness concerning Mr. Dew's role in the chapel assault and burglary. The jury never heard even a minimal explanation as to what "just like I did . . . down there in chapel" meant.

The other defense witness presented at trial was Chester Bettis, Mr. Dew's co-defendant in the chapel case. Despite Mr. Ossman's knowledge of Mr. Dews' and Mr. Bettis' involvement in the chapel case, and despite the fact Mr. Bettis testified in Mr. Dew's case, Mr. Ossman again failed to adduce any testimony concerning the chapel crime. Mr. Ossman only asked Mr. Bettis about a conversation he had with Mr. Dew as Mr. Dew was being transferred to Mr. Zeitvogel's cell:

Q. Did he say why he was going to 5C?
A. Yeah.
Q. What did he say?
A. That he was going to take care of somebody down there.
Q. Did he tell you who that was?
A. Yes.
Q. Who was it?
A. Rickie Zeitvogel.
Q. By take care of him, what do you mean?
A. By killing him.
Mr. Ossman: I have no further questions.

During cross examination Mr. Bettis made two other vague references to the chapel incident with no follow up by Mr. Ossman:

> **Bettis:** No, he [Dew] was upset because he didn't get his time yet, he was pretty upset because of people telling on him; that's—you know, he got some evidence reports from somewhere, I think it was his attorney, or somewhere, and as soon as he got that, he seen everybody's statements, and he was pretty uptight. And he had some violations for dangerous contraband, and I know Crazy pretty well, he's not at all sane, you know, and that's the reason why he got the nickname of Crazy. I know him pretty good.

Mr. Bettis further testified about Mr. Dew's conviction on the chapel burglary and assault:

> **Bettis:** Yeah, when he got busted. He told me he was going down, I tried talking him out of it but he wouldn't listen to me. You know, when he makes up his mind he does what he wants to do. He had a lot at time, and he was only doing seven years before this big time. I don't even think he got his time for the assault that he was charged with, and he was pretty upset about what happened, a jury found him guilty, and me and him was real good friends, and after he found out that, you know, well, I made my little statement on the stand there, "Yeah, I'm guilty I was there," and all this stuff, and he got pretty upset about that. And that's the reason why I came to him, I wanted to get it straightened out. I told him if he wanted to kill me because I was a snitch, then, I'm not going to stop him; but he didn't do that, because we used to be cellies together, and we was real cool to each other.
>
> **Q.** Okay.
>
> **A.** Then he's also threatened—he's not only threatened me, he's threatened Methfessel, and that guy right here (indicating Zeitvogel).

Even though Mr. Bettis referred to the chapel crime, and Mr. Ossman had personal knowledge of that crime and Mr. Dew's involvement, no other questions were asked of Mr. Bettis. Ironically, Mr. Ossman was the attorney Mr. Bettis referred to as having given the reports of witnesses' statements to Mr. Dew.

In a subsequent sworn statement, recalling the events in the chapel that night, Mr. Bettis states: "After we were arrested Gary Dew found out that Zeitvogel had rolled on him and he vowed to kill Zeitvogel." Mr. Bettis remembers Mr. Dew showing him copies of Mr. Zeitvogel's statements "snitching" on them that they were provided by Mr. Dew's attorney. Mr. Bettis recalls the day in March 1985, when he learned an inmate was dead:

[A]fter I heard an inmate was dead, I knew it was Zeitvogel because Gary Dew was determined to get him. I was surprised when I heard it was Dew who got killed and even more surprised when Zeitvogel got charged. Everybody, inmates and guards alike knew it was self-defense and nobody would have died if the guards hadn't put Dew in Zeitvogel's cell.

Another co-defendant in the chapel crime, John Methfessel admitted "he and Dew . . . agreed that we were going to take Chester and Zeitvogel out for rolling over on us." Mr. Methfessel remembers Mr. Dew getting himself transferred to Mr. Zeitvogel's area of the penitentiary and Mr. Dew telling him "Don't worry about Zeitvogel, I know what I have to do." Mr. Methfessel recalls that when he heard an inmate had died he believed Mr. Dew had kept his word and "took out Zeitvogel."

Mr. Zeitvogel was convicted of capital murder and sentenced to death without Mr. Ossman ever disclosing his conflict of interest and without Mr. Ossman ever presenting the evidence he was personally familiar with concerning Mr. Dew's motive to attack Mr. Zeitvogel. After Mr. Zeitvogel's conviction and sentence were affirmed on appeal, he filed a 27.26 state post-conviction motion. Dennis Gooden was appointed to represent Mr. Zeitvogel on that motion. In an affidavit, Mr. Gooden states he was never told Mr. Ossman previously represented Mr. Dew, nor did he have any reason to suspect Mr. Ossman ever represented Mr. Dew.

During the hearing on the 27.26 motion, Mr. Ossman testified of his conversations with Mr. Zeitvogel in preparation for trial. Mr. Ossman voluntarily brought to the 27.26 hearing a transcript of one meeting he had with Mr. Zeitvogel. The transcript was marked as a Respondent's exhibit and admitted into evidence. The transcript conclusively demonstrates that Mr. Zeitvogel (RZ) told Mr. Ossman (JJO) that Mr. Dew was out to get him for having been an informant on the chapel crime.

> **RZ.** Gary Dew is known as Crazy and I got arrested for the case that they got arrested on.
>
> **JJO.** That's Dew and Methfessel?
>
> **RZ.** Yea and Animan. They turned me loose, Roundhead and Dew and all of them sent word out that I snitched on them because I said I'd seen them when I was going to the lower yard.
>
> **JJO.** Who were they accused of . . . same guy?
>
> **RZ.** No, they're accused of kidnapping this dude in the Catholic Church.
>
> **JJO.** What's his name?
>
> **RZ.** I don't know . . . they assaulted. They kidnapped this dude down there and tied him up and beat him. . . .

Later in the meeting the following exchange occurs:

> **RZ.** Now if I can prove that I had a conflict between these people.
> **JJO.** But you're going to have to take the stand to do it.
> **RZ.** No, the man knows it. If this so called statement is in there that I was supposed to have made saying that I seen Dew and them and Methfessel and them by the Chapel . . .
> **JJO.** Why do those names ring a bell with me.

At no time did Mr. Ossman ever disclose to Mr. Zeitvogel or to the court that he had a conflict of interest by having previously represented Gary Dew. Mr. Ossman's failure to disclose his conflict of interest and withdraw from the representation of Mr. Zeitvogel, constitutes ineffective assistance of counsel. Not only did Mr. Ossman have an actual conflict, he was the very person who provided Mr. Dew the motive to kill Mr. Zeitvogel. The only reason Mr. Dew ever knew Mr. Zeitvogel had been the confidential informant against him was because Mr. Ossman gave Mr. Dew the report containing Mr. Zeitvogel's statements.

There is no doubt Mr. Ossman had an actual conflict. Instead of reporting the conflict, Mr. Ossman continued to represent Mr. Zeitvogel and hid the fact that he, Mr. Zeitvogel's own attorney, had provided the motive to Mr. Dew. Mr. Ossman's actions in representing Mr. Zeitvogel, despite his conflict, prevented the jury from ever hearing any competent evidence that Mr. Zeitvogel indeed acted in self-defense and is innocent of capital murder. By pretending to be ignorant of the chapel crime and Mr. Zeitvogel's role implicating Mr. Dew in that crime, Mr. Ossman deprived Mr. Zeitvogel of his only defense to Mr. Dew's murder.

Mr. Zeitvogel has always maintained he acted in self-defense when he strangled Mr. Dew. Mr. Zeitvogel told prison authorities this immediately after the murder and told Mr. Ossman the same when he was initially appointed to represent him. Incredulously, Mr. Ossman already had personal knowledge that Mr. Zeitvogel indeed acted in self-defense. However, only indirect and minimal evidence of self-defense was presented at trial. The jury convicted Mr. Zeitvogel without ever hearing about the chapel crime, Mr. Dew's involvement in that crime, or Mr. Zeitvogel's role as an informant against Mr. Dew. Under Missouri law, this evidence would have been admissible and supportive of Mr. Zeitvogel's claim of self-defense.

2. The Courts Have Refused to Consider Mr. Zeitvogel's Evidence That He Acted in Self Defense Solely Because of Mistakes Made by His Court-Appointed Lawyers

Mr. Zeitvogel attempted to present the above evidence to the courts in his petition for writ of habeas corpus. However, the courts failed to consider the evidence because of the doctrine of procedural bar, which prevents the court from considering evidence which is not presented in the first appeal. Since the case of *Coleman v. Thompson*, even where the failure to present evidence in the first state post-conviction hearing is clearly due to incompetent appointed counsel, the prisoner is forever bound by the lawyer's mistakes. That is exactly what happened to Mr. Zeitvogel—the most compelling evidence that he acted in self defense was not presented by any of his attorneys in the state court. The 8th Circuit Court of Appeals was not the least bit reticent to point out that the reason it was denying Mr. Zeitvogel's plea was the deficient performance of the lawyer appointed for him by the State of Missouri:

> Post-conviction counsel could have obtained the state hospital and prison records if he had acted reasonably and diligently, but he made no effort to obtain them. . . . In our view, the blame for Zeitvogel's procedural default falls squarely on Zeitvogel's post-conviction counsel rather than counsel for the state. . . . [P]ost-conviction counsel failed to follow through on the information handed to him on a silver platter.

Following the Supreme Court rule that the prisoner is bound by the mistakes of his court-appointed post-conviction lawyer, the court of appeals refused to even consider the persuasive evidence that Mr. Zeitvogel acted in self defense. Thus, Mr. Zeitvogel is to be executed because his attorney screwed up his case.

In justifying the courts' adherence to this unforgiving rule, Justice Rehnquist declared, "Clemency is deeply rooted in our Anglo-American tradition of law, and it is the historic remedy for preventing a miscarriage of justice where judicial process has been exhausted." The Governor is not restricted in his clemency powers. He can grant or deny clemency for any reason, or for no reason. He is not bound by the doctrine of procedural default. Indeed, in being able to freely review the facts of the case, he holds "a court of equity in his own breast, to soften the rigor of the general law, in such criminal cases as merit an exemption from punishment," W. Blackstone (Commentaries).

Mr. Zeitvogel has always insisted that he acted in self defense when he killed Gary Dew; substantial credible evidence indicates that he is telling the truth. The courts have refused to even consider the irrefutable facts which indicate that his trial was a sham and a mockery of justice, primarily because the attorneys appointed by the state of Missouri performed incompetently. The courts have as much as said so. The fundamental miscarriage of justice that has taken place, and the refusal of the Court to correct it, create a powerful justification for the exercise of the governor's power of clemency.

▼▲▼

In Richard Zeitvogel's case, the trial attorney had a conflict of interest that interfered with his effective defense of Mr. Zeitvogel. He offered only indirect and minimal evidence at trial to support Mr. Zeitvogel's claim of self-defense. The state also bears some responsibility for the crime, given that it was the prison guards who put the two prisoners together after it was well known that the victim planned to kill Mr. Zeitvogel. Richard Zeitvogel was executed December 11, 1996.

CASE STUDY:
NO WITNESSES PRESENTED

Kelvin Malone, CP#146

Kelvin Malone was convicted of the 1981 fatal shooting of William Parr, a St. Louis cabdriver. Mr. Malone's trial lawyer did not seriously work on his case until about two weeks prior to the jury trial. He presented no evidence during the trial's guilt phase. Some of his mistakes include: not calling material witnesses from the scene who would have cast doubt on the prosecution's case; a total failure to prepare and address the sudden in-court identification of Mr. Malone as being a man near Mr. Parr's cab; overlooking the inconclusiveness of ballistic reports that allegedly connected Mr. Malone with Mr. Parr's death; and the omission of presenting mitigating evidence during Mr. Malone's penalty phase. Mr. Malone passed a polygraph indicating he truthfully stated he did not kill the victim.

▼▲▼
Petition for Clemency[14]

You, Governor Carnahan, are the last resort for justice and mercy for Kelvin. Kelvin's life should be spared because . . .

1. Ineffective Trial Counsel
No one insists that Kelvin should have received a perfect trial or have been represented by a "dream team" of lawyers. However, everyone insists Kelvin deserved fairness. He's entitled to a fair trial and adequate representation. He didn't get either.

Kelvin's miserable representation began November 23, 1983, a mere four months before the start of his capital murder trial, when lawyer William Aylward entered his appearance to defend Kelvin. Mr. Aylward did not get the prosecution's evidence in pre-trial discovery until January 17, 1984—68 days before the trial! In that time, Mr. Aylward tried a capital murder trial from February 27, 1984–March 10, 1984. Before that, he tried an armed robbery of an armored car case in the City of St. Louis. Kelvin's trial counsel did not seriously work on his case until about two weeks prior to the jury trial. Mr. Aylward put it best when he told the trial judge at the start of this case that, "I do not feel I am adequately prepared to begin trial on this case at this time." At this point, Mr. Aylward tried to blame Kelvin for the case proceeding to trial that day, stating Kelvin insisted that the trial go on at that moment. Any competent attorney would have known that this was not sound reasoning, and would not have acceded to Kelvin's stated desire at that time. As you will see in the second part of the petition, Kelvin had a history of mental difficulties. If Mr. Aylward had done his homework, he would have known that about Kelvin. (As you will soon realize, Mr. Aylward didn't do his homework.) Therefore, to take this unsound reasoning to go ahead and proceed to trial unprepared was not reasonable or fair on Mr. Aylward's part. As the trial progressed, Kelvin sadly discovered just how woefully unprepared Mr. Aylward was for any trial, let alone a capital trial. Kelvin suffered miserably through the mistakes Mr. Aylward's unpreparedness caused.

Kelvin's lawyer's many mistakes include, but are not limited to:

A. Not calling material witnesses from the scene who would have cast doubt on the prosecution's case;

B. A total failure to prepare and address the sudden and unfair surprise in-court identification of Kelvin as being a man near victim William Parr's cab;

C. Overlooking the inconclusiveness of ballistic reports that allegedly connected Kelvin with Mr. Parr's death;

D. A complete lack of knowledge of Kelvin's California testimony. This failure caused the California prosecutor to mislead the St. Louis County jury to believe Kelvin made admissions about Mr. Parr's death;

E. The potentially fatal omission of presenting true mitigating evidence during Kelvin's penalty phase;

F. The failure to convey to the jury that this is a weak circumstantial case rather than one built solidly on direct evidence;

G. Not realizing that the cumulative effect of his many errors would lead Kelvin to the gas chamber (now lethal injection).

Kelvin's lawyer presented no evidence during the trial's guilt phase. This certainly indicated to the jury that Kelvin had no defense. Nothing could have been further from the truth. Steven Ferrell told the police he saw someone in Mr. Parr's cab that night. They had him look at five photographs in what the police call a photo spread. Kelvin's photograph was one of the five photographs Mr. Ferrell reviewed. He could not identify any of the persons in the photographs as the person he had seen in the cab. Michael Holloran worked as a security guard in a bank lobby and may have seen Mr. Parr shortly before his death. The police had Mr. Holloran hypnotized and he related that he spoke to a "real black man," age 28–32. Had Kelvin's lawyer bothered, he could have found some official document with Kelvin's description at or near the time of Mr. Parr's death. A police report dated February 6, 1981 gives a description of Kelvin as NMA, 20, 6–2, 155, Blk/Brn. That is nowhere near the man Mr. Holloran describes, and Mr. Aylward never presented this. These witnesses who saw Mr. Parr's killer and remembered the man in detail but could not identify Kelvin cast doubt on Kelvin's guilt. A minimally competent attorney would have offered the exculpatory testimony from Mr. Ferrell who saw the killer in the cab, looked at Kelvin's photograph, and stated Kelvin was not the man. When the prosecution rested its case without calling on-scene witnesses Mr. Ferrell and Mr. Holloran, a light should have gone on in Mr. Aylward's head. A competent attorney who had prepared his case would have realized the State knew its case was weak and these witnesses would have cast doubt that the right man was on trial.

This would have been readily evident to any mindful attorney in light of the surprise in-court identification by Mr. Richard Elder. On the day the trial commenced, the prosecutor in open court told the judge twice that he knew of no witnesses who would be able to come into court and identify Mr. Malone. However, a short time later the prosecutor advised that Mr. Parr's friend, Richard Elder, would identify Kelvin as the man he saw outside the bank shortly before Mr. Parr's death. Had Kelvin received competent representation, trial counsel would have investigated prior to trial whether any of the witnesses could identify Kelvin. By neglecting this elemental task, Mr. Aylward was left with asking for long shot remedies like a mistrial or a continuance. No trial judge will grant a lawyer these extreme remedies when a lawyer fails to prepare his case as did Mr. Aylward. Though the fault belongs to Mr. Aylward, it is Kelvin who has suffered the consequences. Mr. Elder stated that he identified Kelvin by looking through the courtroom doors' window during the afternoon before he testified. How was Mr. Elder permitted to look through this window prior to his testimony? Who allowed this to occur? Was Mr. Elder guided to this place? In every criminal trial, both parties invoke the rule of sequestration. This means the witnesses do not sit in the courtroom to view prior testimony and they do not talk to other witnesses in order to get their stories straight. When sequestration is violated, you have results like the tainted, suggestive evidence that led to Kelvin's conviction.

The questions posed remain hanging because Mr. Aylward never asked them. Any competent lawyer could have done so. This prejudiced Kelvin because the prosecutor's weak circumstantial case included Mr. Elder's suggestive in-court identification of the man he thought he saw near his friend's cab. In this weak case, the prosecutor needed every weak link in their chain in order to connect Kelvin to the scene. Mr. Aylward's oversight here contributed to Kelvin's condemnation.

Along with Mr. Aylward's failure to investigate the witnesses, Mr. Aylward failed to review adequately the physical evidence. In a circumstantial case like this one, a reasonably competent attorney would have examined thoroughly the physical evidence. A glaring example here rests with the ballistics report. The prosecutor tried to establish a connection between a gun found with Kelvin in California with the ballistics here. Four firearms examiners reviewed the ballistics. Though FBI Firearms Examiner Dillon claimed there was a positive link between the gun and the St. Louis County ballistics, he's the only one of the four who made that claim. Only through his cross-examination of Examiner William Crosswhite did Mr. Aylward bring out the fact that not every expert agreed that the ballistics linked Kelvin with the crime.

In fact, the majority of the firearms examiners who reviewed the evidence stated that the link was inconclusive. Mr. Aylward failed to take the necessary steps to bring in Examiner Stubits and the business records of Senior Examiner Reeder whose testimony would have corroborated that of Examiner Crosswhite that the ballistics results were inconclusive. Indeed, given the fact that Mr. Aylward called no witnesses, it's logical to believe the jury would have never heard about the inconsistent results but for the fact the State called Examiner Crosswhite and Mr. Aylward bothered to cross examine him. Had the prosecutor not called Examiner Crosswhite, given Mr. Aylward's record on this case, the jury would never have even received the fleeting hint it received about the ballistics reports' inconclusiveness. This point became critical because the prosecutor argued that FBI Agent Dillon, who claimed the results conclusively tied the weapon found near Kelvin to the bullet removed from Mr. Parr's brain, was the more credible witness. (Given what we know today about the inconsistencies and the inaccuracies from FBI laboratories,[15] is that really a convincing argument to send a man to the death chamber?) Had Mr. Aylward not been ineffective, the defense could have countered Mr. Dil-

Ion's opinion with Examiner Stubits and the business records reflecting the findings of Senior Examiner Reeder, who was unavailable, having suffered from a massive heart attack. Again, but for his lawyer's ineffectiveness, Kelvin would not be facing Potosi's death chamber.

Also, yet another of Mr. Aylward's mistakes was his complete and total lack of knowledge about what transpired during Kelvin's trial in California. The Missouri prosecutors called Gary Admire, the lawyer who prosecuted Kelvin's case in California, to the stand to advise what Kelvin testified about during his California trial. Mr. Aylward's lack of knowledge of Kelvin's California testimony allowed this California prosecutor to mislead the St. Louis county jury to believe that Kelvin made admissions about Mr. Parr's death. Though this is not the time to recount every inaccuracy that Mr. Aylward missed, there are two crucial inaccuracies that Mr. Aylward missed which led directly to Kelvin's Missouri death sentence.

First, Mr. Admire recounted that before the police apprehended Kelvin, he fled from the San Jose police officers. Mr. Admire stated that Kelvin testified that he indicated that for various reasons he was afraid of being identified and apprehended for his activities. Mr. Admire coyly did not say what charges Kelvin was "afraid about." Clearly, Mr. Admire's testimony in this murder trial implied that Kelvin admitted murder. However, that's not true. In California, Kelvin testified that when the police came to his car in San Jose he was wanted in Monterey County for "burglary, parole violation, possession of stolen property, reckless driving, evading arrest, and resisting arrest"—no admission of any murder. Kelvin testified that he "stepped on the gas" because "I was wanted in Monterey County, and . . . there was the weapons in the car, and I knew that it would be another charge"—again, no admission of any murder. Mr. Admire's insinuation was wrong: Kelvin did not flee the San Jose police because he was wanted for murder, and Mr. Aylward did nothing useful to clear that up.

Second, Mr. Admire misled the jury when he said that Kelvin admitted arriving in St. Louis at the Greyhound Station near the bank when and where Mr. Parr was last seen alive. Mr. Admire testified that Kelvin told the California jury that he arrived in St. Louis on March 18, 1981 on a Greyhound bus. The specificity with which Mr. Admire testified clearly placed Kelvin in the area of the crime scene at the appropriate time. Yet, this was not Kelvin's testimony. With disregard for the truth, the prosecutors led the jury to believe that by his own California testimony, Kelvin put himself at the crime scene at the time it happened. This was very powerful evidence and yet it was blatantly false. Nonetheless, Kelvin's lawyer failed to point this out during cross-examination. In this, his performance was grossly deficient.

Though Kelvin's lawyer failed to recognize how crucial Mr. Admire's testimony had been, it was not lost on the prosecutors. This distortion was repeated in their closing arguments several times and emphasized over and over again, giving it more weight. Kelvin's lawyer's failure to point out effectively that it was untrue that Kelvin made these blatant admissions is crucial because other than Mr. Admire's false and misleading testimony, there was only weak circumstantial evidence that Kelvin arrived by Greyhound on March 18, 1981. Again, but for Kelvin's lawyer's ineffectiveness, the outcome of Kelvin's trial would have been different.

As these examples clearly show, Kelvin did not receive effective assistance of counsel as is everyone's guarantee. In order to provide effective assistance of counsel to a person facing the death penalty, the attorney must conduct a thorough investigation of the circumstances surrounding the offense. The attorney must become thoroughly familiar with the facts the prosecution will present at trial. This familiarity comes through obtaining all the police reports, lab reports, experts' reports, and all documentary evidence the State has in its possession. It comes from interviewing and deposing the State's crucial witnesses. It comes from extensive communications with the client and conducting investigation to determine whether any defenses exist for the guilt phase of the trial. It certainly does not come from working on the case for a few days and does not magically occur overnight. It comes through work and preparation. That's the least that Missouri could have offered Kelvin in trial. Instead, without your mercy, Governor Carnahan, Kelvin faces execution after receiving terrible assistance of counsel.

2. Kelvin Received a Horrendously Deficient Penalty Phase

During the penalty phase, Kelvin continued to receive ineffective assistance of counsel. As was readily evidenced by reviewing the guilt phase, Mr. Aylward proved that two weeks is not enough time to prepare an adequate penalty phase. For Kelvin's penalty phase, Mr. Aylward presented no witnesses to humanize Kelvin or to explain the circumstances of his life. He called only one witness, an academic who testified that there was no evidence to support the view that the death penalty is an effective deterrent. You can just hear the jury say "Big Deal." His lack of investigation, preparation, and presentation for his client showed Mr. Aylward was in no way mindful of the basic philosophy for all capital cases articulated in *Lockett v. Ohio:*

> In capital cases the fundamental respect for humanity underlying the Eighth Amendment requires consideration of the character and record of the individual and the circumstances of a particular offense as a constitutionally indispensable part of the process of inflicting the penalty of death.

The entire penalty phase—*including* jury deliberation on the appropriate punishment—lasted only four hours. The only aggravating evidence introduced by the prosecutors were Kelvin's prior convictions and sentences from California which the prosecutors read to the jury from the certified court records.

Again, Mr. Aylward would blame Kelvin for insufficient penalty phase. He stated that Kelvin told him not to bother his family because Kelvin did not want to put his family through the trauma of another trial. However, Kelvin was on trial for his life. A lawyer's actions in serving his client must be reasonable. If Mr. Aylward had reviewed the California transcripts, he would have realized that Kelvin had, in fact, a loving support system of family and friends who readily would have assisted Mr. Aylward in Kelvin's defense. . . .

3. The Lack of a Proper Signature Served as a Procedural Bar to Having Kelvin's Claim of Ineffective Assistance of Counsel Heard by the Courts

Governor Carnahan, one would easily, but mistakenly, assume that these claims have already been meaningfully addressed by the courts. After all, Missouri has remedies for postconviction relief claims of ineffective assistance of counsel, and executive clemency is usually the court of last resort. Governor Carnahan, you are Kelvin's only *real* chance for review and help. Carefully reviewing this case's sad, twisted procedural history clearly demonstrates this. In Kelvin's case a Dickensian adherence to the rules and procedures (over substance) has caused Kelvin to slip through our safeguards.

Kelvin's attempt to have the performance of his trial counsel reviewed started on July 3, 1986, when Kelvin's postconviction attorney, Dorthy Hirzy, filed a motion pursuant to Missouri Supreme Court Rule 27.26 alleging ineffective assistance of trial counsel. That motion was neither signed nor verified by Kelvin personally, but rather was signed and verified by Ms. Hirzy in the following manner, "Kelvin Malone by Dorthy Hirzy." On March 13, 1987, an amended motion was filed by Ms. Hirzy. Again, that motion was neither signed nor verified by Kelvin, but was signed by Ms. Hirzy. Circuit Court Judge Kenneth Weinstock dismissed this motion because Kelvin was incarcerated in California, and therefore was not in the custody of Missouri as required by the rule and thus could not invoke his rights until he was actually in the custody of Missouri. On March 8, 1988, the Missouri Court of Appeals affirmed the circuit court's dismissal holding that Kelvin could not pursue the motion at that time since he was still incarcerated in California, but that the dismissal was without prejudice to the filing of further postconviction relief under the new Missouri Supreme Court Rule 29.15. Under the change in the law, his lawyer had until June 30, 1988 to have everything in order for Kelvin to pursue his claim of ineffective assistance of trial counsel. On May 24, 1988, Ms. Hirzy filed another postconviction motion as his Rule 29.15 motion. This motion was also neither signed, nor verified by Kelvin as required by the Rule; rather it was signed by Ms. Hirzy even though the clear language of the Rule required that Kelvin sign and verify the motion. On July 19, 1988, Ms. Hirzy filed an amended motion. This proved fatal to Kelvin's motion because the clear language of Rule 29.15 required verification of amended postconviction motions.

Following an evidentiary hearing on January 12, 1989, the circuit court denied Kelvin's claim. He appealed to the Missouri Supreme Court. During the appeal, the State challenged *for the first time* Kelvin's original and amended motions as insufficient per Rule 29.15(d) because the motions were unverified. The Missouri Supreme Court ruled that it was faced with an incomplete record on the verification issue and remanded the matter to the circuit court to conduct an evidentiary hearing and determine whether Kelvin complied with the verification requirements. On January 19, 1990, the circuit court dismissed Kelvin's Rule 29.15 motion, holding that the failure to file a properly-verified motion on or before June 30, 1988 deprived the court of jurisdiction to consider the merits of the claims. The circuit court dismissed the motion and the Missouri Supreme Court affirmed that holding and the reasoning. In effect, this denied Kelvin review on the merits of his claim regarding the denial of effective and adequate assistance of trial counsel. Kelvin pursued his remedy of habeas corpus through the federal courts, but the federal courts lacked the power to provide relief because the failure to comply with the verification provision served as a procedural bar to the federal courts granting Kelvin relief.

Governor Carnahan, you must grasp the uniqueness of Kelvin's situation. First, verification is no longer required by Rule 29.15 so no one filing an amended motion under the current version of the rule will be barred by the technicality of not having the client's signature verified. Second, the courts have now dropped the rigidness of the adherence to the rules at all costs. After *Sanders v. State,*[16] there is a remedy for the rare instances when a person may file a claim that may be out of time through no fault of their own. The Missouri Supreme Court has established explicit guidelines for counsel to follow in future cases where fairness demands a person be allowed to file a claim out of time:

> At such time counsel may seek leave to file pleadings out of time, the motion shall set forth facts, not conclusions, showing justification for untimeliness. Where insufficiently informed, the Court is directed to make independent inquiry as to the cause of the untimely filing. The burden is on the movant to demonstrate that the untimeliness is not the result of negligence or intentional conduct of the movant, but is due to counsel's failure to comply with Rule 29.15 (*Sanders,* 1991: 495).

No court has applied the *Sanders* case retroactively to Kelvin. It's not Kelvin's fault that the law changed for the better after it was too late for the courts to help him. Given the way lawyers that Missouri had thrust upon Kelvin treated his case as if it were some afterthought, it's unreasonable to believe anyone here had much interest in looking out for Kelvin and pursuing this matter. Yet, it's not too late for you, Governor Carnahan. It's your duty with the supreme power of executive clemency to correct this manifest injustice. It's not fair to deny Kelvin full review and then kill him. The law must serve Justice, not merely slavishly adhere to heartless rules.

It is ironic in this time when many in the general public assume that defendants are always "getting off" on technicalities, Kelvin, who has suffered serious and grave mistakes at trial and other state court proceedings, will be killed on the technicality that he suffered ineffective assistance of trial counsel and was unable to show that miscarriage of justice to the Missouri Supreme Court because his post-conviction attorney failed to comply with the clear requirements of the post-conviction rules in effect at the time. The only remedy for these serious mistakes rests with you, Governor Carnahan, and your executive clemency power.

4. Kelvin's California Appeals Are Not Concluded

It would be unfair to execute Kelvin on January 13, 1999 because his California appeals are not concluded. The only aggravating evidence the prosecutor used during the penalty phase were certified records that Kelvin had a death sentence in California. Obviously, Kelvin's jury used that as a justification for their imposition of a Missouri death sentence. If that

California sentence is reversed, it would be unfair for Missouri to kill Kelvin for an aggravating circumstance that no longer exists.

Attorney Peter Giannini filed a habeas corpus petition in the U.S. District Court for the Central District of California. A Motion of Summary on all claims has been fully briefed, and was taken under submission by the district court on December 9, 1998. The claims which should result in a reversal of Kelvin's conviction rest on two issues: substantial jury misconduct and false testimony from a jailhouse snitch.

As to the jury misconduct issue, Kelvin's sentence violated Ninth Circuit precedent relating to fair trials tried by impartial jurors. Kelvin had taken a polygraph which showed that he was not the actual killer of the victim. The trial court granted the admissibility of these results. Counsel for both sides conducted individual voir dire (jury selection questioning) of each potential juror regarding their knowledge of polygraphs, their experience with it, and their opinions about it. Dr. Diane Irwin was one of the potential jurors questioned about it. All previous jurors who had expressed an opinion regarding polygraphs and stated they could not fairly consider the matter had been excused by peremptory challenge by one side or the other. Dr. Irwin intentionally lied on voir dire that she had no experience with polygraphs and that she had formed no opinion regarding them. Dr. Irwin was a psychologist. She was ultimately selected as the jury's foreperson. During the deliberations, one of the jurors stated that he had read in the newspaper that Kelvin's case was the first time a trial court in San Bernadino County had admitted polygraph evidence. The polygraph examiner had testified that Kelvin's responses were truthful when he denied killing the victim. Other members of the jury solicited Dr. Irwin's opinion regarding the validity of polygraph results during their deliberations. Dr. Irwin later admitted that she told the other jurors during deliberations that she had reviewed substantial research on polygraph reliability, and that contrary to the trial testimony, polygraph results were accurate only about half the time and could be manipulated. She told the other jurors that polygraphs were not reliable. According to Dr. Irwin, the discussion concerning polygraphs was extensive and it weighed heavily upon the deliberations. Her contribution to these deliberations also was enormous. Since the other jurors treated this juror-psychologist as an expert, they followed her opinions and disregarded the polygraph evidence.

. . . The polygraph was crucial to the defense in both the guilt phase and the penalty phase because it supported Kelvin's contention that he did not kill the victim. . . . Dr. Irwin's lies on voir dire completely destroyed Kelvin's defense because she, as the foreperson, introduced extrinsic evi-

dence into the deliberations. . . . Dr. Irwin's misconduct is in direct violation of California legal precedent. . . . In California, the presence of a
biased juror cannot be harmless error and it requires a new trial. . . .

The second major issue that will result in Kelvin's California conviction
and death sentence being reversed rests with the testimony of the prosecution's key witness, Charles Laughlin, the jailhouse snitch. Mr. Laughlin
claimed to have spoken to Kelvin on numerous occasions when they were
in jail together. Mr. Laughlin testified that Kelvin admitted to committing
murders in California and Missouri. In the years since the trial, it has been
shown that Mr. Laughlin's testimony about Kelvin's confession was false.
The California Supreme Court has determined that Mr. Laughlin believed
he had a deal on unrelated charges in exchange for testimony in Kelvin's
case and he fabricated his testimony about Kelvin's confessions to him.
At the federal district court level, Kelvin's lawyers have asserted that Mr.
Laughlin's testimony violated Kelvin's rights under the Fifth, Sixth, Eighth,
and Fourteenth Amendments to the United States Constitution. Mr.
Laughlin has conclusively been shown to be an opportunistic liar, who has
been willing to say whatever is necessary to get himself off from his latest
legal mess. Since Kelvin's conviction was obtained in large part due to
Mr. Laughlin's false testimony, Kelvin will be entitled to a reversal of the
California conviction and death sentence.

If the California death sentence is overturned, it will be gallingly unfair
for Missouri to kill Kelvin over a legal aggravating circumstance that no
longer exists. Even the conservative United States Supreme Court ruled in
Johnson v. Mississippi,[17] that a death sentence based at least in part on a
prior invalid felony conviction violated the Eighth Amendment prohibition
against cruel and unusual punishment. If the federal district court grants
Kelvin relief, that California conviction will be invalid, and it would not be
fair to kill Kelvin over a major aggravating circumstance which the jury
considered in sentencing Kelvin to death when that aggravating circumstance no longer exists. . . .

5. Conclusion

Kelvin's case is a classic example of the process failures that can occur
in death cases—failures at trial, failures at postconviction stage. These failures cost lives. But Kelvin's life can be saved. This case provides you, Governor Carnahan, a unique opportunity to show that Missouri does care
about the Justice of the process. By taking action to correct the injustice
of Kelvin's Missouri case, you, Governor Carnahan, can show compassion,
concern, and mercy. Here, the wrongs and mistakes are so egregious and

the consequences so severe that you, Governor Carnahan, are fully justified in taking a positive action and granting executive clemency.

Most Missourians are unaware of Kelvin and the issue of whether he will
die on January 13, 1999. It just takes too much time to grasp the details,
too much effort to understand the developments that make Kelvin's execution a grave wrong. Some may argue that the politically astute decision
allows the execution to go on and lets Kelvin die. However, you, Governor
Carnahan, are not known for the politically expedient decision, especially
when that decision is not the just one.

Even those who favor the death penalty, if fully advised about the
wrongs and mistakes in Kelvin's case would agree that Kelvin's death is
not the decision that a careful consideration of the facts compels. Careful
consideration compels belief that no one in Missouri be put to death after
a trial with terrible representation from a lawyer who readily admits in
open court on the record that he is not prepared to go to trial. Careful
consideration requires that no one in Missouri be put to death after a
penalty phase that offered sparse to no mitigation despite a wealth of
mitigating evidence that would have weighed against a sentence of death.
It also requires that no one in Missouri be put to death after full review of
the terrible representation one received in trial is denied over the technicality that a proper verification was not obtained. It's frightening to confront how badly the Justice system has failed Kelvin Malone and the
citizens of Missouri who have a right to fair court procedures to test the
correctness of its decisions. Someone must stand up, rather than hide
behind legal technicalities and say this is wrong. Our liberty, all of our
liberty, depends on the criminal justice system's ultimate fairness. In rare
cases such as this, it's the governor who is fairness' final arbiter. Today,
you, Governor Carnahan, are the last and final hope.

We respectfully request you, Governor Carnahan, to commute Kelvin's
sentence from the Missouri death sentence to a sentence on his Missouri
case to life in prison without the possibility of parole and remand Kelvin
to California in order to complete his California proceedings. As a gesture
of good will, two weeks prior to the arrival of Pope John II, you, Governor
Carnahan, should grant clemency to a fellow human whose case is con-
taminated with serious errors. This historic and courageous human rights
gesture will impress a watching world.

▼▲▼

In Kelvin Malone's case, the trial lawyer's admitted unpreparedness
was directly responsible for not being able to counter the prosecutor's

use of a flawed witness identification and repeated restatements of the testimony of another witness's false testimony in closing arguments. In addition, the courts were unwilling to allow Mr. Malone's appeals in his California case to be completed before rushing to execute him. Kelvin Malone was executed January 13, 1999.

CONCLUSIONS

This chapter presented four cases that illustrate the major problems encountered with trial attorneys in Missouri death penalty cases. Generally the attorneys assigned to these cases had little or no experience with capital murder trials. Other problems involved inadequate preparation for trial and little or no pretrial investigation. This lack of investigation led directly to not presenting readily available evidence at trial. Hence the trial attorneys were not prepared to defend against prosecutors who were able to derive maximum benefit from very questionable evidence. The adversary system was not a contest between equally prepared opponents. Then, in each case, procedural barriers limited the appellate courts from considering the substantial merits of the prisoners' appeals. Thus, new evidence uncovered by competent counsel (appointed too late in the process) was never considered by a jury and only considered by the governor.

Michael Mello has said that "[t]he illusion of having a lawyer is worse than having no lawyer" (1997b: 256) because it gives the appearance that justice is being done and that due process is functioning as it should. These cases suggest that serious questions about the reliability of the trial process are grounded in the lack of effective assistance of counsel. Clearly all lawyers are not equally qualified to handle the defense of a capital case. Surprisingly, courts have permitted the prisoner to be his own attorney.[18] Despite the reasonableness of the language of the *Strickland* standard, it has not been a remedy for the many behaviors that the public would equate with ineffectiveness of counsel.[19] "*Strickland's* emphasis on the 'ends' (i.e., the outcome of the trial), and not the 'means' (i.e., the process that led to the conviction), may prove to be a most unfortunate precedent" (Klein, 1986: 645). The courts' assumption of adequate representation at the trial level can lead the courts to be deaf to the serious claims being made by death row prisoners, with fatal results. Supreme Court Justice Blackmun reminds us in his dissent in *McFarland v. Scott* (1994: 2787) that "[e]vidence not presented at trial cannot later be discovered and introduced; arguments and objections not advanced are forever waived."

Although there is no constitutional requirement for assistance of counsel at any stage of the criminal process except for the trial and direct appeal (*Murray v. Giarrantano*, 1989), states have recognized the need for counsel at all stages. The ABA guidelines recommend the appointment of counsel for appeals and postconviction work. In Missouri, as in twenty-two other states with the death penalty (Mello, 1997b: 160), the initial appointment of counsel is now managed by the state public defender's office.

The Missouri public defender system provides counsel for all stages of state appeals, relying on the specialized capital litigation unit to represent poor defendants in proceedings. The Missouri Supreme Court has established minimal eligibility standards for the appointment of attorneys to state appeals in death penalty cases in its Rule 29.16: attorneys must have at least three years of litigation experience in the field of criminal law; have participated as counsel or cocounsel to final judgment in at least five postconviction motions involving class A felonies; and have participated in at least three felony jury trials or five direct criminal appeals in felony cases. Notice that these standards do not require death penalty experience as recommended by the ABA standards and others (Ogletree, 1998). In Missouri, two attorneys are assigned to handle the capital trial, just one to do the direct appeal work (which is one less attorney than the ABA guidelines call for in the direct appeal).

These standards rely on criminal trial experience to be the criterion for appointment of counsel. However, we have seen that experience is not necessarily a guarantee of effectiveness. Kelvin Malone's attorney did not spend the time necessary for the investigation and preparation for trial. Richard Zeitvogel's attorney had experience with death penalty cases, but he did not possess the competency to defend his client effectively. What is needed is the combination of death penalty experience with recognized competency.[20]

Despite the aforementioned problems associated with police, prosecutors, and trial attorneys, ultimate responsibility for ensuring due process and a fair trial rests with the trial judge. We turn next to consider the role of the judge in the capital trial.

CHAPTER FIVE

THE TRIAL JUDGE

Although the Missouri Supreme Court had developed a limiting construction for the phrase "depravity of mind" in *State v. Preston* (1984), four years prior to Mr. Feltrop's trial, the jury in this case was not instructed in accordance with *Preston*'s guidelines, nor was it given any other limiting construction.

Any presumption that the trial judge knew the narrowing definition is just plain wrong. It is impossible to conclude otherwise. If the trial judge knew of the required narrowing definition, he would have given the correct instruction to the jury.

Furthermore, there is absolutely nothing in the record that remotely suggests that the trial judge in pronouncing sentence applied any of the narrowing criteria required by *Preston*. One of the most fundamental rights a criminal defendant has in Missouri—sentencing by jury properly instructed in the law—was denied to Ralph Feltrop.

> FROM THE CLEMENCY PETITION
> *for Ralph Feltrop*, CP#67,
> executed August 6, 1997[1]

THE PROMISE OF JUDICIAL NEUTRALITY

Many expectations are associated with the role of judge during the trial stage of a death penalty case. Death penalty trials take place in two phases separating the determination of guilt from the sentencing decision. The courtroom in which these decisions are made is under the management of the judge, who is given wide latitude in fulfilling the legal responsibilities. The judge decides questions of the admissibility of evidence and of procedure; assists in the selection of the jury and guides the questioning of witnesses; and is responsible for maintaining an environment in which all parties are given the opportunity to present their side of the case, while maintaining respectful and appropriate decorum in their conduct. The American Bar Association has developed *Standards for Criminal Justice* (1980), which address these expectations of the judge: "The trial judge should require that every proceeding before him or her be conducted with unhurried and quiet dignity and should aim to establish such physical surroundings as are appropriate to the administration of justice" (Standard 6-1.1[b]). Once both adversaries have presented their case, the judge formally charges the jury by instructing its members on what points of law and evidence they must consider in reaching a decision, receives the jury's decision, and then formally imposes the sentence. Guiding the judge throughout the trial is the general responsibility "for safeguarding both the rights of the accused and the interests of the public in the administration of criminal justice" (Standard 6-1.1[a]).

It is a basic understanding that judges "are entrusted with the duty of ensuring that the trial is conducted within the boundaries of legal fairness" (Senna and Siegel, 1998: 35). The ethical Code of Judicial Conduct (Redlich, 1984) adopted by the American Bar Association describes the professional expectations for judges, emphasizing words such as integrity, independence, propriety, and impartiality of the judiciary. Three of the rules are particularly relevant to this discussion:

> *Canon 3:* A judge should perform the duties of his [*sic*] office impartially and diligently. A1. A judge should be faithful to the law and maintain professional competence in it. He should be unswayed by partisan interests, public clamor, or fear of criticism.
>
> *Canon 4:* A judge may engage in activities to improve the law, the legal system and the administration of justice—if in doing so he does not cast doubt on his capacity to decide impartially any issue that may come before him.
>
> *Canon 5:* A judge shall not (i) make pledges or promises of conduct in office other than the faithful and impartial performance of the duties of the office; [or] (ii) make statements that commit or appear to commit the candidate with respect to cases, controversies, or issues that are likely to come before the court (Redlich, 1984).

THE REALITY

The promise of the ideal judge is difficult to achieve in death penalty trials because judges are typically elected to their positions and as such are likely to be sensitive to public opinion, especially if a death penalty case receives a lot of media attention. This awareness interferes with the judicial expectations for independence and impartiality. In some jurisdictions, judges who are initially appointed are also later subject to the election process in order to be retained in office. While the professional ideals mandate that judges "follow the law, not the election returns" (Bright and Keenan, 1995: 776), the activity of "campaigning" for office is fraught with pitfalls.[2] For example, candidates who make statements to the media promising to be "tough on crime" are likely surrendering their impartiality and appear to be violating Canons 3 and 5 of the Code of Judicial Conduct (Bright and Keenan, 1995: 823). Frequency of judicial elections is another factor that can affect judicial independence. A longer term gives a judge distance from controversial cases before the next election or retention vote, which means that the judge will have many more cases that could be balanced against one or two controversial cases.

Whether appointed or elected, judges cannot escape the political dimension of their work. Stephen Bright has observed that in "some instances, political considerations make it virtually impossible for judges to enforce the constitutional protections to a fair trial for the accused, such as granting a change of venue or continuance, or suppressing evidence" (1995: 793). Sensitive to the public's intense interest in capital murder cases, judges are more likely to sentence a defendant to death than are juries hearing the same evidence (Bright and Keenan, 1995). It is not hard to understand why trial judges would be more likely than jurors to favor executions.

> Justice John Paul Stevens put his finger on the problem in a dissenting opinion to the United States Supreme Court ruling upholding the Alabama provisions for judicial override in death penalty cases: "the 'higher authority' to whom present-day capital judges may be 'too responsive' is a political climate in which judges who covet higher office—or who merely wish to remain judges—must constantly profess their fealty to the death penalty" (Uelmen, 1997: 1,141–42).

Gerald Uelmen (1997) has called this political factor the "crocodile in the bathtub" and urges attention to these issues to preserve the independence and impartiality of the judiciary.

In Missouri, most circuit court (trial) judges are popularly elected (except in Kansas City, St. Louis, Platte County, and Clay County, where the nonpartisan Missouri court plan applies) (Johnson, 1999–2000: 190, 191, 217). All other judges are appointed by the governor when a vacancy on the bench occurs (Missouri Constitution, Article V, section 25). This Missouri Plan, a model for other states, is known for its attempt to eliminate partisanship. One person to be appointed to a judgeship is selected by the governor from a three-person panel, which is chosen by a nonpartisan judicial commission of laypersons, lawyers, and judges. A judge appointed in this way must then stand for retention in office at the first general election occurring after the judge has been in office for twelve months. The judge's name is placed on the ballot without political party designation, and the voters must vote either for or against retention. If the judge is voted out of office, the vacancy is filled through the appointive process described earlier. State appeal court judges and supreme court judges are retained for twelve-year terms; circuit court judges serve six-year terms (Missouri Constitution, Article V, section 19). Although the appointment/retention process of the Missouri Plan shuns party affiliation, the feature of facing the ballot keeps political influences ever present in the courts' environment.

It is an unusual feature of Missouri law that the judge may impose the death penalty if the jury is unable to decide upon punishment. This procedure became law in 1981, a change which made it easier to obtain a death sentence. Prior to 1981, when a jury could not decide on recommending a death sentence, the law required that a life without parole sentence be imposed. Since the law changed, the trial judge imposed death in every case in which the jury was unable to decide between life without parole or death. This change in the law was significant in four (8 percent) of the clemency petitions presented to the governor.

In thirteen of the Missouri clemency petitions (26 percent), the trial judge's actions became an issue that was raised to the governor as one source for mistaken conviction or capital sentencing (or both) (see table 5.1). The judicial behavior that was challenged included: not permitting the defense to present evidence of an alternative theory of the case; not permitting the defense to present certain mitigating evidence; denying the right of defense experts to offer evidence; failing to order a psychiatric examination prior to trial; prejudging the case; incorrectly finding fact; refusing to give certain jury instructions; deliberately giving a defective instruction to the jury; failing to admonish the prosecutor for an improper closing argument; allowing a highly prejudicial photograph during the penalty phase; failing to permit withdrawal of a guilty plea; and not having jurisdiction. These are serious allegations which bear on the jurors' ability to decide cases with full and complete information and which indicate unseemly judicial partiality and bias in the courtroom. The case presented next

TABLE 5.1
Judicial Complaints

Alleged Misconduct	Cases
Not permitting the defense to present evidence of an alternative theory of the case	Winford Stokes, Jessie Wise
Not permitting the defense to present certain mitigating evidence	Frederick Lashley
Refusing expert testimony	Milton Griffin El
Failing to order a psychiatric examination prior to trial	Sam McDonald
Prejudging the case	Sam McDonald, Andrew Six
Incorrectly finding fact	Bert Hunter, Darrell Mease
Refusing to give certain jury instructions	Milton Griffin El, Bobby Shaw, Jessie Wise
Giving a defective instruction to the jury	Ralph Feltrop, Jeff Sloan
Failing to admonish the prosecutor for an improper closing argument	Emmitt Foster
Allowing a highly prejudicial photograph during the penalty phase	David Leisure
Failing to permit withdrawal of guilty plea	Bert Hunter
Not having jurisdiction	Glen Sweet

alleges judicial impropriety that reflects the influence of the local political environment in which capital cases are too often immersed.

CASE STUDY:
THE APPEARANCE OF BIAS

Andrew Six, CP#70

Andrew Six and his uncle, Donald Petary, were convicted of the killing of twelve-year-old Kathy Allen in northern Missouri in 1987. The jury that found Mr. Six guilty of first degree murder was unable to agree that he be sentenced to death. The decision whether Mr. Six should live or be put to death fell into the hands of the trial judge, who had urged the bankrupt county to go ahead with the capital trial. Judge Webber imposed the death sentence just an hour and a half after the jury announced their impasse.

▼▲▼
Application for Commutation
of a Sentence of Death[3]

Andrew Six may become the first person in the modern history of this state to be executed even though he was not sentenced to death by the jury which heard the evidence of his participation in the crime. Rather, after the jury which heard the prosecution's case against him was unable to agree upon the punishment, Andrew Six was sentenced to death by a single elected trial judge after a mere eighty two minutes of deliberation. In the typical death penalty case, officials of the State of Missouri can contend that the imposition of the death penalty upholds the trial jury's enormous decision to render a verdict of death and that the jury's decision reflects the conscience of the community in making this weighty decision.

Mr. Six is the first person to come before this Governor who faces execution without a unanimous jury's decision that he deserves to be put to death. In the early 1980's, prosecutors persuaded the Missouri legislature that it should be easier for the state to obtain death sentences. Legislation was passed which changed the law to permit the trial judge to decide the sentence if the jury was unable to unanimously agree on the appropriate punishment—death or life imprisonment without parole. Prior to this important change in the law, unless the penalty phase jury was unanimous on the death sentence a sentence of life imprisonment without parole was imposed. Presumably prosecutors were concerned about the possibility of a single "hold-out" juror frustrating the state's desire for the death penalty. In this case, Mr. Six's attorneys have contacted at least three jurors who have indicated that they were not convinced beyond a reasonable doubt that Mr. Six deserved the death penalty. Thus, the standard in this state for determining whether a person shall live or die is now the functional equivalent of the standard in civil cases, for Mr. Six may be executed even though at least three jurors disagreed.

In Mr. Six's trial several serious errors occurred which contributed to the jury's inability to be unanimous that his life should be spared. In the absence of those errors, the jury would likely have returned a verdict of life imprisonment without the possibility of probation or parole.

Mr. Six was found guilty of first degree murder by the jury at the guilt phase of his trial. However, the state has never conclusively established whether it was Mr. Six or his co-defendant and uncle, Donald Petary, who actually committed the murder. The jury was given standard instructions on accessorial liability which gave the jury the ability to find Mr. Six guilty even if it did not find that he was the actual killer. Mr. Six's jury never specifically found that he was the killer, not did it make any findings at the penalty phase which would support such an inference.

Mr. Six's penalty phase portion of the trial was plagued with numerous errors, including ineffective assistance of counsel for failing to present substantial mitigating evidence and a confusing jury instruction on mitigating evidence that has been revised since his case. Unfortunately for Mr. Six, his trial lawyers knew little of the investigative techniques pertaining to mitigation evidence which are now considered routine in capital cases. These lawyers limited their penalty phase strategy to a plea for mercy based upon the brief testimony of family members. These lawyers neither investigated nor presented the full range of mitigating evidence which was available to them. These lawyers ignored a unique window into Andy's upbringing and mental health history which was created by various social services' extensive involvement with the Six family throughout Andy's childhood. Although his trial lawyers later offered as an excuse for their failure to investigate and present the mitigating evidence that their strategy was to only present "positive" things about Mr. Six, they failed to present evidence that Andy had worked from an early age on newspaper routes, selling cards, and in the corn fields and was recognized as a good employee. Combined with other issues, including the existence of residual doubt regarding who the killer actually was, there is a reasonable possibility that the misinformed jury would have returned a verdict of life imprisonment without the possibility of probation or parole instead of being deadlocked. It is important to note that under Missouri law the trial judge may not override a jury's recommendation of a life sentence.

In order to uphold the important role of the jury in protecting the rights of citizens against the unbridled power of prosecutors and to carry out what would have been the trial jury's true verdict, Andrew Six respectfully requests this Honorable Governor to grant commutation of the sentence.

1. Political and Economic Factors May Have Influenced the Judge's Decision That Mr. Six Should Be Put to Death

It is undisputed that the sole reason Mr. Six's trial was ever even conducted in Schuyler County was to obtain the death sentence. Mr. Six had already received a 200 year sentence without the possibility of parole for at least 66 years from the federal district court in Iowa for the kidnapping of the victim in this case. After the federal trials, and in spite of the fact that Schuyler County, Missouri was nearly bankrupt at the time, Mr. Six and his uncle, Donald Petary, were tried in Schuyler County, Missouri for the stabbing death of Kathy Allen which had occurred on or about April 10, 1987. Both men were convicted of first degree murder in separate trials and sentenced to death in Missouri courts in 1988.

The prosecution occurred during the time of the worst financial crisis in the history of Schuyler County, MO. In November of 1987, the Schuyler County courthouse was actually closed for a period of time because of a lack of operating funds. Considerable debate took place within the Schuyler County Commission on whether the County should expend precious scarce resources for the trials of the two men in view of the costs and the fact that both men had already been effectively sentenced to life imprisonment without parole in federal court. During the debate, the Commission consulted with the popularly elected circuit court judge for Schuyler County about the potential costs of the trials. Judge Webber, who would later make the decision that Mr. Six should be put to death after the jury deadlocked, also commented about the cost of the trials in the local press. After several votes, the Schuyler County Commission decided to spend the money in the hope of obtaining death sentences.

. . . Unlike the jury in Mr. Petary's case, the jury in Andrew Six's case did not return a finding of the existence of any aggravating circumstances after the penalty phase of the trial, and was otherwise unable to agree on punishment. Against the backdrop of a County Commission determined to spend precious funds if death sentences would result, Judge Webber, who in Schuyler County faced re-election every six years,—not the jury— made the decision that Andy should be put to death. In making this momentous life-or-death decision, the trial judge considered aggravating circumstances that were never found by the jury. Instead of waiting for a pre-sentence investigation, the judge retired to his chambers, read the Bible and announced his decision in the courtroom only eighty-two minutes after the jury's announcement that it could not reach a verdict.

2. Residual Doubt in the Minds of the Jury Regarding Who Was the Perpetrator

Andy's defense at trial was that his uncle, Donald Petary, was the actual killer. Andy's uncle was older than Andy and had an extensive criminal history, including several long periods of imprisonment. Mr. Petary was a known pedophile. Without an appropriate role model, Andy turned to his uncle for companionship. He was easily led astray as a result of the domination and control of his uncle. Despite the terrible fact that a twelve year old girl was killed, the jury was unable to sentence Andy to death. The detailed information concerning the location of Ms. Allen's body came from Mr. Petary. From the beginning Andy has always maintained that it was Mr. Petary who killed Ms. Allen. There is no tangible evidence in this case proving that Andy Six was the actual killer. At best the state was able to prove that Andy participated in Ms. Allen's abduction. A reasonable inference can be made that the jury had doubts regarding whether Mr. Six actually killed Kathy Allen.

3. Substantial Mitigating Evidence Was Not Presented to the Jury

It is undisputed that Andy was treated by mental health professionals from the time he was a toddler. He grew up in a seriously dysfunctional and culturally deprived home environment that was monitored for many years by social service agencies. Andy suffered from a hearing loss that went untreated for three years while he was in elementary school. To a reasonable degree of medical certainty, he suffers from an organic brain disorder which most likely was more pronounced during his formative years and at the time of the crime.

Andrew Six's father was a functionally illiterate man who was seldom gainfully employed, shunned Andy, and was never significantly involved in the boy's life. When Andy was five years old, his mother divorced his biological father and remarried Leo Mott, who had nine children of his own. This union resulted in Andy's spending his fifth year in an impoverished home with thirteen other siblings. It is a fact that Mr. Mott, an alcoholic, repeatedly physically abused him during this period. Andy never had an acceptable role model in the home while he was growing up.

Unfortunately, his trial lawyers knew little of the investigative techniques pertaining to mitigation evidence which are now considered routine in capital cases. These lawyers limited their penalty phase strategy to a plea for mercy based upon the brief testimony of family members. These lawyers ignored a unique window into the child's upbringing and mental health history which was created by various social services' extensive involvement with the Six family throughout Andy's childhood.

Andy's long history of hyperactivity and attention deficit disorder was first documented in a pre-kindergarten head start program. The condition was aggravated by his home life, described by social service agencies as "truly culturally deprived." This disorder was noted throughout evaluations of Andy in Head Start, kindergarten, and elementary school. The disorder was severe enough for a physician to prescribe Ritalin when Andy was four. A psychiatrist described Andy as "very hyperactive" and noted there was a family environment component to Andy's problems. The "family environment component" became more and more pronounced throughout Andy's upbringing and compounded the child's problems. He also was found to possess low verbal abilities and problems with visual perception, which is typical for a child with learning disabilities and attention deficit disorder.

The Six family, as was their pattern according to the various social service agencies involved with the family, did not seek further appropriate care. The pattern of inattentiveness to their children's basic needs is seen in the family's treatment of Andy's sister Amanda, who is profoundly retarded. Amanda has never been able to walk or talk. Professionals described it as "striking" that the family never really attempted to deal with Amanda's problems or use available community resources. An evaluation from 1969 notes that Andy's mother "could benefit from some guidance in child rearing practices," and describes the Six home as "a rather chaotic home environment." Additional evaluations of Amanda Six indicate that several maternal relatives are mentally retarded and that there were allegations that the parents of Amanda and Andy were related.

Head Start program reports reveal concern that the Six family needed assistance in nutrition and hygiene. The pattern of neglect included evidence Andy's mother failed to continue him on the Ritalin, despite documentation that the medication improved his behavior. Medical records from the Gilfillan Clinic in 1976 mention Andy had a hearing loss. School officials did not detect it until 1978, when he was near the end of his seventh grade. In the fall of 1978 an assessment report recommended that Andy receive a hearing aid and that the family utilize the services of the Itinerant Teacher of the Hearing Impaired, a free program of home visits and counseling for poor families with hearing impaired children. The family did not avail itself of the program and did not obtain a hearing aid for him until three years after the hearing problems were first detected. The neglect of Andy's hearing problem coincided with the deterioration of his performance in school, which declined markedly beginning in the sixth grade. . . .

Unfortunately for Mr. Six, however, none of this evidence was presented to the jury for its consideration of what punishment to impose. Trial counsel was ineffective in failing to present this evidence to the jury. It is undisputed that trial counsel testified in support of their plea for a continuance, that they had been unable to review all psychological materials regarding

Andy and were not sufficiently aware of the above mentioned matters. Evidence from Andy's upbringing, portraying a troubled youth with very low self esteem would have been entirely consistent with the defense theme that young Andy had been led astray by his uncle Donald Petary and that Donald Petary was the real killer. Even with the scarce mitigation evidence presented, and even in the face of the disturbing facts of this crime, the jury was unable to recommend that Andy should be put to death. Had Mr. Six's trial lawyers investigated adequately and given the jury an accurate portrayal of his mental health background and the circumstances of his upbringing, there is a quite reasonable possibility that the jury would have returned a unanimous life verdict instead of being deadlocked.

4. Mr. Six's Penalty Phase Jury Was Not Properly Instructed Concerning Mitigating Evidence

Because of the jury's deadlock at the penalty phase, a crucial issue in this case is whether the jury was correctly instructed concerning how it was to consider mitigating evidence. This process was seriously flawed in Mr. Six's case in two important regards.

First, Mr. Six's lawyers failed to request that the jury be instructed on available statutory mitigating circumstances. Had they been requested, the trial court would have been required to give the jury the following mitigating circumstances for consideration:

A. Whether the defendant was an accomplice in the murder in the first degree committed by another person and his participation was relatively minor; and

B. Whether the defendant acted under extreme duress or under the substantial domination of another person.

Both of the circumstances were appropriate in Andy's case. The Missouri Supreme Court recognized that Andy's defense was that his uncle Donald Petary had committed the murder. If the jury had been given these circumstances for consideration, there is a reasonable probability that the divided jury would have returned a unanimous verdict of life imprisonment.

Second, the instruction which was given to the jury on mitigating evidence was seriously flawed because it incorrectly told the jury that the finding of any mitigating circumstances must be unanimous. This instruction has been revised since Mr. Six's trial to no longer require unanimity. The instruction given to Mr. Six's jury stated: "If you unanimously find that one or more mitigating circumstances exist sufficient to outweigh the aggravating circumstances found by you to exist, you must return a verdict fixing defendant's punishment at life imprisonment for life by the Division of Corrections without eligibility for probation or parole." The term "unanimously" modifies the adjoining phrase, "find that one or more mitigating circumstances exist." A reasonable juror would interpret this to mean that, before the jury can consider a mitigating circumstance, that circumstance must first be found to exist by all twelve jurors.

The United States Supreme Court found a Maryland jury instruction requiring the jury to unanimously agree as to the existence of mitigating circumstances was unconstitutional in *Mills v. Maryland* (1988). The Supreme Court expressed concern that a unanimity requirement might result in a situation in which a single juror could prevent the remaining jury panel members from finding and weighing any mitigating circumstances. The instruction submitted in Mr. Six's case is almost identical to the Maryland and North Carolina instructions found to be constitutionally infirm in *Mills* and *McKoy v. North Carolina* (1990).

In 1989, after Mr. Six's trial and in response to the *Mills* decision, the instruction was changed. The revised instruction now states:

> If you decide that one or more sufficient aggravating circumstances exist to warrant death . . . each of you must then determine whether one or more mitigating circumstances . . . outweigh the aggravating circumstances. . . . It is not necessary that all jurors agree on the existence of the same mitigating circumstances.

Mr. Six's jury, however, did not receive the clarification now found in the revised instruction. . . . The inference that Mr. Six's jury was confused by the instruction is quite strong because of the fact that the jury was unable to agree on the punishment. There is a quite reasonable probability that the jury was misled into the mistaken belief that it must be unanimous on the existence of any mitigating circumstance before it could return a verdict of life imprisonment. The correction of the very flaw in the instruction which prevented the jury from returning a life sentence verdict will be of little consolation to Mr. Six as he lay on the gurney at Potosi awaiting lethal injection. No matter how the Missouri Attorney General attempts to "spin" this issue, it is an undisputable fact that if Mr. Six's case were tried today the jury would not be given the fatal instruction on mitigating evidence that was given to his jury in 1988.

5. Defects in the Penalty Phase Verdict Form

Mr. Six's case is the first Missouri case to reach this stage wherein the decision in favor of execution over life imprisonment without parole was made by the trial judge and not by the jury. The Missouri death penalty sentencing procedure at the time of Andy's trial conferred the original responsibility of "the finding of [at least] an aggravating circumstance" on the trier of fact, which is a jury unless a jury is waived. The jury was to consider the facts supporting the existence of at least one aggravating circumstance and the jury also had the responsibility to determine which aggravating circumstances warranted the imposition of the death penalty. However, in the event the jury deadlocks on the question of punishment, no provision is made to ensure that the jury found any aggravating circumstance beyond a reasonable doubt or that any aggravating circumstance, if so found, warranted the imposition of the death sentence beyond a reasonable doubt. Thus the problem which results in such cases is that there is no assurance that the jury ever found the defendant to be eligible for the death penalty in the first place. Another serious problem is that in such cases, a defendant may be sentenced to death after the trial judge includes in the sentencing calculation aggravating circumstances which the jury in fact rejected; the verdict form in a hung jury case simply provides no guidance for the sentencing judge or for a reviewing court. It is a great irony that only those defendants whose juries are in enough doubt to be unable to return a death verdict are then subjected to aggravators being weighed by the trial judge which may have been rejected by the jury.

Former Chief Justice Charles Blackmar of the Missouri Supreme Court recognized the deficiencies in the verdict form soon after its adoption. "There is no provision for polling to make sure the jury has made the essential findings" (*State v. Sandles*, 1987: 181). Chief Justice Blackmar proposed a simple remedy for the problem: "the jury should return into court the aggravating circumstance which it has found" because this would be a "guarantee of the integrity of the verdict."

Due to the faulty verdict form, there is no assurance that Andy's jury ever found the existence of an aggravating circumstance warranting the death penalty beyond a reasonable doubt. It may be legal, but it is fundamentally unfair and contrary to the principles upon which this nation was founded to allow a single trial judge—in this case an elected public official—to determine the alleged existence of aggravating circumstances when the individuals entrusted with making such a determination—the jurors—did not.

Prior to 1981, if the jury could not agree on punishment in a capital case, the defendant was sentenced automatically to life imprisonment without parole. It is noteworthy that the Missouri capital punishment procedure does not permit a trial judge to override a jury's verdict of life imprisonment and impose a death sentence, while conversely, the trial court may override a death verdict and impose a life sentence. Thus Missouri is about to join a small group of states such as Florida, Alabama and Arizona which permit a single elected trial judge to override the decision of a jury of twelve and impose a death sentence. Even a state such as Texas, where the death penalty is carried out most frequently, requires a unanimous jury of twelve to agree that society's most exacting and severe punishment is called for. The name of "Show Me State" is about to become a euphemism. Mr. Six doubts that this Governor would have permitted this change in the law—which will now cost him his life—to occur had he been in office when prosecutors sought to ease their burden when they seek to exert the power of the government in taking a citizen's life. . . .

The Governor is the last resort for justice and mercy for Andrew Six. For the reasons set forth above, we implore you to grant Mr. Six relief from his sentence of death and for Mr. Six to be sentenced to life imprisonment without the possibility of probation or parole.

▼▲▼ ──────────

We have seen in the Andrew Six clemency petition several problems that put a spotlight on the critical role of the trial judge. Before the trial even began, the judge appeared before the county commission, which was considering whether to even have a capital trial. Although his testimony evidently concerned the cost of a death penalty trial in general and did not directly address the specifics of the Six case, the judge's participation demonstrates that he was well aware of the county's expectations for a death penalty verdict. Speaking to the media on the issue also betrays his cognizance of the politics of the death penalty. Thus, in this case it appears that the political environment determined the death penalty result, whether or not it actually did. It is only conjecture that the judge's brief penalty deliberation, which contrasted with the jury's difficulty in reaching a decision, reflected these political influences. It is the appearance of arbitrariness that raises questions of fairness in the Six case. One of the institutional mechanisms that should have limited arbitrariness, the verdict form, was flawed in that it did not require the jury to report the basis for their guilty decision. So despite the myriad complicated death penalty procedures that purportedly protect the rights of the defendant, the reality is that oftentimes the rules do not work that way.

Other problems presented in the clemency petition compound the questionable image of the trial judge's behavior. Particularly disturbing is the lawyers' ineffectiveness in doing no background investigation and in failing to request jury instructions on mitigating circumstances. Tragically, the judge did not see the need to give these relevant instructions. Again, the impression is given that the judge was not vigilant in "safeguarding the rights of the accused." As a result of these errors, the jury did not have full information or adequate guidance by the judge to reach a fair determination of punishment. Andrew Six was executed August 20, 1997.

CONCLUSIONS

It is difficult to establish that political influences interfere with impartiality and fairness. Yet, when trial judges are more willing to impose the death penalty than are juries, the appearance of bias is powerful. Stephen Bright has represented persons facing the death penalty at trials, on appeals, and in postconviction proceedings since 1979. He chastises the judiciary for "following elections rather than the law":

> Judges have failed miserably to enforce the most fundamental right of all, the Sixth Amendment right to counsel, in capital cases. And many judges routinely abdicate their judicial responsibility and allow the lawyers for the state to write their orders resolving disputed factual and legal issues in capital cases (Bright and Keenan, 1995: 793).

Bright challenges judges to reclaim the integrity of their professional ideals. Ultimately, the legitimacy of the criminal justice system is dependent on the appearance of being fair.

In death penalty litigation, if mistakes are made by trial judges, they are very difficult to overcome. Although the defendant has an automatic review by the state supreme court, higher courts typically grant a great deal of deference to the decisions of the trial court. The appellate courts are reluctant to find "fatal" error—that is, error so serious that the defendant did not have a fair trial. One wonders if such conservative decisions are an institutional cover-up or a method of institutional preservation. Minimally, the role of the reviewing courts is to assure the community that the death penalty was not imposed unfairly. The next chapter examines the quality of review given by the higher courts.

CHAPTER SIX

APPELLATE COURTS

David [Leisure] was represented [at trial in 1987] by a collections attorney who used a law student as his conduit of information to and from David, and whose thinking he relied on for grand strategy. David's present counsel did not learn until February 1999 that this law student had been laboring under the adverse psychological effects of untreated chemical dependency. When they brought this fact to the attention of the federal courts, the representatives of the State of Missouri said David couldn't be killed quickly enough, that it didn't matter that his trial counsel's "brains" was a drug addict.

By the time of this discovery, the federal district court had already denied relief, the Eighth Circuit had denied a certificate of appealability, and the matter was before the Supreme Court of the United States on a petition for certiorari. When the Supreme Court denied certiorari, David's counsel filed a motion for relief from judgment under the Federal Rules of Civil Procedure 60(b) based on this newly discovered evidence. They alleged that trial counsel's failure to detect the law student's mental problems stemming from past or present illegal drug use elevated trial counsel's already ineffective assistance to the level of gross negligence, and thus satisfied the "extraordinary circumstances" test of the Federal Rules of Civil Procedure 60(b)(6).

The federal courts should have granted relief, or at least held a hearing, on this grievance. The district court denied relief on the basis that the Rule 60(b)(6) motion was "really" a second petition, and required the permission of the Eighth Circuit under AEDPA. David's counsel sought to appeal this ruling or, in the alternative, to obtain the Eighth Circuit's permission to file a second petition to raise this grievance. On August 24, 1999, the Eighth Circuit panel to which David's most recent pleadings were directed denied relief, once more without giving any reasons. At this writing, the Eighth Circuit en banc, the Missouri Supreme Court, and the United States Supreme Court still have the opportunity to grant relief on this ground or at least to grant a stay of execution to allow David to litigate it. Counsel submit this application for clemency in an abundance of caution, so that the Executive Branch may review the evidence and authorities supporting this grievance, and may either commute David's sentence for this and the other reasons advanced or appoint a board of inquiry to review this grievance and any of the others concerning which the courts have failed and refused to give David the time of day.

FROM THE CLEMENCY PETITION
for David Leisure, CP#76,
executed on September 1, 1999[1]

In *Caldwell v. Mississippi* (1985), the U.S. Supreme Court stated that "the qualitative difference of death from all other punishment requires a correspondingly greater degree of scrutiny of the capital sentencing determination." This scrutiny happens in three different steps at the appellate stage in death penalty litigation.[2] The first step is known as the direct appeal because the appeal is made directly to the state supreme court. This appeal is guaranteed in all death penalty convictions and is intended to ensure that the death sentence was not imposed arbitrarily or randomly. At the direct appeal, the state supreme court is to determine whether any errors jeopardized the fairness of the trial, leading either to a wrongful conviction or to an unjust sentence of death. A second, and equally important, function of the direct appeal is to conduct a "proportionality review." A proportionality review assesses whether the imposition of the death penalty is "disproportionate to the penalty in similar cases, considering both the crime and the defendant."[3] This is the only appeal with a constitutional guarantee of appointed counsel.

The second step in the appeals process is known as the state habeas or postconviction review. This step generally involves the courts in reviewing the trial transcript for constitutional violations of procedure or evidence, such as giving the jury wrong instructions. In addition, claims that could not have been raised at trial or on direct appeal, such as ineffective assistance of counsel or failure to provide exculpatory evidence, may be raised and decided on their merits. In the postconviction proceedings, the prisoner is trying to prove "fatal, or reversible, error"—that is, the existence of a seriously flawed legal procedure, or the accumulation of errors, during the trial that substantially and adversely affected the outcome of the trial.

The final step of review in a death penalty case is known as the federal habeas corpus review. Historically, the writ of habeas corpus has been called the "Great Writ" because of its importance in protecting constitutional rights. Like the state habeas review, this appeal is a civil action brought against the prison superintendent or the director of corrections on the grounds that the conviction or sentence under which the prisoner is being held was obtained in violation of the Constitution of the United States. Entering the federal habeas arena means that the prisoner has completed, or exhausted, all of the state reviews.

The scope of federal habeas corpus has changed over time. Originally recognized in the Constitution and specified in the Judiciary Act of 1789, the writ of habeas corpus was limited to challenges in the court that sentenced the prisoner. But after the Civil War, along with the growth in federal authority generally, the Judiciary Act of 1867 expanded federal judicial authority to "issue writs of habeas corpus in all cases where any person may be restrained of his or her liberty in violation of the Constitution or any treaty or law of the United States" (Rivkind and Shatz, 2001: 599–600). This trend of widening jurisdiction continued until the mid-1970s when the Supreme Court began to make decisions that drastically restricted federal habeas corpus and limited the growth of procedural rights. The political climate in the country was also shifting in the 1970s. Crime was elevated to a national issue and reflected a "law and order" conservative agenda. During this time, the nation's conservatism was reflected in President Nixon's Supreme Court appointments of Justices William Rehnquist and Warren Burger,[4] who reshaped the Court by favoring state law enforcement over the individual rights of criminal defendants.

The cutback in federal habeas corpus review responds to two concerns that came out of the changing political environment. The first was to address the perception that prisoners were "abusing the writ" (Amsterdam, 1999) delaying the finality of their sentences, and the second was to give more respect and deference to state decisions than previously granted. These concerns also were reflected in the Antiterrorism and Effective Death Penalty Act of 1996, which "codifies and extends the Supreme Court's restrictions on the scope of habeas corpus review" (Rivkind and Shatz, 2001: 607). We will discuss some of the details of this law and its impact later in this chapter.

THE PROMISE OF APPELLATE COURT REVIEW

Traditionally, the role of appellate courts has been to discover serious trial errors and to correct those errors. We have seen in chapter 5 that trial judges can be pressured by political concerns in doing their work. At the appellate level, state judges have longer terms than the trial judges and federal judges have lifetime appointments, all in the expectation that these appellate judges will be more insulated from common political concerns and be better able to uphold the neutral principles of justice and fundamental fairness. After all, the mark of our legal system is the high value we place on the due process of law as applied through judicial procedures. The implication behind these various levels of review is the recognition that judges will make mistakes but that in the "doing of justice," serious errors will be corrected. The importance given to these reviews presumes that the merits of the cases will be thoroughly considered. When the public gets frustrated with the length of time between sentencing and execution, they are at least comforted by the belief that the prisoner has had his "day in court." We expect that any wrongful convictions will be discovered and overturned. If the case has not been reversed, then it must be true that the trial judgment is correct and the sentence is just. Executions are conducted unless the appellate courts see a problem. If they do not stop it, all must be right. In this sense, the appellate courts give legitimacy to the implementation of the death sentence.

When the state supreme court is addressing the proportionality of the death sentence, the court should compare the death sentence with other cases that are similar. The National Center for State Court Proportionality Review Project recommends that a meaningful review would use a pool of cases for comparison that included all cases in which the criminal *charge* included a death eligible offense and in which a homicide conviction was obtained (Wallace and Sorensen, 1994: note 129). Then, in assessing whether the particular death sentence is proportional, the review should be able to display rationally based differences between those defendants who receive death sentences and those defendants who do not.

After the proportionality review, the death row prisoner asks the courts for a writ of habeas corpus. The writ of habeas corpus has been known as the Great Writ because it is "a bulwark against convictions that violate fundamental fairness" (*Engle v. Isaac*, 1982). Concerned with the potential abusive power of government, the state and federal habeas reviews give important protection to individual rights. "As Justice Fortas observed, 'There is no higher duty of a court, under our constitutional system, than the careful processing and adjudication of petitions for writs of habeas corpus' " (*Harris v. Nelson*, 1969: 292).

The significance of the habeas review of death penalty cases, particularly at the federal level, can be seen in the high rates of reversals. Research indicates that as many as two-thirds of the capital cases have been overturned at the federal levels (Liebman et al., 2000). Virtually all capital judgments reviewed on federal habeas had previously been given two state court inspections: one review on state direct appeal (at which 41 percent of the judgments were rejected) and a second review on a state postconviction appeal (after which, the state courts together had rejected 47 percent—or almost half—of the capital judgments they reviewed). Federal courts found additional serious error in 40 percent of the capital judgments they reviewed at this third inspection point. In two-fifths of the states in the study, federal courts detected error rates of 50 percent or more at this third review.

THE REALITY

Throughout the Liebman et al. (2000) study of reversal rates in capital cases, Missouri is consistently ranked at the low end of the states. Whereas nationally 41 percent of the capital cases were reversed on direct appeal, Missouri was second lowest of twenty-eight states, at 17 percent of the capital cases reversed on direct appeal. And again, whereas the national composite of direct and postconviction appeals was a 47 percent reversal rate, Missouri's reversal percentage was just 20 percent of the capital cases being reviewed. At the federal habeas corpus stage, the national composite indicates that 40 percent of the death penalty cases were reversed because serious reversible error was found. For Missouri, just 15 percent of the cases were reversed at the federal habeas corpus stage. Only Virginia was ranked lower than Missouri.

Defenders of the legal status quo in Missouri argue that these significantly low reversal rates indicate that there is a lack of serious error to be found in Missouri death penalty cases and that the appellate courts are doing a good job in identifying those relatively few cases in need of remedy. In contrast, critics argue that Missouri's low reversal rates reflect the inability or unwillingness of the appellate courts to recognize the weaknesses that pervade the criminal justice system in adequately safeguarding constitutional rights of fundamental fairness. In previous chapters, serious claims were raised about the problems throughout the criminal justice system. In this chapter, we present complaints by death row prisoners concerning the inadequate appellate review given to them by the courts.

In reality, the two most probable explanations for the low reversal rates in Missouri have nothing to do with the merits of the cases decided. In many death penalty cases, the appellate courts do not consider the merits of the case.

The first explanation for Missouri's low reversal rates concerns the review policies of the state supreme court. In Missouri the direct appeal must be filed within ninety days of the sentencing (Mo. SCT

Rule 29.15) and must include all issues. Any issue not included in the direct appeal is barred from being raised later. The purpose of this rule is to eliminate the filing of an infinite number of appeals. Unfortunately, if the same trial attorney handles the direct appeal, it is likely that any trial errors will be compounded in the appeal because the lawyer may not be aware of all the errors or be able to critique his or her own performance. In such a situation, the appeals court would affirm a death penalty case without considering all the substantive issues in the case because of timing or attorney error.

State courts vary in the scope of cases they use to conduct the proportionality review. There has been considerable criticism of the proportionality review conducted by the Missouri Supreme Court (Suni, 1982; Wallace and Sorensen, 1994). The state supreme court has defined the pool of comparison cases narrowly—that is, the court includes cases that "resulted in either a life or death sentence, but only if they advanced to a penalty trial and have been appealed" (Wallace and Sorensen, 1994: 291). These criteria do not include cases in which the death penalty was waived or in which the jury could not reach a recommendation on the sentence. With a smaller pool for comparison, the result is that the court rarely finds a death sentence that is disproportionate to other cases. "The Missouri Supreme Court has reversed only one case out of 70 reported cases on a proportionality review basis" (Wallace and Sorensen, 1994: 286). Even with a smaller pool of cases, the basis for comparison appears to be designed to affirm the death sentence.[5] The proportionality review conducted in Missouri has been described as "little more than allowing the reviewing court to justify a death sentence" (Wallace and Sorensen, 1994: 313). This impression, coupled with allegations of judicial misconduct, give the Missouri Supreme Court the reputation of an "execution-happy state judiciary" (Taylor, 1994: 70).

We have already seen that there are serious questions raised at every stage of the trial which might merit reversal. In Missouri, there are six clemency petitions (12 percent) that claim the punishment was disproportionate to the condemned's action in the crime (see table 6.1). Claims of self-defense might fit this category. In nine clemency cases (18 percent), petitioners made the claim that their sentence was disproportional to the sentence received by another perpetrator in the same crime.

The second probable explanation for the low reversal rates in Missouri death penalty cases is attributed to the retroactive application

TABLE 6.1
Claims of Disproportionality

Type of Disproportionality	Frequency	Cases
To other perpetrators	9	Emmitt Foster, Milton Griffin El, Bruce Kilgore, Leonard Laws, David Leisure, George Mercer, Robert Murray, Richard Oxford, Robert Walls
To crime	6	A. J. Bannister, Thomas Battle, Martsay Bolder, James Chambers, George Harris, Frederick Lashley

of the federal Antiterrorism and Effective Death Penalty Act of 1996 (AEDPA). Before the AEDPA, the federal courts had full authority to examine all constitutional violations and could ignore state court decisions that interpreted the Constitution differently. The AEDPA provides that federal constitutional claims that were "fully and fairly adjudicated" in state court should be dismissed by the federal courts even if the state courts decided such claims contrary to federal law. The emphasis of the changes in the new habeas law is on speeding up the appeal process and limiting federal review. It legislates deference to state courts by presuming that state courts are not making mistakes and do not need to be reviewed.

Traditionally, an evidentiary hearing has allowed a prisoner to introduce in federal court facts that were not developed adequately in state court. Now under AEDPA, a federal court will be allowed to grant an evidentiary hearing *only if* the prisoner's claim relies on a *new rule* by the Supreme Court and on *new facts* that show by clear and convincing evidence (a most difficult standard) that *no* reasonable judge or jury would find the prisoner guilty. This new standard to obtain a hearing reverses the trial standard for conviction by a unanimous jury. At trial, if there is just *one* juror with reasonable doubt, then the defendant would not be convicted of capital murder. But at the federal habeas stage, the standard is that *all twelve* jurors must be convinced that the prisoner is not guilty before a hearing will be held. So AEDPA greatly limits the possibility that a review will be granted, much less that a conviction will be reversed.

Although most of the cases considered in this book were decided under the "old" federal habeas corpus law, the Eighth Federal Circuit Court of Appeals is alone in the country in applying the AEDPA retroactively. Six of the Missouri clemency cases lost opportunities to make appeals because the new procedural rules were applied to their cases when other jurisdictions would not have imposed them. This unique application of AEDPA produces decisions that result in fewer reversals than in other jurisdictions.

The focus of this chapter is the role of the appellate courts and how they become an issue in clemency appeals. In twenty-seven of the Missouri clemency petitions (54 percent), there were claims that the appellate courts made errors in the interpretation of law or in applying procedures (see table 6.2). In fact, in twenty-one of the cases (42 percent of the total clemency petitions), procedural bars that did not permit consideration of substantive matters resulted in executions. These sorts of issues are particularly difficult for the governor to reverse, as a rejection of a court's decision can appear to be "interfering" with the

---

TABLE 6.2
Issues of Appellate Review

Type of Issue	Frequency	Cases
Proportionality review	5	James Chambers, Ralph Feltrop, Milton Griffin El, Frederick Lashley, Robert Walls
Interpretation of law	10	Ralph Feltrop, Milton Griffin El, Bert Hunter, David Leisure, George Mercer, James Rodden, Gary Roll, Jeff Sloan, Robert Walls, Jessie Wise
Procedural bar	21	A. J. Bannister, Walter Blair, Martsay Bolder, William Ted Boliek, James Chambers, Ralph Davis, Milton Griffin El, Frank Guinan, Bert Hunter, Bruce Kilgore, Anthony LaRette, David Leisure, Kelvin Malone, Sam McDonald, Robert Murray, Richard Oxford, Reginald Powell, Jeff Sloan, Robert Walls, Jessie Wise, Richard Zeitvogel
General	3	Emmitt Foster, Larry Griffin, Darrell Mease

judicial process. However, the governor could draw support for clemency from the dissenting opinions of other judges—when they are available. Petitioners often support their claims by referring to appellate judges who disagree with their colleagues' conclusions in ruling against the death row prisoner. In twenty-one of the clemency petitions (42 percent), there is legal dissent by appellate judges indicating their disagreement with lower court decisions as well as disagreement with their colleagues who support the lower court.[6]

As in other chapters, all the cases considered in this chapter present multiple issues, but we want to focus particularly on the decisions made at the various stages of appellate review. First we read a portion of a clemency petition that criticizes the proportionality review in the case of James Chambers, the last person to be executed in Missouri in 2000. The second clemency petition (Jeff Sloan) presents the issue of a higher court's mistaken interpretation of law which remained uncorrected. The third clemency petition (Milton Griffin El) is an example of both postconviction errors and the retroactive application of AEDPA.

CASE STUDY:
DIRECT APPEAL AND
THE PROPORTIONALITY REVIEW

James Chambers, CP#22

James Chambers was convicted of killing Jerry Oestricker on May 29, 1982, outside a lounge in Arnold after an argument in the bar. Both men had been drinking. A review of factually similar Missouri cases, involving tavern homicides, have all resulted in lesser sentences.

▼▲▼

Application for Executive Clemency and/or
Commutation of a Sentence of Death[7]

Introduction

James W. Chambers has been on Missouri's death row for over 17 years as a result of a barroom argument which culminated in the shooting of Jerry Oestricker outside the Country Club Lounge in Arnold, Missouri in 1982. James Chambers has had three trials, but he has not had three fair trials. Due largely to the incompetence of his different trial counsel, Mr. Chambers' story that he lawfully acted in self defense against a larger man who was the initial aggressor and had a reputation as a violent barroom brawler, has never been effectively told and properly presented to a Missouri jury.

By all accounts, the facts of this case, essentially involving a barroom brawl resulting in a homicide, would not seem to warrant the imposition of the ultimate penalty of death by execution. Sadly however, the Supreme Court of Missouri, in the words of former Chief Judge Charles Blackmar in his dissent in *State v. Reuscher* (1992), in its eagerness to affirm death penalty convictions in Missouri, has "continually refused to face up to its responsibilities in proportionality review."

Apart from the disproportionality of the penalty to the severity of the crime, there are many other compelling reasons to spare Mr. Chambers' life. Because of the incompetence of his trial attorneys, the jury did not hear compelling evidence regarding the true facts surrounding the crime which, at a minimum, would have resulted in a conviction for a lesser included offense of manslaughter or second degree murder. In this regard, the comments of jury foreman, Eric Chism are particularly appropriate. Mr. Chism, in a sworn affidavit, has stated that the experienced and skilled prosecutor Richard Callahan totally out performed and out classed the defense counsel at the third trial. Mr. Chism now states that he does not believe that Mr. Chambers should be executed and has provided powerful evidence and insight indicating that if the case had been properly tried by competent counsel that Mr. Chambers would not be on death row.

It is inescapable that there has never been a case in the post-*Furman* era where a state has executed a convicted murderer for a homicide that occurred in the context of a bar fight. If Mr. Chambers' execution is allowed to proceed as scheduled, the fairness of Missouri's criminal justice system will be forever tarnished by this aberration of justice. Effective counsel could have persuaded the jury that this homicide was a culmination of a barroom fight instigated by Jerry Oestricker, a violent man with a reputation as a barroom brawler, whose violent acts precipitated his own death. The jury that convicted and sentenced Mr. Chambers heard nothing of Mr. Oestricker's background. It was also not pointed out to the jury that the prosecution's star witness, Fred Ieppert, gave a drastically different account of the shooting in Mr. Chambers' third trial. Mr. Ieppert's change in his story went virtually unchallenged by the defense, who incompetently failed to point out to the jury the inconsistencies between Mr. Ieppert's account of the crime at the third trial and his previous testimony. Mr. Ieppert's changed story at the third trial, whether motivated by intentional perjury or his own lack of memory and overall credibility, made this homicide appear much more premeditated than it actually was. In particular, Mr. Ieppert's testimony at the third trial falsely suggested that Mr. Chambers lured Mr. Oestricker out of the tavern, checked his gun as he was exiting the tavern, and then shot Mr. Oestricker a "split second" after he walked out the door. In fact, Mr. Ieppert had previously testified that there was a ten to twelve second lapse between the victim's exit from the bar until the shot was fired. This would have provided plenty of time for Mr. Oestricker to attack Mr. Chambers before he was shot, thus bolstering his claim of self-defense.

The other glaring failure of trial counsel in the third trial was their utter failure to put on any evidence regarding Mr. Chambers' borderline mental retardation, which could have rebutted the mental element necessary to convict of capital murder and provided powerful mitigating evidence to the jury that would have convinced them to spare his life at the penalty phase. Counsel's failure in this regard was inexcusable. For all these reasons elementary principles of justice demand that, at a minimum, Mr. Chambers' disproportionate and unfairly imposed sentence of death be commuted.

James Chambers' Sentence of Death Is Grossly Disproportionate to the Circumstance of His Case

"[A]n ordinary barroom altercation" was the description given to this case by Judge Welliver of the Missouri Supreme Court in his dissent in State v. Chambers,[8] after the second trial. The imposition of the death penalty in such a case is simply disproportionate to the gravity of the crime committed. The facts of this case clearly do not warrant the death penalty and justice demands that this travesty be rectified.

A. No Other Defendant Has Ever Been Executed for a Barroom Killing in Modern Times

The imposition of the death penalty in this case was arbitrary and fundamentally unfair. The only case counsel has been able to find in any state, including Missouri, where on similar facts the defendant was given the death penalty was reversed by the Supreme Court of the State of Nevada as disproportionate. The description by the Nevada court of the facts of that case fits this case almost perfectly.[9]

The most factually similar Missouri cases, involving tavern homicides, have all resulted in lesser sentences. In 1998, for example, the Missouri

Court of Appeals, Western District affirmed Larry McCoy's conviction for second degree murder and armed criminal action and his sentence of concurrent terms of twenty years for shooting a man in an altercation which had spilled out of a bar.[10] The Southern District in 1993 affirmed Ronald Hill's conviction of second degree murder and sentence of fifteen years imprisonment for shooting an acquaintance in a barroom argument.[11]

B. The Penalty Review Procedure by the Missouri Supreme Court Was Inadequate

In order to prevent the arbitrary, and therefore unconstitutional, use of the death penalty, the Supreme Court of Missouri must, by law, independently review all cases where the death penalty has been imposed. The Court must consider: *"whether the sentence of death is excessive or disproportionate to the penalty imposed in similar cases, considering both the crime, the strength of the evidence and the defendant."*[12] The court must also cite references to those similar cases which it has taken into consideration in its proportionality review. This process is intended to ensure that a fair and consistent distinction is made between those crimes for which the death penalty is deemed suitable and those for which it is not.

The starting point for a proper proportionality analysis, therefore, should be those cases which are factually similar to the case under review in terms of the crime committed, the evidence and the personal characteristics of the defendant. A comparison should then be made between the penalty imposed in those other similar cases and the case under review.

The seven cases cited by the Missouri Supreme Court as similar to Chambers' case clearly are not, under any stretch of imagination, remotely comparable to this tavern homicide. *State v. Wilkins* involved a stabbing of a store clerk committed during the course of a robbery. *State v. Lingar* involved a murder of a young man during a kidnapping that had sexual overtones. *State v. Rodden* was a double murder where the victims' bodies were set on fire after they were stabbed to death. *State v. Grubbs, State v. Reuscher,* and *State v. Feltrop* also were particularly gruesome homicides that are categorically different from this case.

The monstrous injuries inflicted by these defendants on their victims in these purportedly comparable cases are of a wholly different character from the homicide in this case. In *Reuscher,* the victim suffered multiple head wounds including a fractured skull and stab wounds to the chest, throat and testicles. In *Rodden,* the two victims died from multiple stab wounds and an attempt was made to burn the bodies; and in *Grubbs* the victim had thirteen broken ribs, a cracked sternum, lacerations to face and liver, a broken nose and a brain hemorrhage. The victim in *Wilkins* suffered multiple stab wounds. In *Lingar*, the victim was shot, beaten, and run over by a car. In *Feltrop*, the victim bled to death after being repeatedly stabbed by the defendant, who then dismembered and disposed of the body in a pond.

C. The Federal Courts Did Not Address This Issue

Apart from the Missouri Supreme Court, no other court has considered the proportionality of the death penalty in this case. The District Court acknowledged that it was bound to reject the proportionality claim without consideration because of prior case law. However, Judge Sachs noted that *"a tavern related homicide may be an unfamiliar context for capital punishment."* The Eighth Circuit was also unable to fully consider the question of proportionality because precedent precluded them from independently examining the determination by the Missouri Supreme Court that the sentence was proportionate.[13]

All similarly-situated defendants in Missouri, who have committed homicides in tavern fights have received sentences of imprisonment. James Chambers, therefore, has been given a death sentence for a crime for which no other person either in Missouri or anywhere else in the United States has been executed in modern times.

The last word on this subject should be heard from Judge Welliver of the Missouri Supreme Court:

> I am unable to see any new or additional evidence that changes the case from a barroom altercation. Under these circumstances, I cannot impose the death penalty. I would reduce the sentence from death to life imprisonment without parole for fifty years; otherwise proportionality in Missouri is reduced to totally meaningless.[14]

If This Case Had Been Properly Tried with the Assistance of Competent Counsel, Mr. Chambers Would Not Have Been Convicted of Capital Murder

The State claimed the shooting of Jerry Oestricker was a premeditated attack in contrast to Mr. Chambers' claim that he acted in self defense. At trial the State had the burden of proving beyond a reasonable doubt that James Chambers *did not* act in self defense. The key issues in every self defense case involve whether the defendant (a) reasonably believed it was necessary to use deadly force, and (b) to protect himself from what he reasonably believed to be the use of unlawful force that placed him in imminent danger of serious injury or death from the victim. Vital witnesses and evidence which established that Mr. Oestricker had attacked Mr. Chambers with a pair of pliers were not presented to the jury. As a result, the defense's contention that James Chambers reasonably believed he was in danger of serious injury when he shot Mr. Oestricker was not effectively presented. Independent evidence and impeaching information, which undermined the prosecution's case that this was a premeditated attack, was also not utilized. Finally, the fact that Mr. Chambers was advised by counsel not to testify meant that it was almost impossible for a jury to determine what he reasonably believed at the time of the shooting, thus dooming his claim of self-defense.

A. Mr. Chambers' Lack of Premeditation Could Have Been Proven by Effective Counsel

The prosecution's theory that the shooting was premeditated and therefore deserving of the death penalty was largely unsubstantiated and incredible. Because he had incompetent attorneys, Mr. Chambers had no opportunity to effectively advance his version of events. The true reason Mr. Chambers wound up at the tavern that night was to obtain a boat with which to fish on the river. It is for this reason that he traveled first to the Turners' house and then to the bar. When he discovered that the Turners' boat was unavailable, Mr. Chambers proceeded to the Country Club Tavern to see Jerry Hardesty about a boat. There were many witnesses who could have attested to this and, therefore, undermined the prosecution's argument that Mr. Chambers was on a mission to kill Jerry Oestricker at the behest of the Turner family. None of these witnesses was called at the guilt phase of trial.

Even more pertinent is the fact that there was no grudge between Jerry Oestricker and Jackie Turner at the time of the shooting and hence no motivation for a premeditated killing by Mr. Chambers to "avenge" Jackie Turner. There was a fight that had occurred earlier that day between the victim and Mr. Turner, but the two men reconciled. The reconciliation was verified by an independent witness, Beverly Melton. In a police interview, she stated she saw the two men "*shaking hands and patting each other on the back and Jackie went his way and Jerry went back to the pool table and so I assumed well they just figured they had both been drinking and that was it.*" This evidence was never heard and, as such, the jury was left with little choice but to believe the unsubstantiated and incredible "retaliation" theory advanced by the prosecution.

The other glaring shortcoming of defense counsel, apart from their failure to discredit the state's theory of motive and premeditation with credible evidence, was their utter failure to present to the jury the fact that the victim, Jerry Oestricker, had a notorious reputation for violence. The jury that convicted Mr. Chambers and ultimately sentenced him to death heard nothing about Jerry Oestricker's background and reputation as a barroom brawler. Available evidence could have been presented to show that Mr. Oestricker had prior convictions, had a reputation for violence, and was known to frequently engage in barroom fights. In fact, some of the injuries noted on Mr. Oestricker's body by the coroner after he was killed were inflicted upon him in a fight the previous night with a man named Russell Humphrey. Because of counsel's failure to provide the jury with a true picture of Mr. Oestricker's violent tendencies, the result of the third trial was inherently unreliable and unjust.

In this regard, it is interesting to note that counsel for Mr. Chambers was recently contacted "out of the blue" by a man from Arnold, Missouri, named Bill Lee. Mr. Lee, after reading of Mr. Chambers' upcoming execution in the local newspaper, contacted counsel to provide information about a similar barroom confrontation that he had with Jerry Oestricker in 1969. Mr. Lee has stated in a sworn affidavit that he was subjected to an unprovoked attack by Jerry Oestricker outside a bar in south St. Louis that was strikingly similar to Mr. Oestricker's confrontation with Mr. Chambers that led to his death some thirteen years later. Mr. Lee's account of his confrontation with Mr. Oestricker in 1969 speaks volumes as to the victim's true character and history of violent behavior while intoxicated. Although no barroom brawler deserves to die, Mr. Oestricker's violent and belligerent nature and actions undoubtedly contributed to his death. Had the jury known of Mr. Oestricker's character and propensity for violence, there is little doubt that they would not have convicted Mr. Chambers of capital murder, nor sentenced him to death. The fact that Mr. Oestricker's violent behavior contributed to his own death also significantly bolsters Mr. Chambers' argument that the facts of this case are not appropriate for capital punishment.

The death penalty, in theory, in order to be constitutionally imposed, is supposedly reserved for a small percentage of the most heinous and atrocious murders. A common thread of the overwhelming majority of death penalty cases that have come before the Governor and the courts for review is that the victim was innocent and helpless. Never before in the modern history of this state's capital punishment system has a man been executed where, as here, it is clear that the victim's violent and provocative behavior contributed to his own death. For this reason alone, the death penalty is an aberration in this case that cries out for correction.

Fred leppert was the star witness for the State and his testimony was vital to the State's case for capital murder. He testified at the preliminary hearing and all three trials. Mr. leppert's testimony was critical to the issue of whether Mr. Chambers was acting in response to a perceived risk of serious injury or death. Mr. leppert testified at the third trial that Mr. Chambers shot Mr. Oestricker, without provocation, a split second after they exited the tavern.

Even the most cursory look at the transcripts of the three trials and the preliminary hearing reveal that Mr. leppert's testimony is totally inconsistent and self contradictory. Mr. leppert not only gives contradictory testimony between each trial but also contradicts himself within the same trial, sometimes within a few lines. Mr. Chambers' trial attorney did little to impeach Mr. leppert regarding the inconsistencies between his testimony at the third trial and his previous statements and testimony. If trial counsel had effectively challenged Mr. leppert as to these inconsistencies in his testimony, the jury would have reached the inescapable conclusion that his testimony was unworthy of belief. It is James Chambers' grave misfortune that Mr. leppert's credibility was not effectively challenged.

To execute James Chambers after he has spent 17 years on death row would constitute cruel and unusual punishment.

▼▲▼ _____

Professor Suni concludes about Missouri's proportionality review that "the last vestige of protection against inappropriate sentencing has proven largely ineffective" (1986: 577). The clemency petition for James Chambers highlights some of the problems with the state's proportionality review. The petition questioned the comparability of the cases chosen by the state supreme court to decide the appropriateness of the Chambers death sentence. Higher courts deferred to the state's evaluation without testing whether the procedures for proportionality review actually result in an effective distinction between cases that receive the death penalty and those cases that do not. The judicial presumption of correctness goes unexamined, despite dissenting judicial opinions. In addition to the questionable process of proportionality review, the Chambers petition raised concerns about ineffective counsel and its effects upon the resulting trial verdict. Ironically, James Chambers had three trials because of the court's recognition of serious error, but the quality of counsel Mr. Chambers received never improved. Thus, Mr. Chambers was still deprived of due process and fundamental fairness. In the end, no appellate court would admit to the seriousness of the flaws in the delivery of legal justice in his case. James Chambers was executed November 15, 2000.

CASE STUDY:
MISINTERPRETATION OF MISSOURI LAW:
IS MISSOURI A "WEIGHING" STATE?

Jeff Sloan, CP#55

Jeffrey Sloan admitted to killing his father, his mother, and his two younger brothers in December 1985. The jury never heard significant mitigating factors including substantial physical and emotional abuse that was perpetrated upon Jeff by his father. Neighbors, although alarmed by the abuse, declined to alert authorities. Although new evidence was discovered that could have affected the jury's deliberation, appellate courts would not permit a retrial. The courts concluded that Missouri is not a "weighing" state, and despite the fact that all agreed an unconstitutional jury instruction was used, Mr. Sloan was not entitled to a reconsideration of his case. Mr. Sloan's attorney was disbarred shortly after Jeff's trial, having been convicted of laundering drug money.

▼▲▼

Application for Commutation of a Sentence of Death[15]

Jeff Sloan did not receive adequate representation at trial. His lawyers, both of whom have since been disbarred, failed to put on any meaningful evidence in mitigation of the crime for which Jeff was convicted. The criminal justice system has exacerbated that failure through procedural barriers that have prevented every court from deciding on the merits (based upon the evidence we now have) whether Jeff Sloan's trial lawyer fulfilled his constitutional duty to provide effective assistance of counsel.

The trial court instructed the jury on two aggravating circumstances. They were whether the murder was committed "while the defendant was engaged in the commission of another unlawful homicide . . ." and "whether the murder . . . involved depravity of mind and that as a result thereof it was outrageously or wantonly vile, horrible or inhuman." The jury found that both aggravating circumstances applied.

The Eighth Circuit's decision concludes, and there is no dispute, that the depravity of mind instruction as given is unconstitutionally vague because it had no qualification to temper the jury's discretion. The Eighth Circuit theorized that a state appellate court may cure an unconstitutionally vague instruction by establishing and then later applying a valid limiting instruction. However, the Eighth Circuit expressly recognized that the Missouri Supreme Court had not cured the instruction's vagueness on direct appeal.

The Eighth Circuit—recognizing that the depravity of mind instruction on aggravating circumstances was unconstitutional and that the state supreme court had failed to cure this unconstitutional flaw in the procedure—nevertheless, they determined that the sentence passed muster.

The only possible avenue to permit the conclusion that the procedure in Jeff's case is constitutional concerns the analysis of whether Missouri requires the weighing of aggravating and mitigating circumstances. The Eighth Circuit recognized that the "outcome depends" on this single, crucial question.

The structure of analysis is basically agreed upon. If Missouri is a non-weighing state, then the loss of an aggravating circumstance does not require a re-weighing of aggravating and mitigating circumstances. However, if Missouri is a weighing state, as it clearly is based upon the language of the applicable statute, the decisions of the Supreme Court applying other similar statutory schemes and the Missouri Supreme Court's own analysis concerning its statute, then it is constitutionally necessary that a trier of fact re-weigh aggravating and mitigating circumstances so that the unconstitutional thumb of the "depravity of mind" instruction is not holding down the scales in favor of the death penalty.

The applicable Missouri statute[16] reads as follows:

> The trier shall assess and declare the punishment at life imprisonment without eligibility for probation, parole, or release except by act of the governor.
>
> (a) If the trier does not find beyond a reasonable doubt at least one of the statutory aggravating circumstances set out in subsection 2 of section 565.032; or
>
> (b) If the trier does not find the evidence in aggravation of punishment, including but not limited to evidence supporting the statutory aggravating circumstances listed in subsection 2 of section 565.032, warrants imposing the death sentence; or
>
> (c) If the trier concludes that there is evidence in mitigation of punishment, including but not limited to evidence supporting the statutory mitigating

circumstances listed in subsection 3 of section 565.032, *which is sufficient to outweigh the evidence in aggravation* of punishment found by the trier; *or*

(d) If the trier decides under all of the circumstances not to assess and declare the punishment at death.

If the trier is a jury it shall be so instructed (emphasis added).

The statute specifically and expressly *requires* that unless the trier of fact determines there is insufficient evidence in mitigation to "outweigh the evidence in aggravation . . . found by the trier" the penalty *must* be life imprisonment. It is therefore required under the clear language of the statute that the jury must weigh mitigating circumstances against aggravating circumstances before it can determine that the death penalty is appropriate.

This conclusion is clear from the structure of the statute. The statute provides that the sentence is to be life imprisonment *unless* all the subparagraphs (1) through (4) are resolved in favor of the death penalty conclusion. This is accomplished by providing that the sentence is required to be life imprisonment if any of the listed four possibilities occur. The four points are listed disjunctively. The failure of the trier of the fact to resolve any one of them on the side of the death penalty means the sentence must be life in prison. Thus, the jury *must* conduct a *weighing* exercise before it can reach the verdict of death under the statute. The jury is required to determine that mitigating circumstances do not "outweigh" aggravating circumstances before it can complete the verdict form sentencing a defendant to death.

The Eighth Circuit asserts that in the Missouri scheme the finding of an aggravating circumstance merely is a "threshold requirement" to imposing a death sentence. In short, the Eighth Circuit concludes that the finding of at least one aggravating circumstance is a condition precedent, or a qualifier, that is needed before the jury can go on to sentence a defendant to death.

The structure and language of the statute shows this conclusion is simply wrong. The language of the statute shows that the process of weighing mitigating circumstances against aggravating circumstances is *equally* a threshold requirement to adopting a death sentence as is the finding of an aggravating circumstance. Both must happen before a sentence of death is proper. That is, the jury must find beyond a reasonable doubt that one or more aggravating circumstances exist *and,* equally as important and equally as qualifying, the jury must conclude that there is insufficient mitigating circumstances to *outweigh* aggravating circumstances before the death penalty can be imposed.

The Eighth Circuit notes that the jury found one valid aggravating circumstance and "was free then to consider all evidence in aggravation and mitigation." Again, this is wrong because it is contrary to the statute and contrary to the instructions given to the jury. As noted, the statute requires the jury to weigh mitigating circumstances against aggravating circumstances not simply to "consider all evidence in aggravation and mitigation."

The Eighth Circuit agrees that the "depravity of mind" instruction as given in this case is unconstitutionally vague and it agrees that the Missouri Supreme Court did not apply a limiting instruction in this case. In considering whether the sentence should be invalidated, the Eighth Circuit then states:

> The outcome depends on how Missouri uses aggravating circumstances in deciding whether to impose the death penalty. In some states, aggravating circumstances are expressly weighed against any mitigating circumstances. If the former outweigh the latter, the death penalty is applied. *In those jurisdictions, the invalidation of an aggravating circumstance is of tremendous import because the removal of that factor from the equation might change the result.* (emphasis added)[17]

The correct analysis is that in Missouri "aggravating circumstances *are* expressly weighed against any mitigating circumstances" (emphasis added). Accordingly, in Missouri, the removal of an aggravating circumstance "is of tremendous import because . . . [it] might change the result."[18]

The Missouri Supreme Court has repeatedly recognized that juries in this state *must* weigh aggravating and mitigating circumstances.[19] The key point in all of this analysis with regard to the Missouri case law is that in each opinion the Missouri Supreme Court recognizes that a weighing process is required in each case. It is simply unavoidable under the Missouri statutory scheme because weighing has to occur between mitigating and aggravating circumstances. While there are other elements in the statutory scheme, it is admitted repeatedly by the Missouri Supreme Court that a weighing process relative to mitigating and aggravating circumstances is required in each case. And where a weighing process is required, removal of one of the factors that is necessarily utilized in that weighing process "is of tremendous import" and certainly could "change the result." Because it is impossible to change this logical chain of analysis that flows directly from the statute, it is apparent that Missouri is a weighing state.

The suggestion that Missouri is a weighing state is also supported by the observation that the 1984 amendments to the Missouri statutory scheme were a clear attempt to adopt the Model Penal Code approach (Suni, 1986: note 8). It is recognized that the Model Penal Code is considered a weighing/balancing statute. The Comment to Model Penal Code sec. 210.6 expressly indicates that it is a weighing scheme. The Comment also states that the Model Penal Code "is a balanced judgment of one or more [aggravators] against any mitigation that constitutes the ultimate decision."

The courts have concluded in Jeff Sloan's case that Missouri is not a "weighing" state and, despite the fact that all agree an unconstitutional instruction was used, Mr. Sloan is not entitled to a re-weighing of the circumstances of his case. The unfairness and blatant injustice is apparent. A greedy, distracted and unprepared lawyer failed to properly investigate and present the mitigation evidence that would have balanced against the aggravating circumstances. By effect of the legal machinery, an acknowledged unconstitutional aggravating circumstance instruction is used to tip the scales even further against Mr. Sloan.

Jeff Sloan did not receive adequate representation at trial. If his lawyer had done something resembling even a mediocre job the jury would not have sentenced Jeff Sloan to die. The jury could have learned about the violent and abusive practices of Jeff's father and the general dysfunctional nature of his family. The jury also could have learned that Jeff suffered brain damage about seven years before the crime took place and that his cognitive skills were drastically stunted such that his ability to reason and his judgment were affected. The jury did not hear this. . . . No state or federal court has considered the facts below but instead has ignored them because the claims were procedurally barred. There is no such restriction on the decision-making process of the Governor.

The key question in this case has always been why did Jeff kill his parents and his two brothers. Attorney Michael Lerner never explained anything to the jury. The jury did not know:

1. that Jeff is brain damaged—most likely as a result of a blow to the back of his head when he was 12 years old. He was struck by his father wielding a weighted pool cue. The blow left an indentation about the size of a quarter in Jeff's skull and is about an inch to an inch-and-a-half deep.

2. that Jeff has significant cognitive deficiencies that compromise his ability to think and judge. Although now 29 years old, his basic skills achievement is equal to the early elementary grades.

3. that Jeff, although living in as horrific and disturbed family situation as

most of us could imagine, chose to stay at home in order to protect his mother and his brother, Jason.

4. that other members of his family still care about him and do not want him executed.

5. independent evidence of Jeff's mother's scheme to end the cycle of abuse and her own bout with cancer by urging Jeff to kill all the members of the family, including herself.

6. that Jeff was represented by a lawyer who was involved in a drug money laundering scheme and would later be disbarred.

7. that Jeff's lawyer had done virtually nothing to investigate and establish all of the possible evidence in mitigation in the good side of his character such as his caring attitude toward his mother and brother Jason and his good work record.

8. that they utilized a "depravity of mind" aggravating circumstance instruction that is recognized by both the Federal District Court and the United States Court of Appeals to be unconstitutional.

9. that Jeff was a teenager (19 years old) at the time of the crime.

A written report prepared by Dr. Marilyn Hutchison, Ph.D. states:

Significant mitigating factors that were present in Jeff's commission of the murder of his family include:

1. Intense psychological distress that resulted from substantial physical and emotional abuse that was perpetrated upon Jeff by his father. This abuse was significant enough to elicit concern from neighborhood observers. Bruises and signs of beatings were noted. He expressed an intense fear of his father as well as making extreme efforts to please him. Acquaintances noted Jeff was anxious all the time and his hands frequently shook.

2. Significant cognitive deficiencies that were the result of a learning disability and/or profound head trauma. Testing indicates an inability to process information and remember it, impaired cognitive flexibility (unable to shift to another problem solving strategy when confronted with failure) and evidence of long standing learning problems as revealed by current basic skills achievement equal to early elementary grades. There was a strong likelihood of left hemispheric damage, the area of the brain responsible for logical sequential thinking.

3. Serious psychological difficulties compromise his ability to think and judge. Psychological testing endorses a possible diagnosis of paranoid schizophrenia and clear evidence of disordered thinking. He has difficulty perceiving reality and uses fantasy as a defense against unresolved emotions.

4. An uncommonly close relationship with his mother who appears to have had substantial psychological problems including suicidal wishes. Jeff was strongly influenced by his mother's repeated requests that he not leave her and her other sons. He always obliged these requests. Jeff reports she also wanted the family killed and had reasons why each specific member should be killed. It is not unreasonable to believe that he also complied with that request.

5. A particularly emotionally distressing week preceded the incident in question: Jeff's mother told him he was not his father's son; Jeff stole some checks from his father; due to weather he was not able to work to repay his father; and his mother received a medical diagnosis that concerned her. The last straw seemed to have been that his father did not react to the checks being returned from the bank. Jeff and his mother discussed what it could mean that he was not behaving in his usual abusive manner. It appears that the stress and distress of these situations was significant enough for Jeff to murder his family.

The jury heard none of this. Mr. Lerner called only two witnesses in the penalty phase. The entire defense case on mitigation covers less than 20 pages of the trial transcript. The first witness was Carolyn Streeter, Paul Sloan's sister and the paternal aunt of the petitioner. Her most telling comment was that she did not believe that Paul had physically abused his children. Thus, she contradicted a key part of Jeff Sloan's case without adding any corroboration to what should have been the petitioner's main themes. It is apparent that her testimony hurt the petitioner's case, as opposed to providing any mitigation whatsoever. The second and final witness in the penalty phase was Betty Sloan, a sister-in-law to Paul Sloan. Mr. Lerner asked her questions about Jason Sloan (Jeff's brother) and then had her recount cleaning the Sloan's house after the murders. There is nothing in her testimony that is in any way mitigating. The State had no cross examination. The defense then rested at the penalty stage.

Mr. Lerner gave the jury *absolutely nothing* to mitigate against the horrible offenses that had been presented to the jury in gruesome detail.

Mr. Lerner's failure to provide any semblance of the available evidence to this jury is nearly unfathomable. However, the record is replete with information that suggests why Mr. Lerner did not perform his constitutionally mandated preparation. Mr. Lerner's own personal, financial and criminal problems prevented him from performing his duties. Mr. Lerner was involved in a drug money laundering scheme that began sometime in 1984 and continued throughout the entire time of his representation of Jeff Sloan. Mr. Lerner pled guilty on June 30, 1988 in the United States District Court for the District of Kansas to a felony charge of aiding and abetting income tax evasion in order to "launder" drug money. As a result of this event, Mr. Lerner was disbarred January 24, 1989.

In the mid-1980s, Mr. Lerner was experiencing financial problems as a result of his law practice and other business interests. Mr. Lerner contacted Jeff Sloan and agreed to represent him without cost basically as a marketing technique. Mr. Lerner testified in his deposition that he volunteered his services with the anticipation of attracting future death penalty cases because he believed that Kansas was soon to adopt a death penalty law.

Mr. Lerner was experiencing significant personal difficulties during his representation of Jeff and these problems directly impacted Mr. Lerner's performance on behalf of Jeff. Specifically, these problems prevented Mr. Lerner from effectively and adequately investigating Jeff's case in the guilt and penalty phases as well as adequately understanding the relevant case law on death penalty litigation defense during the pre-trial, trial, post-trial and direct appeal time periods.

Testimony at the Rule 29.15 hearing demonstrated that Mr. Lerner had "absolutely no knowledge" of the refinements of death penalty litigation and was not familiar with the most basic principles necessary in a death penalty case.

It is understandable to wonder that although Mr. Lerner's behavior before, during and after his representation of Jeff Sloan was despicable and contrary to law with regard to the money laundering scheme, what impact did Mr. Lerner's illegal activities and personal problems have upon Jeff's trial. The answer is that the footprints of Mr. Lerner's confused, disjointed experiences are everywhere in this case. From the complete failure to investigate mitigation evidence, at the same time professing that this part of the trial was the primary issue, as well as demonstrating approximately a week before trial a complete lack of knowledge concerning the most fundamental issues in a capital punishment trial. The crux of the matter, however, is simply Mr. Lerner's failure to investigate. And, as noted in the legal discussion herein, when the attorney's performance is based upon a lack of investigation, it is not part of a strategy choice.

The importance of this failure is even more evident because of the jury's uncertainty. The jury returned a guilty verdict after about an hour of deliberation. The same group of twelve people spent approximately six hours considering the appropriate sentence. The jury also asked to review certain medical records during the sentencing phase deliberation. This was a jury that was troubled by the task before them.

If the jury would have learned of the violent and twisted nature of the defendant's home life and, that despite the environment, the many examples of his love for the members of his family, his good character, contributions to society and positive work record, the sentencing result would have been different.

▼▲▼

In Jeff Sloan's petition, the legal debate that is highlighted is whether Missouri is a "weighing" or "nonweighing" state. This controversy directly impacts whether the appellate court will require a new sentencing hearing. The clemency petition to the governor argues that the Eighth Circuit Court made a mistaken interpretation of the law, which is never reversed. The outcome of the legal debate endorses a procedural barrier that blocks the consideration of Mr. Sloan's substantive claim of ineffective assistance of counsel. The detailed legal argument is presented to the governor in hopes that he will overrule all the courts that decided otherwise and commute the death sentence to life imprisonment without parole. Significantly, nine other clemency petitions (20 percent of the total) claim that a misinterpretation of law adversely affected the fundamental fairness of their death penalty convictions and sentence. Jeff Sloan was executed February 21, 1996.

CASE STUDY:
POSTCONVICTION APPEAL AND
PROCEDURAL BARRIERS—AEDPA

Milton Griffin El, CP#57

Milton Griffin El was convicted of the killings of Loretta Trotter and Jerome Redden in 1986 during an apartment robbery that involved five men. The jury that convicted Mr. Griffin El sentenced him to life imprisonment for the murder of Ms. Trotter, but could not decide on the penalty for the murder of Mr. Redden. The sentencing decision passed to the trial judge, who sentenced Mr. Griffin El to death for the murder of Mr. Redden. The codefendant, who was identified by all involved as the instigator of the crime and who also participated in the stabbing, received a life sentence.

▼▲▼
Application for Commutation
of a Death Sentence[20]

In the late evening of August 14 or the early morning hours of August 15, 1986, a black woman named Loretta Trotter and a white man named Jerome Redden were killed in their St. Louis apartment during a robbery which involved five men. Milton V. Griffin,[21] a black man, was arrested and gave a statement implicating himself and Antoine Owens as the two who had gone into the apartment. Antoine Owens, who planned the burglary, brought a gun to the crime, talked about killing the victims to leave no witnesses, and repeatedly stabbed both victims, was tried separately. He was convicted of both murders and received a life sentence for each. It is undisputed that Antoine Owens was the instigator of the crimes as Milton and the three others identified him as such.

A major issue developed in the jury selection at Milton's trial. The state used five of its ten peremptory challenges to strike five black women from the jury. When Milton's lawyer complained, the trial judge said he found the issue "difficult and confusing."

Another circumstance compounded the issue as to whether Milton was truly guilty of deliberating before killing Mr. Redden and thus eligible for the death penalty. The jury was instructed on first degree murder and conventional second degree murder. Milton's trial lawyer asked the judge to give a felony murder instruction also. The judge refused. That instruction would have informed the jury that it had the option of finding Milton guilty on a murder theory which did not involve the death penalty. The Missouri Supreme Court agreed that it was error for the trial court to refuse the instruction. However, the Court found that there was no showing that Milton was legally prejudiced (seriously harmed) by the error. Had the jury been instructed on felony murder, which the Supreme Court found to be a viable theory based on the evidence, perhaps it would have found him guilty of that charge. The jury may have found that the facts as perceived by its members fit with the felony murder theory better than the other two theories. Perhaps the jury was not comfortable with applying the facts to the two legal theories on which it was instructed and it chose first degree murder as the closer fit. If the jury had all three options, each of which was supported by the facts of the case, it would have had the ability to make a more informed choice. Proper instruction to the jury would have cut Milton's odds on being eligible for the death penalty from 1 out of 2 to 1 out of 3.

The trial judge imposed the death sentence for the murder of Jerome Redden after the jury could not decide on the penalty. Prior to a statutory change in 1984, that indecision would have resulted in a life sentence for Milton. In Milton's appeal to the Missouri Supreme Court, dissenting Judge Blackmar wrote that allowing a judge to determine whether a death sentence was appropriate was an "unprecedented" delegation of the "right of trial by jury. . . ." Currently pending in the Missouri Legislature is legislation which would require the imposition of a life sentence when the jury "hangs" during the sentencing phase of a capital case. That would result in a reversion to the pre-1984 situation, in which Milton would have received a life sentence. Should that legislation pass without the Governor intervening in this case, then Milton may die simply by virtue of his trial date. We must protect against such an arbitrary application of the ultimate punishment.

State Appeals

The Missouri Supreme Court has established a 100 page limit on briefs submitted by appellants. That limit may be exceeded by seeking permission of the court. While one would presume that cases of the magnitude of capital appeals should be granted that permission upon reasonable request, that was not done here. Milton's brief was due in the Supreme Court on March 31, 1988. A week before the appeal was due, Milton's attorney requested leave to exceed the 100 page limit. She pointed out in her motion that the transcript contained a total of 1969 pages; that there were a total of 47 allegations of error; that she had carefully reviewed the issues to make sure they were not frivolous; that she avoided long quotations and string citations to keep the brief as short as possible; and that this was a capital case. That motion was denied. She then asked the court to reconsider its denial and argued that for her to delete any more of the brief would violate her duties to her client under the Rules of Professional Conduct to which all Missouri attorneys must adhere and would also constitute ineffective assistance of counsel. Again, the court denied her request. Counsel then petitioned the Supreme Court en banc pointing out the things she had presented in her previous motions; noting that she had made reference to prior arguments in the brief at all possible times to avoid reiterating anything; stating that she had reduced the brief from its original 201 pages to 132 pages; and that the court's own rules, requiring her to set forth in full any instructions at issue, consumed a large part of the brief as four separate instructional issues were being raised on appeal. The court denied that motion also.

The last 33 pages of her brief were stricken by the court from the brief. Thus, the brief was submitted without a reasonable process to select which issues should have been deleted or which arguments should have been shortened. This was the first capital appeal that Milton's attorney had been involved in. She now realizes that her failure to adhere to the rule by shortening her brief in a judicious manner cost Milton the right to have important issues reviewed on appeal. One issue that was stricken pertained to the trial court's failure to instruct on three mitigating circumstances. The second stricken issue had to do with insufficient evidence of aggravating circumstances and imposition of the death sentence as a result of passion and prejudice. The third went to the lack of proportionality in giving Milton the death sentence and the impropriety in the statutorily mandated review of proportionality. While the Supreme Court was required by statute to consider proportionality, it was done without any information or argument being offered by Milton's lawyer. The latter issue is especially cogent in this application for clemency because the instigator, Antoine Owens, received life sentences. This is galling as Mr. Owens knew the victims, came up with the plan, provided the transportation, took a gun to the apartment, reneged on a commitment that there would be no killing, and stabbed both victims over Milton's protests that he would not do that. We will never know whether Milton would have prevailed on one of these issues if the Supreme Court had granted the motion to exceed the limit or if his attorney had been reasonable in prioritizing the issues for that court.

This problem was compounded in the litigation of Milton's request for post-conviction relief following Supreme Court Rule 27.76. The 100 page limitation issue was raised in the trial court without any relief being granted. In affirming the lower court, the Missouri Supreme Court stated that:

> Movant [Mr. Griffin] offers no explanation for the excess length of his brief in the direct appeal of his criminal case nor is an explanation offered as to why, during the course of his direct appeal, prior leave to file a brief of greater length than was permitted by Rule 30.06(i) was not requested.[22]

Whether Milton's post-conviction attorneys failed to present properly the factual background or whether the Missouri Supreme Court was inept in reading the record is academic. The bottom line is that Milton never received any kind of a hearing on those issues through no fault of his own.

We will never know whether any of those deleted issues would have provided relief. That they were deleted meant not only that the issues could not be considered by a Missouri court of review but also that they could never be considered by a federal court in a petition for a writ of habeas corpus. Issues not presented to state courts are deemed waived when presented for federal habeas corpus review. The refusal of the Supreme Court to allow an oversize brief was clearly arbitrary. The court's own rule provides for consideration of over-length briefs. The Missouri Supreme Court commonly grants such requests. Our state is sending a man to his death without a full and fair review of the facts and circumstances attending his processing in the criminal justice system.

Denial of Federal Appellate Rights

In 1991, Milton filed a petition for a writ of habeas corpus in the United States District Court for the Eastern District of Missouri. The petition raised twenty six issues. The case was assigned to Judge Clyde Cahill. Counsel was appointed and his petition was amended in December, 1991. In early 1993, an evidentiary hearing on one issue raised in the petition was held and subsequently denied. Later that year the case was transferred to Judge Carol Jackson. The case languished in the district court as the new judge and her staff reviewed the voluminous records of the state court proceedings and the documents filed in support of the habeas petition. In February of 1996, Judge Jackson denied several motions that had been pending since 1993. The only thing left was her final judgment on the petition.

On April 24, 1996 the federal Anti-Terrorism and Effective Death Penalty Act of 1996 (AEDPA) became effective. AEDPA changed several of the procedures pertaining to petitions for habeas corpus relief. One of the changes was to require a habeas petitioner to obtain a certificate of appealability (COA) before appealing the denial of habeas corpus relief by a federal district court. Previously a petitioner denied relief at the federal district court level had to obtain a certificate of probable cause (CPC) before filing an appeal. The practical difference between the two certificates is that in issuing a COA, a court must specify those issues which it believes merit appellate review. The CPC had no requirement of specificity. Once it was issued, the petitioner could raise any issues on appeal which had been adversely decided by the lower court. The CPC was generally issued by the district court. Because of poor drafting, there was initial confusion in the federal courts as to whether a district court could issue the new certificate or whether it had to be issued by an appellate judge or supreme court justice. Nationwide litigation has settled that issue and it is now widely-held that a district court can issue the COA.

On July 31, 1996, Judge Jackson denied the petition for a writ of habeas corpus. She also issued a certificate of probable cause. As Milton's attorney had left the private practice of law, Judge Jackson appointed new counsel. A notice of appeal to the United States Court of Appeals for the Eighth Circuit was filed on September 27, 1996. An issue immediately developed as to which type of certificate Milton needed to appeal. Milton's attorney took the position that the old law should apply and that all he needed was the certificate of probable cause issued by Judge Jackson. This was because the case was filed and processed under the old law and all that remained to be done on April 24, 1996 was for the judge to render her decision. At that time, application of the new law was in its infancy.

The Eighth Circuit entered an order stating it would treat Milton's notice of appeal as an application for a COA. The state then moved to quash the notice of appeal and alleged that there were no issues worthy of appeal. Milton's attorney filed a pleading asking the Court to accept Judge Jackson's CPC as the petition was filed prior to the change in law. Alternatively, he asked the court to remand the case to Judge Jackson for her to determine which issues were meritorious. The court denied those requests but allowed him to submit a memorandum in support of the application for a COA. On March 21, 1997, the court denied the application for a COA. A petition for rehearing was submitted on May 13. The court then amended its March 21 order to delete a portion which stated that a United States District Court Judge had no authority to issue a COA. The court also allowed Milton to re-file a petition for rehearing in light of the change in its order denying him a COA. The revised petition was filed on June 25, 1997.

On June 23, 1997, the United States Supreme Court decided *Lindh v. Murphy* holding that the new habeas procedures set forth in AEDPA generally apply to those cases filed after April 24, 1996. In spite of *Lindh*, the Eighth Circuit refused to allow Milton to proceed with his CPC and denied the petition for rehearing on August 11.

As a result of the *Lindh* decision, the other circuits of the United States Court of Appeals have held that a habeas petitioner who filed a petition before April 24, 1996 must always be treated under the old law.[23] The Eighth Circuit is the only circuit to consider the question and to decide otherwise. In *Tiedeman v. Benson* (1997), the Eighth Circuit grasped on to the word "generally" in the *Lindh* opinion to mean that the federal courts may make a case by case determination as to when to apply the particular parts of AEDPA law to the cases filed before April 24, 1996. The Eighth Circuit is alone in that interpretation as all other circuits which have decided the issue interpret *Lindh* to be an *absolute* prohibition on such a practice. Were Milton on death row in any other circuit in the country, he would be allowed the right to appeal.

As an alternative to his argument that he should have been allowed to appeal upon the issuance of a CPC, Milton, through his attorney, suggested that the Court of Appeals send the case back to Judge Jackson with instructions to apply the new law and to specify which issues were worthy of appellate review. Several federal courts had adopted that tactic.[24] Their reasoning was that the district courts had spent a lot of time familiarizing themselves with the facts and the law applicable to a particular case and were therefore in the best position to decide on which issues a petitioner should be allowed to appeal. When Milton's case was pending before the Eighth Circuit, that court had never ruled on this issue and there was no guidance as to how attorneys should proceed.

The Eighth Circuit took the position that a COA was required and that it would determine whether there were issues deserving of review. It refused to send the case back to Judge Jackson in spite of the fact that she had studied the case for more than two years, had developed an intimate familiarity with it, and would have been in the best position to determine which issues had enough merit to appeal.

As in any federal habeas case, the district court looked at all of the prior records of the state courts who previously had Milton's case before them. That record included the charging document; the motions and orders in all of the Missouri courts; the transcripts of jury selection, trial testimony, and sentencing; the motion for a new trial; the briefs to the Missouri Supreme Court for Milton's direct appeal and from the denial of the motion for a new trial; the two decisions of the Missouri Supreme Court; and all of the pleadings and other documents filed in the district court during the pendency of the case there. The Eighth Circuit did not review any of those documents. The docket entries from the United States District Court state that all that was transmitted to the Court of Appeals were the notice of appeal, the docket entries, Judge Jackson's order, and a transcript from the single issue evidentiary hearing before Judge Cahill. The Eighth Circuit reviewed none of the state court documents in spite of the fact that those records are what Milton's habeas corpus petition was based on. The Eighth Circuit ruled that it would not issue a COA and dismissed Milton's appeal. A petition for a rehearing was filed and it was denied over the dissent of four circuit judges. This made Milton the first person to ever be denied a certificate of appealability in a capital case and the first person to be denied the right to appeal from the denial of a first habeas corpus petition in the Eighth Circuit.

The Eighth Circuit has not been consistent on this issue. The denial of Milton's petition for rehearing came on August 11, 1997. On August 18, 1997, the same court sent the case of Roy Ramsey, another death row inmate who was initially denied a COA, back to the district court for a determination of which issues merited a COA. The turnabout in *Ramsey* was predicated on the *Tiedeman* decision. Since *Tiedeman* was handed down five days before Milton's denial and twelve days before Mr. Ramsey's remand, the disparate treatment is inexplicable.

Further inconsistency is demonstrated by the Eighth Circuit's order in *Rodden v. Delo*, No. 97-2100, where the court granted a CPC after April 24, 1996. Presumably the reason behind this inconsistency is the newness of applying the procedures in AEDPA and the lack of a body of precedent. However, that newness does not excuse the disparate treatment and the denial of the right of a first appeal for a death row habeas petitioner. Those who oppose the death penalty complain of the arbitrary processing of the individual through the criminal justice system. Those who support the death penalty must guard against such arbitrariness. Milton Griffin El would not have a date with death if he were in any other circuit.

Given the probability that Milton was incapable of deliberating before killing Jerome Redden, that the safeguards enacted to protect against the arbitrary use of capital punishment were abused to such an extent that we should not in good conscience execute Milton, and that Milton Griffin El is a different person than Milton Griffin, the Governor should commute his sentence to life imprisonment. Alternatively, the death sentence should be stayed until the Governor is assured that Milton has received the judicial review that the law provides for all citizens.

▼▲▼

Milton Griffin El's clemency petition pleaded with the governor to ignore the procedural barriers he encountered and to consider the merits of his case. As in other cases, the ineffectiveness of his attorneys directly contributed to his death sentence and its affirmance, with the additional burden of the application of the AEDPA aggravating his problems.[25] Because of the courts' willingness to deny his appeals on technicalities, the merits of his complaints were not addressed. The clemency petition raises multiple issues of fundamental fairness and arbitrariness as the courts appear to conspire to deny him the careful scrutiny due death penalty cases.[26] Milton Griffin El was executed March 25, 1998.

CONCLUSIONS

This chapter is *not* a thorough survey of all the complex legal issues concerning death penalty litigation. Law review articles are abundantly available which examine the nuances of the ever-changing and complicated domain of such litigation. What is presented here are examples of some of the criticisms of the appellate process that are raised in the Missouri clemency petitions. These claims primarily focus on procedural matters that have real consequences for the substantive protection of fundamental fairness. These problems are the kinds of issues that are likely raised in the majority of states with the death penalty.

Jurists have said repeatedly that compared with other possible legal punishments, the death penalty is different, meaning that the irrevocability of the death sentence requires special procedural protections to ensure that an innocent person is not executed.[27] Although none of the cases presented earlier claims actual innocence, each would claim that they were legally innocent of capital murder—that is, that they were not guilty beyond a reasonable doubt of "knowingly" and "deliberately" committing murder. Each would claim that the procedural protections that exist on paper do not function in reality to ensure fairness or reliability in the result, nor do they overcome the systemic problems that pervade the criminal justice system. These kinds of claims are difficult to communicate to a public that is focused on quick fixes and on punishing the guilty.

The public's perception is that some sort of "super due process" exists for the death row prisoner, which he or she then manipulates by multiple appeals in order to evade execution. This impression is fostered by politicians. Johnny Sutton, the criminal justice policy director for then–presidential candidate George W. Bush, said, "We have a system in place [in Texas] that is very careful and that gives years and years of *super due process* to make sure that no innocent defendants are executed and that the defendant received a fair trial" (Mills, Armstrong, and Holt, 2000). With statements such as this, the "public develops a strong but false sense that many levels of safeguards protect against unjust or arbitrary executions. They are thus likely to accept any executions that finally make it through the system as being more than fair enough" (Steiker and Steiker, 1995: 436).

The due process procedures approved by the U.S. Supreme Court in *Gregg v. Georgia* (1976) focused on structural forms, not substantive distinctions. The protections include separate trials for the conviction and sentencing phases; the automatic appellate review by the state supreme court; the enumeration of categories of crimes as capital offenses; mandatory considerations of aggravating and mitigating circumstances by the sentencer; and the finding of at least one statutory aggravating circumstance before death may be imposed (McGill, 1990: note 48). These protections were intended to narrow the class of cases eligible for the death penalty; to remove passion, prejudice, and arbitrariness from the jury's decision making; and to provide individualized sentencing. But the reality is that these procedural protections for fairness are empty promises and insufficient to ensure reliability in the trial results. The courts and the Congress actually give *fewer* protections to death penalty cases than to ordinary criminal cases.

The direct appeal is meaningless for three major reasons. Not only is the scope of the proportionality review questionable, the Supreme Court has ruled in *Pulley v. Harris* (1984) that such a review is not constitutionally required. The Court defers to states that conduct proportionality reviews and does not inquire whether they actually distinguish between death penalty cases and not others (Liebman, 1985: 1,433). Second, the failure to consider the cumulative impact of numerous errors indicates a court that is fully in tune with the political climate of the time and eager to affirm death sentences.[28] The court is more responsive to the public's inclinations than to its theoretical legal responsibility as one ultimate umpire or conscience of the criminal justice system and of society in general. Third, because jurisdictions expand the list of aggravating factors to cover most murder situations (Missouri has seventeen aggravating factors), having the requirement that one aggravating factor must be found before imposing the death penalty does not provide any limitation on arbitrariness. Steiker and Steiker conclude that "this approach is essentially indistinguishable from the standardless discretion embodied in the pre-1972 statutes" (1995: 378).

> Instead of achieving the narrowing functions suggested in the *Furman* and *Gregg* decisions, these aggravating factors merely give the sentencer the illusion that the offense at issue truly falls within the select set of crimes that justifies imposition of the death penalty (Steiker and Steiker, 1995: 375).

Supreme Court decisions have continually cut back on providing different scrutiny for prisoners awaiting the death penalty. Instead of providing extra-careful scrutiny to death penalty cases, legal doctrines have developed to limit the courts' review functions by ignoring errors that may have occurred. We have already seen in chapter 5 that the vagueness of the *Strickland* standard for ineffective assistance of counsel has very rarely identified poor lawyering that would overturn a capital conviction and death sentence, in large part because of the strong presumption for the effectiveness of the counsel that is built into the standard. To compound the problems that can arise when operating from this presumption, the Supreme Court stated in *Coleman v. Thompson* (1991) that prisoners are bound by any errors made by their postconviction lawyers.

Supreme Court unwillingness to overturn state court decisions is grounded in four other legal doctrines:

1. **Presumptive correctness.** The factual findings by the state court benefit from a presumption that they are correct.[29]
2. **Exhaustion.** The exhaustion of remedies rule requires a federal court to dismiss an appeal that presents claims that have not yet been litigated in state court.[30]
3. **Procedural default.** If the petitioner misses a deadline or does not file a motion or brief properly, the appellate issue cannot be considered.[31]
4. **Nonretroactivity.** A new constitutional rule generally may not be applied to cases that have already had their habeas review.[32]

Through the invocation of these doctrines, the courts have limited their reviews of death penalty cases to matters of procedural correctness, rather than to addressing issues of substantive justice. While the courts appear to conduct a careful review, in fact, through these doctrines they have given states the means to justify whatever they want to do (Steiker and Steiker, 1995). The clearest statement of the Court's narrowing focus may be when, in *Murray v. Giarrantano* (1989),

> Chief Justice Rehnquist rejected the argument that "death is different," reasoning that the capital inmate's special protection under the eighth amendment is limited primarily to the trial stage and does not extend to the post-conviction stage (McGill, 1990: 214).

Congressional legislation limits the death row appeal process. The developing consensus regarding the new habeas corpus law (AEDPA) is that now death penalty prisoners have fewer protections than in ordinary criminal cases. Title I of the habeas corpus reform puts severe limitations on federal appeals in death penalty cases (Latzer, 1998). Two of the most significant changes are as follows:

Time Limits

The AEDPA imposes a *one-year* time limit for filing the federal habeas petition after the state appeals are final. The problem with this time limit is that it is usually necessary for the petitioner to find (or to request to have and be appointed) a new attorney at this stage. The new attorney needs to read all the previous records, do investigation, and then write and file the petition all within the one-year deadline. Because death penalty appeals are complex, an attorney would likely have to stop all other work to meet this deadline. This time constraint makes it very difficult for a new attorney to do thorough work in representing the prisoner on death row.

Deference to State Courts

Although the doctrine of "presumptive correctness" was available to courts to employ before the AEDPA, the law now *requires* deference by the federal habeas judges to state court rulings. "An application for a writ of habeas corpus . . . shall not be granted with respect to any claim that was adjudicated on the merits in State court proceedings . . . and a determination of a factual issue made by a State court shall be presumed to be correct." Because of the mandatory language of these clauses, there is no need to review the state judgments. Notice that the statute requires merely an examination of the procedural considerations of the state review. If issues were raised "properly" at the state level and the state court made a decision, that decision is not reviewed on its merits by the federal court. Since the federal courts will not be looking for reversible error, it is very unlikely that the federal courts will find reversible error. Thus, if serious problems with lower court decisions exist, they will be ratified rather than reversed.

Other than the mandatory direct reviews, courts have discretion in accepting cases for review. The statutory changes and legal precedents make it likely that the habeas corpus appeals will be denied without a consideration of the merits of the case, and the affirmance of death penalty convictions and sentences will increase.[33] Such increases in affirmance rates would not mean that death penalty trials are more fair. To the contrary, given the poor quality of lawyering discussed in chapter 4, such increases may mean that lawyers are increasingly unable to deal with the procedural rules that have developed in death penalty litigation. Any increase in the rates of affirmed death sentences would be in dramatic contrast to the findings of the Liebman et al. (2000) research that witnessed to the overall importance of appellate review for detecting errors. That Missouri has a very low reversal rate does not mean that these cases are free of fundamental error.

The intentional limiting of review results in an institutional contradiction. In some cases, the Supreme Court has lifted stays of execution that a lower federal court had permitted in order to proceed with the execution. Anthony Amsterdam (1999: 148) describes those Supreme Court decisions as

> offend[ing] humanity and reason. They forsake fairness, orderly procedure, intelligence, and judicial efficiency for no stated reason and no rational purpose. Insofar as their results are explained in opinions, the opinions are delusory in the double sense of being built upon delusion and promoting it. . . . This [delusiveness] involves a kind of warping of reality that can allow civilized people to conceal from themselves and others that they are engaging in atrocities.

It is remarkable that the Supreme Court is so willing to reach down and interfere with its own lower federal court decisions in the name of reaching finality of sentence, when all its other opinions avoid involvement by *deferring* to state courts.

The Great Writ of habeas corpus is no longer. Increasingly, voices of dissent are being raised within the judiciary and within the legal profession:

> In closing, I would observe that the miscarriage of justice that is about to occur is the product of the federal judiciary's elevation of procedure over justice, of speed and efficiency over fairness and due process. I regret that we have chosen that course in recent years, and believe that in doing so, we have severely tarnished our nation's justice system. It is the courts that should engender in all of the people an enduring commitment to liberty and fairness" (*Thompson v. Calderon,* 1998: 937 [Circuit Judge Reinhardt, concurring and dissenting]).

And in a dissenting opinion, Chief District Judge Bennett states that

> the current status of federal *habeas* law, in my view, increasingly elevates tortuous and tangled procedural impediments over fundamental fairness

(*Lee v. Kemna*, 2000: 1038). . . . The Supreme Court once recognized that "habeas corpus is not a 'static, narrow, formalistic remedy' . . . , but one which must retain the 'ability to cut through barriers of form and procedural mazes.'" . . . This large and increasingly complex web has now virtually obscured the core purpose of the Writ. . . . The vast majority of federal habeas petitioners find themselves entangled in this omnipresent and perplexing procedural web, which effectively precludes federal courts from ever reaching the merits of their constitutional claims (*Lee v. Kemna*, 2000: 1047–48).

This chapter began by suggesting that appellate judges would be less vulnerable to political pressures than the trial judges because of the length of their terms. Could one explanation for the appellate courts' self-limiting and conservative decision making be that they, too, are unable to resist the strong political pressures that have been loosed by raising crime to the national agenda? There have been instances of voter rejection of individual justices. In California, Rose Bird and two other California Supreme Court justices lost their positions on the bench in elections because of their opposition to the death penalty (Korengold, Noteboom, and Gurwitch, 1996: 363). This also happened in Mississippi, Texas, and other states where judges "have been voted off the bench upon accusation that they were 'soft on crime' and replaced with judges who would give the voters what they want" (Bright, 1996: 1,077). These election outcomes jeopardize the independence and impartiality of the court. It may be that the only way the courts will avoid losing their integrity and survive as an institution is to take the issue out of existence by finding the death penalty inherently unconstitutional.

The problems with the death penalty appellate review process are clearly systemic. The Supreme Court has tied its own hands through its decision making and Congress has encoded these legal doctrines in the AEDPA. We have seen that the appellate courts did not respond to the serious errors disclosed by Missouri death penalty prisoners. Perhaps as an institution, the judiciary has needs that depend on public acceptance more than on its actual independence and fairness. Steiker and Steiker (1995: 429) contend that the institutional need of the Court for legitimacy is satisfied by appearing to do justice and at the same time, moving quickly to fulfill the popular desire for executions. Increasingly, however, the Supreme Court is justifying its legal actions by making presumptions that are not based in reality.

The Supreme Court's decision in *Herrera v. Collins* (1993) absolves the Court of responsibility in its relinquishment of duty to preserve constitutional protections of fundamental fairness by relying on the governor as a fail safe in the death penalty process to prevent miscarriages of justice. The burden of protecting the innocent has been intentionally shifted away from the courts and onto the governor's desk. We turn next to the last step in the administration of the death penalty: the governor's decision-making process. The relinquishment of the Court's role depends entirely on the integrity of the governor's consideration. Knowing that the office of the governor is a political role, we look to see if the reliance of the U.S. Supreme Court on executive clemency is misplaced.

CHAPTER SEVEN

GOVERNORS' DECISIONS
Fail Safe or Fiction?

"While there is guilt for Ronald Monroe, in an execution in this country the test ought not be reasonable doubt; the test ought to be is there any doubt."— Louisiana Governor Buddy Roemer, quoted in J. Wardlaw & J. Hodge, "Execution Halted by Roemer," *New Orleans Times-Picayune,* Aug. 17, 1989. . . .

"There was more than sufficient evidence to show he was guilty, but there were some questions as far as I was concerned. I was able to get some information that I know the judges and jurors did not necessarily receive. Some of the evidence came in after the trial."—Virginia Governor George F. Allen, quoted in, the *New York Times,* Nov. 10, 1996 (commutation of the death sentence of Joseph Payne).

> FROM THE CLEMENCY PETITION
> *for Roy Roberts,* CP#44,
> executed March 10, 1999[1]

We have seen systemic problems alleged at every stage of the death penalty process. In each instance, the petitioner looks to the governor to prevent a miscarriage of justice. The last stage in the process before an execution takes place is the appeal for executive clemency made to the governor. Clemency is a broad power of the executive branch and is intended to serve as a check on the judiciary. The need for such a check has been amply demonstrated in the previous chapters. In *Herrera v. Collins* (1993) the Supreme Court expressed its reliance on the governor to be the fail-safe mechanism in the capital punishment system in upholding the integrity of the administration of justice. As Chief Justice Rehnquist said, "[e]xecutive clemency has provided the 'fail safe' in our criminal justice system. . . . It is an unalterable fact that our justice system, like the human beings who administer it, is fallible" (*Herrera v. Collins,* 1993). This fail-safe function has taken on increasing significance as the AEDPA (discussed in chapter 6) reinforces the Court's trends of deferring to state court decision makers and of relinquishing its modern role to protect the justice interests of individuals from governmental abuse. Unfortunately, the role of governor is too much of a political position to escape the defects of expediency and fallibility. In Missouri only two commutations have been granted since the reinstatement of the death penalty in 1977. This chapter examines what happens when clemency petitions reach the governor's desk. We turn next to an examination of governors' decisions in death penalty clemency requests.

THE PROMISE OF CLEMENCY

Knowing that someone's life is in your hands must be an awesome responsibility. California governor Pat Brown, who decided fifty-nine clemency cases, sending thirty-six to death and sparing twenty-three with life without parole sentences, ends his book perhaps yearning for forgiveness:

> It was an awesome, ultimate power over the lives of others that no person or government should have, or crave. And looking back over their names and files now, despite the horrible crimes and the catalog of human weaknesses they comprise, I realize that each decision took something out of me that nothing—not family or work or hope for the future—has ever been able to replace (Brown, 1989: 163).

Every state that has a death penalty has provision for the governor or a board of advisers to grant clemency (Strach, 1999: 892). Not surprisingly, states differ in their handling of death penalty clemency petitions. In nine states the governor must have a recommendation of clemency from a board or advisory group, in three states the board or advisory group makes the determination, and in three states the governor sits on the clemency board that makes the determination. In the majority of the death penalty states then, the governor has the primary responsibility for granting clemency. Typically, governors do not have formal training or written guidelines that offer instruction about how to make these decisions. They rely on their good judgment and on the advice of staff or of a pardons attorney.

In Missouri, the duties of the governor include taking care that the laws are "faithfully executed" (Missouri Constitution, Article IV, section 2). Granting reprieves, commutations, and pardons is an important power reserved to the governor without limit or constraint. Article IV, section 7 of the Missouri Constitution states that

> [t]he governor shall have power to grant reprieves, commutations and pardons, after conviction, for all offenses except treason and cases of

impeachment, upon such conditions and with such restrictions and limitations as he may deem proper, subject to provisions of law as to the manner of applying for pardons. The power to pardon shall not include the power to parole.

The governor's clemency power is repeated in the Missouri statutes under the Department of Corrections section 217.800:

1. In all cases in which the governor is authorized by the constitution to grant pardons, he may grant the same, with such conditions and under such restrictions as he may think proper.
2. All applications for pardon, commutation of sentence or reprieve shall be referred to the board [of Probation and Parole] for investigation. The board shall investigate each such case and submit to the governor a report of its investigation, with all other information the board may have relating to the applicant together with any recommendations the board deems proper to make.

Additionally, Chapter 552 of the Missouri statutes deals with criminal proceedings involving mental illness and offers another option to the governor in clemency matters. Instead of directly commuting a sentence or pardoning an individual, the governor may appoint a board of inquiry to gather information and make recommendation to the governor concerning whether a person condemned to death should be executed or reprieved or pardoned, or whether the person's sentence should be commuted (section 552.070). Such a board of inquiry has no restriction on what information it can consider, and as such, could be open to evaluate all the new evidence and information discovered by later investigators.

The Supreme Court in *Herrera v. Collins* justified its denial of review even when the appellant was probably innocent by relying on the executive duty to consider clemency. The implied expectation is that miscarriages of justice will be prevented through the clemency process, if not through the courts. Since the governor is able to consider all and any evidence presented, this wide-ranging authority anticipates that a careful and detailed evaluation of the clemency case will be conducted. Additionally, that the Board of Probation and Parole is mandated to conduct an investigation and to make a recommendation to the governor envisions diligence and care in the process.

THE REALITY OF CLEMENCY DECISIONS

Robert Bohm observes that the decline in executions in the United States began in the 1950s "partly as a result of the lingering horrors of World War II and the movement by many allied nations either to abolish the death penalty or to restrict its use" (1999: 7). The number of executions dropped from 1,289 in the 1940s to 715 in the 1950s to 191 in the 1960s. A 1966 Gallup Poll indicated that public support for the death penalty was at its lowest level (42 percent). Between 1967 and 1979, no executions occurred in the United States. After the 1972 Supreme Courts' decision, *Furman v. Georgia*, all death sentences were effectively commuted to life or to life without parole sentences because the Court determined that the implementation of the death penalty was arbitrary and capricious. Four years later, the Supreme Court approved the structure of the new death penalty statutes that were designed to minimize jury arbitrariness and affirm individualized sentencing (in *Gregg v. Georgia*, 1976).

Because of the Supreme Court's recent trend to back away from substantive consideration of the death sentences (discussed in chapter 6), it is ironic that the post-*Furman* trend in executive clemencies has been to grant fewer clemency requests than in the pre-*Furman* period (Bedau, 1990).

> Although the rate of executions is at an all-time high following the Supreme Court's ruling that invalidated most capital punishment statutes, the number of clemency grants has declined to an almost negligible level (Korengold, Noteboom, and Gurwitch, 1996: 350).

"Prior to *Furman*, (1900–1967) clemency was granted with greater frequency and for a greater variety of reasons than in the years following *Furman*" (Korengold, Noteboom, and Gurwitch, 1996: 357). In a classic study of death penalty clemency decisions, Abramowitz and Paget (1964) report on pre-*Furman* clemencies and executions in forty-three states, reporting a range of clemency rates across a variety of time periods.[2] These clemencies from governors' offices were relatively common occurrences in the pre-*Furman* days. According to Palacios (1996: 347), "[t]he heyday of commutations was the early and mid-1940s, during which twenty to twenty-five percent of death penalties were commuted."

Historically, clemency has been granted for a variety of reasons, some of which are grounded in justice concerns, others more related to qualities of mercy (Gross, 1996; Bedau, 1993; Korengold, Noteboom, and Gurwitch, 1996; Kobil, 1991; Abramowitz and Paget, 1964; Radelet and Zsembik, 1993). However, not all states consider the same standards to be important. "Because of its inherently political nature, clemency has been a decision for the executive to make based on any 'wide range of factors' that the executive deems appropriate" (Strach, 1999: 921). Clemencies have been granted for the following reasons:

1. proof of actual innocence;
2. violation of prevailing standards of decency (such as in diminished mental capacity, retardation, intoxication, or minority);
3. an express request by the prosecution;
4. guilt is in doubt;
5. proportionality or equity in punishment among equally guilty codefendants;
6. the public has shown conclusively albeit indirectly that it does not want any death sentences carried out;
7. a nonunanimous vote by the appellate court upholding a death sentence conviction leaves disturbing doubt about the lawfulness of the death sentence;
8. the statutes under which the defendant was sentenced to death are unconstitutional;
9. mitigating circumstances;
10. rehabilitation of the offender while on death row undermines the rationale for carrying out the death penalty;
11. the death penalty is morally unjustified;
12. fairness of trial (such as in eyewitness testimony, perjury by real killers, confessions).

Since 1976, when the Supreme Court gave approval to the new death penalty statutes in *Gregg v. Georgia,* only forty-five death row prisoners have been granted clemency for humanitarian reasons—doubts about the prisoner's guilt, questions about the prisoner's mental capacity, rehabilitation of the prisoner, or the personal convictions of the governor (DPIC, 2001). In addition, between 1973 and 1992, Radelet and Zsembik (1993) report forty-one commutations for judicial expediency—where courts had vacated, or were likely to vacate, the death sentence, and a commutation would save the time and expense of going through a new sentencing proceeding.

One suspects that the decline in granting clemencies is tied to the political agenda of elected officials and their perception that public opinion is strongly in favor of capital punishment. By 1989 public support for the death penalty had increased to 80 percent. To understand the increasing salience of the death penalty since the early 1960s, we can point to the evidence of civil unrest that was plastered across the headlines of all newspapers during this time period. The urban riots in the late sixties merged the political issues exposed through street protests against involvement in the Vietnam War with the socioeconomic issues of racial unrest that erupted after the assassination of Martin Luther King Jr. "Because crime in the streets was an issue in the 1968 elections, concern about crime intensified, with a resultant hardening of attitudes toward criminals and a greater demand for harsh penalties" (Rankin, 1979: 194). Thereafter, every presidential campaign reverberated with the theme of law and order to deal with violence, rising crime rates, and the perceived threats of drug use. "Political conservatives, from Nixon in the 1970's to Reagan and Bush in the 1980's and 1990's, have claimed to be 'tough on crime'" (Cook, 1998: 24). Since Michael Dukakis's defeat in 1988, attributed in part to his opposition to the death penalty, presidential candidates of the Democratic Party have all supported the death penalty. In the 2000 presidential race, the death penalty was actually a minor issue because both candidates supported the death penalty. As governor of Texas, George W. Bush had commuted only one death sentence while not stopping the executions of 131 persons. Because he expressed confidence in the fairness and accuracy of the death penalty process in Texas, the appeals process of Texas's death penalty cases was scrutinized by some, but with no discernible impact on then-governor Bush's presidential campaign. Based in part upon the dual public desires for revenge and safety, the death penalty became a part of conventional political understanding, while the voices for abolition or moratorium (or both) of executions were basically rendered impotent.

For governors, the accepted political wisdom has been that an anti–death penalty position will hurt one's political future (Korengold, Noteboom, and Gurwitch, 1996: 365). For example, California governor Pat Brown believed that he lost his reelection to Ronald Reagan in part because of his death penalty decisions (Palacios, 1996: 350). "Republican Dave Treen challenged incumbent Louisiana Governor

Edwin Edwards in 1979 and used Edwards' clemency record to help defeat him" (Palacios, 1996: 350). Most recently, the New York State gubernatorial elections in 1996 witnessed George Pataki make use of a pro–death penalty platform to overcome incumbent Mario Cuomo.

Despite these examples of the political significance of the death penalty, Korengold, Noteboom, and Gurwitch claim that "there is no evidence to suggest that a large portion of the electorate are single-issue death penalty voters" (1996: 365). They maintain that a candidate's position on the death penalty would not be the only issue to influence most voters. Support for the minimal political impact of holding an anti–death penalty position was uncovered in a public opinion poll conducted in Missouri in 1999, which found that respondents opposed to the death penalty were more likely than respondents who supported the death penalty to say that their vote for a candidate was affected by a candidate's particular stand against the death penalty (CSSPPR, 1999). In other words, respondents in favor of the death penalty were not likely to base their votes on the similarity of the candidate's death penalty position with their own view. Perhaps it is only when an opponent makes an issue of the death penalty that the candidates' positions become salient to voters.

THE MISSOURI SENATORIAL CAMPAIGN OF 2000

The contentious Missouri senate race of 2000 involved two major party candidates who, as governors, had both approved executions. During the campaign, both candidates declared that they were pro–death penalty politicians. Mel Carnahan's statement rested in his "[c]omplete confidence in [the] guilt of those executed . . . beyond a reasonable doubt" (Carnahan, 2000). He explained that

> the essential fact reviewed by my staff is whether or not the individual is in fact guilty of first-degree murder. . . . If either the staff or the board determines that the defendant is actually innocent, I would not proceed with the execution. . . . It must be used in a fair and equitable manner as well so that no innocent person is executed.

John Ashcroft explained that his standard was as follows:

> State law had given me powers as governor to step in and correct any mistaken sentence erroneously imposed by the people through our judi-

cial system. It would have been arrogant and irresponsible of me to second-guess the people and the court system by arbitrarily reversing the decision of unmistaken juries and judges (Ashcroft, 2000).

Senator Ashcroft positioned himself to be stronger on the death penalty issue by alluding to Governor Carnahan's commutation of Darrell Mease in 1999. Senator Ashcroft rejected overturning a death "sentence because of a personal opinion that capital punishment is wrong, or on the basis of a momentary consideration having nothing to do with guilt, or on the basis of a legal technicality unrelated to guilt" as such action would "demonstrate a disrespect for our legal system and lack of compassion for victims."[3] However, the death penalty issue was overshadowed by allegations of racism when, during the close campaign, Senator Ashcroft suddenly refused support for the nomination of Missouri Supreme Court Judge Ronnie White to a federal judgeship by claiming that Judge White was soft on crime because he voted to overturn a death sentence.[4] As a result, the death penalty issue probably did not in and of itself distinguish the two major candidates.

STYLES OF CLEMENCY DECISION MAKING

An inside look at the clemency decision-making process is rarely available to the public. In *Dead Man Walking* (1993), Sister Helen Prejean recounts her conversation with the chairman of the Pardon Board in Louisiana. He admits that the Board of Pardons insulated the governor from public backlash by intentionally never recommending clemency. Indeed, he confessed to Sr. Helen that the major qualification to be appointed to the Pardon Board was the person's willingness to be loyal to the governor despite the possibility of conflicting demands of personal integrity. Such a system results in regular denials of clemency regardless of the merits of the case. In this style of decision making, political position is used to shield the governor from popular criticism.

Another style of clemency decision making is one in which the merits of the clemency case are weighed against the political impact of a commutation of a death sentence. This more open process is described by former California governor Pat Brown, who recounts the death penalty clemency process during his tenure in a book, *Public Justice, Private Mercy* (1989). He confessed that he was always looking for legal and moral reasons to halt executions. His finding of meritorious claims depended on the degree of premeditation, evidence of brain damage, and disparity in the sentencing of a codefendant. The political impact was always factored into the governor's deliberation. Even a personal call from his son prompted Governor Brown to grant a temporary stay in order to pursue a general death penalty moratorium legislatively. When that effort failed, Governor Brown permitted the particular execution to proceed. Whenever he could not find a reason to halt an execution, the sentence was carried out according to the law. After each case, Governor Brown released a statement explaining the basis for his decision. This style of decision making demonstrates a mix of politics and morality, showing a responsiveness to significant others, to political implications for his legislative agenda, and to personal values. While public opinion was considered, it was never the weightiest factor in his deliberation.

A third style of clemency decision making halts all executions, irrespective of the merits of the case. Solie Ringold (1966) collects several examples of this approach, which leads governors out of their personal opposition to the death penalty to commute death sentences as a matter of mercy and grace. Oklahoma governor Lee Cruce commuted every death sentence imposed during his administration (1911–1915); Oregon governor Robert D. Holmes commuted every death sentence that arose during his term (1957–1959); and Governor Peabody of Massachusetts recommended commutation of every death penalty (1962–1964). In 1971 Governor Winthrop Rockefeller commuted all death sentences in Arkansas (Bedau, 1990: 257). More recently, New Mexico governor Anaya commuted all persons on death row before leaving office in 1986. Despite being a supporter of the death penalty, in January of 2000 Illinois governor Ryan declared a moratorium on all executions until he was convinced that the legal system would stop sending innocent persons to death row. Going against the majority opinion, these clemency decisions are made only on the basis of personal morality to do what is "right."

THE MISSOURI PROCESS

Because of the relative silence of the executive office on this subject, it is not known what style of clemency decision making describes that of Missouri governors. According to statute, the governor sends any clemency petition that is received to the Board of Probation and Parole for its recommendation before he considers the appeal. Precedent was established in 1984 for the right of citizens of the state to apply for commutation in behalf of the public welfare when then-governor Bond accepted the application for Reprieve or Commutation for Gerald Smith submitted by religious leaders and others and then referred it to the Board of Probation and Parole for review. Since that time, at least one clemency petition from a citizens' group is always filed with the governor, relying on the comment by Justice Holmes in *Biddle v. Perovich* that "[t]he public welfare, not his (the prisoner's) consent, determines what shall be done" (274 U.S. 486).

The Board of Probation and Parole, made up of seven members appointed by the governor for six-year terms, conducts an investigation of the case, which involves reviewing the documents in their possession. The governing statute (R.S.Mo. 217.800.2) does not specify how the investigation is to occur. Generally, the investigation involves reviewing the clemency petition provided by the prisoner's legal team, the trial transcript, and court decisions provided by the attorney general's office. A personal visit with the prisoner is made several days before the scheduled execution by a local member of the Department of Probation and Parole, who merely asks the condemned if there is anything else he would like to say on his behalf, and who then submits a written report to the board. The board does not meet with the attorneys or hold any sort of hearing, public or otherwise. Rather, the board typically meets in the Jefferson City office (in the state capitol) the Monday before a scheduled execution (scheduled for 12:01 A.M. on Wednesday) to review the case, having an attorney present who is on contract to the board should any legal guidance be needed. However, if the clemency petition arrives late, the board will stay up late on the eve of the execution, sending their recommendation to the governor just hours before the execution. The "investigation" by the board is limited to reading (if they actually do so) the trial transcript, the clemency petition, and the court decisions. Such an investigation provides effective insulation from any personal contact with the condemned. One chairperson of the board said that the members try to make their decisions from the "layman's point of view." The board's written recommendation to the governor is secret.

In most respects, the death penalty clemency process is quite different from regular parole decisions that are held at the prisons. There, the inmate can present his case to a three-person panel (a board member, a parole analyst, and a prison supervisor), victim(s) can be present, and both parties can bring an advocate. If the decision can be finalized by the hearing, it is done. If the decision requires a majority vote of the entire board, a review of the prison hearing file is held in the Jefferson City office until a majority vote is obtained. It appears that regular parole decisions have more elements of due process than do death penalty clemency decisions.

When executions in Missouri resumed in 1989, the clemency process needed to be recreated. There was no tradition or written "protocol" in place to address the last pleas before the governor. Such a procedure only emerged as the executions accumulated. In the early days, before any tradition in clemency reviews was established, filing a written clemency appeal with the governor was not done by the attorneys who were absorbed in working the legal appeals through the courts. However, a civic group of community and religious leaders did file petitions. By 1991, the attorney's practice of submitting a clemency petition and meeting with the governor's legal counsel was normalized.[5] The custom has been that the governor does not meet with any of the parties directly. Meanwhile, when the execution date is announced, the governor's legal advisers "pull down" the court decisions for the case. The entire legal file is obtained from the attorney general's office, although typically, the governor's staff does not consult with prosecutors or judges involved with the case. After digesting the issues in the case, the legal advisers meet with the governor in an "organic process" and talk about the nuances and the legal merits of the case. According to one of the legal advisers, everything that enters the office concerning the case is presented to the governor, including the number of phone calls and faxes received from the public. More significant than numbers of letters from the public, however, is from whom the letters come. More weight is likely given to letters that come from the victim's family, former judges, jurors, or even legislators. After the briefing with his legal staff, the governor waits to announce his decision until all the court litigation is completed, sometimes as late as 10 P.M. or 11 P.M. on the eve of the execution. No doubt the governor waits for the courts' deliberations in the hopes that he will not have to make the life-or-death decision.

Taken in its entirety, this process maximizes the distance between the governor and the prisoner. Without personal contact with the attorneys involved or with the condemned, the governor is able to make the clemency decision without dealing with the raw emotion that surrounds most any death. It is all done on paper, without personal contact with those whose life is in the balance.

Because there is not a right to clemency, there is no appeal from the governor's decision. However, because of the constitutional and statutory provision for clemency, it could be argued that there is a right to make a clemency appeal. As such, questions have been raised concerning what due process is required in clemency deliberations. Due process usually means having notice of a hearing and providing an opportunity to participate in the hearing. To date, "[t]he federal courts of appeals have refused to require that clemency decisions be made in a fundamentally fair manner and in accordance with due process" (Kobil, 1998: 539). However, in *Ohio Adult Parole Authority v. Woodard* (1998), the Supreme Court may have opened the door for future consideration of the due process expectations in clemency decisions. Although Chief Justice Rehnquist reasoned in his plurality opinion that there is *no* continuing life interest in clemency proceedings that requires constitutional due process protection, Justice O'Connor (and four others) wrote that there is a *minimal* due process protection requirement even where clemency is at the discretion of the executive.

Following the lead provided by Justice O'Connor, a brief was filed in 2000 on behalf of James Chambers, CP#22, contending that the investigation conducted by the Missouri Board of Probation and Parole violated minimal due process guarantees. Filed and decided the same day, just hours before the execution, the Eighth Circuit Court of Appeals denied the petition without writing an opinion on the appeal and the execution proceeded.

CASE STUDY: DUE PROCESS EXPECTATIONS IN THE CLEMENCY DECISION

James Chambers, CP#22

▼▲▼

Application for Stay of Execution and Temporary Restraining Order[6]

The District Court relying solely on the holding of *Whitmore v. Gaines* (1994) held that a commutation statute that does not itself impose standards does not create a constitutional right to due process, and that therefore the Due Process Clause does not apply to this proceeding, even to impose minimal standards.

That, we submit, is directly contrary to the majority holding in *Ohio Adult Parole Authority v. Woodard* (1998). . . . As this Court stated in *Young v. Hayes* (2000), the pre-*Ohio Adult* cases in this circuit, such as *Whitmore*, can no longer be regarded as defining the law. The obvious purpose of the Missouri statute requiring the Board of Parole and Probation to investigate the case and report to the governor is to enable the governor to make an informed decision as to whether or not he should grant clemency. Because it involves the life of Plaintiff, the defendant is entitled to an investigation that at least comports to minimum standards of due process.

. . . We attach hereto the Affidavit of Counsel of Plaintiff who filed his Application [for clemency] in September 1999 [fourteen months earlier]. Counsel asserts that the only "investigation" to his knowledge occurred yesterday afternoon when a probation officer talked to the Plaintiff. In addition, counsel for the Religious/Civic Leadership Group that filed an Application for clemency on behalf of Plaintiff have been unable to learn of any investigation into the matters raised in their Application, nor to receive any information from the Board as to its investigation. . . .

In sum, the Board appears to have done nothing with respect to an investigation until yesterday afternoon. And whatever it has done, and whatever it recommends, is clothed in silence. This can hardly be said to constitute even minimal due process. . . . Certainly, a secret Star Chamber-like proceeding, offends the basic concept of due process.

▼▲▼ ────────

James Chambers was executed November 15, 2000.

─────────

ANNOUNCING THE DECISION

A grant of clemency is discretionary. Furthermore, the governor is not required to explain his decision, and usually does not. In Missouri, the governor's office issues the *same* statement after each execution. It is issued over the phone to the Department of Corrections, only changing the names of the victims and the offender. A call is made by the governor's spokesperson to the Associated Press waiting at the Potosi Correctional Center, usually between 8 P.M. and 10 P.M. (after having notified the prisoner and his lawyer), giving the governor's decision. After the execution is completed, the director of the Department of

Corrections or the prison superintendent reads the prisoner's last words and the governor's statement to the media. The statement from Governor Roger Wilson is an example of a typical statement made by each of the governors in clemency decisions.

> James Chambers was charged and convicted of the murder of Jerry Oestricker. I extend my sympathy to the Oestricker family. I also extend my sympathy to the family of Mr. Chambers. Tonight, the process of our judicial system has run its course. The state, on behalf of its citizens, has the right to impose the death penalty for the crime of capital murder. Our Courts and the Department have met their responsibilities under the law. I have examined the history of the judicial proceedings and the applications for clemency that have been placed before me. I find nothing to justify setting aside the result of the judicial proceedings. I reaffirm my solemn oath to uphold the law. It is the duty of my office to do so, on behalf of the people of Missouri.

Notice that the governor's press release does not refer to the recommendations of the Board of Probation and Parole. Nowhere does the governor discuss his interpretation of the specific issues presented in the clemency petition. The focus of this statement, as of so much of the death penalty experience, is on the final result, not on the process in getting to the result. Because the governor's statement does not allude to the specific issues of the particular case being considered, the public has no knowledge about what factors were considered or what was the governor's reasoning.

NEW INFORMATION

The governor who takes seriously the responsibility for executive clemency as a fail safe in preventing miscarriages of justice has a heavy burden. One of the major issues facing the governor in a clemency petition is the significance of newly discovered information that was not available to the trial court or to the jury. It would be imprudent for any governor to overturn a jury's decision because such action would appear to be a blatant use of power diminishing the role of citizens in their civic duties. In the administration of justice there is always great deference given to the decisions of trial participants, since they can draw on nonverbal observations to evaluate evidence and witnesses.

But can the jury's decision be the "correct" decision if it did not have full and complete information on which to base its decision? The basic contention in the thirty-nine (78 percent of the fifty) clemency appeals that offer new information is that this new information would change the outcome of the jury deliberations if it had been available at the time of trial. These clemency petitions are usually not challenging the decision-making process of the jury at the time of trial. But by highlighting the new relevant information, the clemency petitions ask the governor to consider this new evidence as an extra juror or as a fully informed juror. Although to the unaware, it may appear that the governor is being asked to overturn a jury decision, in these cases, the request is actually asking the governor to set aside the jury's decision to make a more reliable one.

Typically, the new information is developed when an investigator is hired by a postconviction attorney. There are several different types of new information that the clemency petitions document: discoveries that the prosecutor withheld information, or that witnesses made false statements during trial; eyewitnesses are now available to swear that the death row prisoner is not guilty of the crime; or the offer of new mitigating evidence that was undeveloped by the trial attorney. In all these situations, the death row prisoner claims the new information would make a difference in the outcome of the trial if the new information was considered.

The public is most troubled about executions when the possibility exists of killing a person who is actually innocent of the crime. A random sample of Missouri residents conducted in 1999 reported that 80 percent of the respondents said their opinion about the death penalty was affected by the fact that some people executed are later found to be innocent. Questionable guilt has been a common basis for commutations in other states. In a study of ten states, Radelet and Zsembik (1993) report that 13 percent of the commutations were for the reason that guilt was doubtful. Obviously, the governor has an immense dilemma when facing questions of actual innocence and legal innocence. Actual innocence means that the person did not do the killing. This category of innocence usually includes both those persons who were not present as well as those persons who were present but did not actually participate in the killing. But the question of guilt involves more than reviewing the conviction of a person who may be actually innocent of the crime. Legal innocence refers to the situation in which the person admits to the killing, but for various defenses claims to be not guilty of first degree capital murder. Claims such as self-defense or diminished mental capacity are acceptable legal excuses when accused of first degree murder. We have seen that much of the evidence to support these contentions is only developed later, when postconviction lawyers get involved. In Missouri, eighteen of the fifty cases (36 percent) claim they are actually innocent of the crime (see table 7.1). Another seven (14 percent) claim they killed in self-defense, and nine (18 percent) claim they are guilty of a lesser offense than first degree murder. Overall, thirty-four of the fifty cases (68 percent) raise concerns of either actual or legal innocence.

Because court rules bar the submission of relevant information if discovered too late, this new information has most likely not been considered by *any* judicial body. Only the governor who has no limitation on his clemency consideration will include it in his deliberations. We have seen the gravity of the legal issues that face the governor.[7] However, it is not clear that the governor is inclined to give this new evidence any weight. The statement issued by the governor after his decision not to stop an execution states, "I find nothing to justify setting aside the result of the judicial proceedings." But the governor offers no explanation in the statement for his nonfinding. How then does the governor decide?

TABLE 7.1
Innocence Claims

Type of Innocence	Frequency	Cases
Actual innocence	18	Thomas Battle, Walter Blair, Maurice Byrd, Emmitt Foster, Larry Griffin, Frank Guinan, Bert Hunter, Bruce Kilgore, Kelvin Malone, George Mercer, Roy Ramsey, Donald Reese, Roy Roberts, Lloyd Schlup, Gerald Smith, Winford Stokes, Doyle Williams, Jessie Wise
Self-defense	7	James Chambers, Ralph Feltrop, George Harris, Robert O'Neal, Reginald Powell, James Rodden, Richard Zeitvogel
Lesser offense	9	A. J. Bannister, Martsay Bolder, William Ted Boliek, Ricky Grubbs, Anthony LaRette, Darrell Mease, Gary Roll, Bobby Shaw, Andrew Six

THE CONTEXT OF COMMUTATIONS

From 1800 through 1937, 246 persons were executed in Missouri (Espy, 1994). State record keeping began in 1938 when executions became the responsibility of the state authority instead of the local counties. From 1938 through 1965, there were thirty-nine executions, seven (probably eight, including a codefendant) commutations, and six cases in which the death sentences were reversed and remanded back to the trial courts. Unfortunately, the archival records do not include the reasons for these commutations. During this pre-*Furman* period then, the Missouri clemency rate was about 15 percent, a rate that situates Missouri in the *top range* of death penalty states, with a ratio of almost five executions for each commutation (Acker and Lanier, 2000).

Since reinstatement of the death penalty in 1977, five governors have served the state of Missouri: Joe Teasdale (1977–1981), who signed the reinstatement legislation; Christopher Bond (1981–1985); John Ashcroft (1985–1993); Mel Carnahan (1993–2000); and Roger Wilson (2000–2001). During this time period the number of persons sentenced to Missouri's death row grew to 162. Usually, cases move through the legal system's maze of appeals only when execution dates are set. It is understandable that unless the condemned is actually facing an execution date, the prisoner is not motivated to file another appeal. Because the prisoner has several appeals to make, many execution dates are "unreal" until all the appeals are exhausted. Thus, executions in Missouri actually began in 1989 and by the end of the year 2000, forty-six persons had been executed in Missouri. Governor Ashcroft permitted the execution of seven persons, giving no commutations and just one stay. Governor Carnahan permitted thirty-eight executions,[8] two commutations, and two stays of execution, including one stay for the purpose of appointing a board of inquiry. Governor Wilson approved the execution of one person. These are relatively high numbers, and by the end of 2000, Missouri ranked fourth in the nation in the number of persons executed since reinstatement of the death penalty. Only Texas, Florida, and Virginia had executed more persons in this post-*Furman* era.

OUTCOMES

An examination of all fifty of the clemency petitions reveals few factors that make any difference in the clemency outcome. Forty-six persons were executed during this time period, three received stays, and two were commuted to life without parole sentences.[9]

Stays

Out of the fifty clemency petitions considered by the Missouri governors, three stays of execution were granted. To date, the three persons involved—Bobby Shaw, Lloyd Schlup, and William Ted Boliek—have not been executed. Mr. Shaw successfully raised the issue of mental competency and was granted a hearing to determine his eligibility to be executed. Missouri is not permitted by state law to execute anyone who does not understand what an execution means (R.S.Mo. section 552.060). However, four others raised this same issue in their clemency petitions and were not granted stays.[10] Apparently, the only difference between the successful and unsuccessful mental competency appeals is found in their attorneys. Two of the three successful death row prisoners (Mr. Shaw and Mr. Schlup) were represented by Sean O'Brien, former director of the now-defunct Missouri Capital Resource Center.[11] In the case of Lloyd Schlup, Mr. O'Brien raised a claim of actual innocence and won a stay in order to argue his case before the U.S. Supreme Court. Mr. O'Brien won at the Supreme Court level and later negotiated a plea bargain for his client. However, seventeen others who raised the claim of actual innocence did not receive a stay or commutation. The third recipient of a stay of execution was William Ted Boliek, who probably benefited from the unusual circumstance of being the fourth execution scheduled within the hot month of August in 1997. During that month, the media were beginning to reflect a growing public resistance to so many executions in too short a time period (Shelly, 1997). Despite a long history of mental disorders, his lawyers did not ask for a competency hearing. Instead, they asked for a new trial of the penalty phase so that a jury could consider Mr. Boliek's mental disorders as mitigating evidence. But the governor had never granted a new trial. In this case, the governor issued a stay so as to appoint a board of inquiry.[12]

Commutations

Bobby Shaw

The first Missouri commutation in the post-*Furman* period was given by Governor Carnahan to Bobby Shaw in 1993. The reason given for the commutation was that Mr. Shaw did not have the mental capacity to understand the execution process. Mr. Shaw's attorney was Sean O'Brien. This case came quite early in Governor Carnahan's tenure— only his second death penalty clemency petition. Sensitive to the potential political fallout of this decision, the governor chose to release his decision the same day that former state attorney general Bill Webster was pleading guilty to conspiracy and embezzlement charges in federal court. Because the bulk of the media attention was diverted from the death penalty commutation, the negative impact of the decision was minimized. Departing from the usual statement, the governor's statement granting the stay offers his explanation. Notice that the statement gave a lot of weight to the recommendation by the Board of Probation and Parole:

> I have decided today to accept the recommendation of the Board of Probation and Parole to commute the death sentence of Bobby Lewis Shaw to life in prison without parole.
>
> In its recommendation, the board said: "Based on the information provided to the Board in a variety of psychiatric and psychological reports, there appears to be little doubt that Mr. Shaw is mentally retarded and suffers from varying degrees of mental illness."
>
> Further, the Board's letter indicates that lingering questions remain about Shaw's mental impairments and the fact that information about those impairments was not provided to the jury during the sentencing phase of Shaw's trial.
>
> "It is the Board's conclusion that Mr. Shaw did not receive the necessary protections he was entitled to and, because of that fact, the sentence of death may be fundamentally unfair."
>
> I concur with the board's recommendations, and have signed the order commuting the death sentence.
>
> I take my role in executive clemency issues very seriously. I analyze these issues personally, and I review them on a case by case basis. The Shaw case brings together a unique set of circumstances that merit a commutation of his death sentence.
>
> It is important to note that I continue to support Capital Punishment, however, circumstances warrant a life sentence for Bobby Lewis Shaw.
>
> I would note that over the last few years, the federal courts have curtailed their review of death penalty cases. Consequently, the role of the governor in reviewing these matters has become more significant.
>
> I want to take this opportunity to remember the victim in this case,

Walter Farrow. I want to extend my sympathies to Walter's family, his friends, and his colleagues at the Department of Corrections. They remember him as an outstanding family man, and fine corrections officer. His loss is truly tragic.

After the commutation, the governor was hit with a hailstorm of protest from Department of Corrections personnel because the victim in this instance was a prison guard. Never again has the governor commuted a death penalty because of mental impairments. Since that time, the governor (and/or his staff) appeared to learn that the same goal could be accomplished (that is, stopping an execution for reason of mental incompetency) without incurring the political cost of public criticism if he granted a stay for a determination of mental capacity. In this way, a board of inquiry or a magistrate in a competency hearing would make the politically sensitive recommendation to stop the execution. Additionally, death row prisoners under a stay would remain eligible to be executed if their mental condition should improve. Consequently, both sides in the death penalty debate would be satisfied. Should the Department of Corrections request a competency hearing before an execution warrant was issued, the pressure on all parties was further reduced.

Darrell Mease

Darrell Mease was granted a commutation of his sentence to life without parole under extraordinary circumstances. Originally, Darrell Mease was scheduled to be executed on January 27, 1999. But four days after receiving his death warrant, the date was changed to February 10 by the Missouri Supreme Court. Because Pope John Paul II was scheduled to visit St. Louis on the January execution date, it is surmised that the state did not want to conduct an execution at the same time as the pope's visit, particularly as the pope was a well-known advocate of abolition. In fact, during his January visit, the pope made a personal petition to the governor for mercy for Mr. Mease. The impact of this personal appeal evidently greatly affected the governor.

The press reports of Governor Carnahan's commutation repeated his statement that he was still in favor of the death penalty, but as a personal gesture of mercy toward the pope, the governor would grant the clemency. The statement announcing the commutation was the second departure from the standard press release:

> I, Mel Carnahan, Governor of the State of Missouri, have had presented personally and directly to me by Pope John Paul II, a request for mercy in the case of Darrell Mease who was convicted of First Degree Murder on April 25, 1990 and sentenced to death on June 1, 1990. After careful consideration of the extraordinary circumstance of the Pontiff's direct and personal appeal for mercy and because of the deep and abiding respect I have for him and all that he represents, I hereby grant to Darrell Mease a commutation of the above sentence in the following respect: This commutation eliminates from the sentence the penalty of death and further causes Darrell Mease to remain incarcerated for the remainder of his life without the possibility of parole.

In Darrell Mease's case the commutation was an act of simple mercy and grace. Opponents of capital punishment, pleased with the outcome for Mr. Mease, nonetheless pointed out that the governor's decision was quite clearly a demonstration of the capriciousness of the death penalty process. As expected, the voices in opposition to the governor's action were louder than the supporters. Polls showed that Governor Carnahan lost four potential votes for every one he gained by sparing the prisoner (Lifton and Mitchell, 2000: 7). It was suspected that to reaffirm his "tough on crime" image, the governor would not likely commute the death sentences of the next prisoners seeking clemency. In fact, it was believed that the consequence of the governor's act of mercy actually "accelerated the execution assembly line in the state" (Lifton and Mitchell, 2000: 9).

In Mr. Mease's case, the governor had not had any recommendation from the Board of Probation and Parole; in fact, the governor had not had time to send the clemency petition to the board for its "investigation." Perhaps the strongest argument in Mr. Mease's clemency petition did not even address the merits of the case, but rather criticized the due process of changing the execution date. The clemency petition argued that the Court had no authority to amend the first execution date because there was no notice given and no opportunity to be heard. In an ironic complaint about the extension of the opportunity to live, Mr. Mease's attorney argued that "the failure of the Missouri Supreme Court to follow its own procedure has rendered the administration of the death penalty arbitrary and capricious and cruel and unusual punishment."

EXTRALEGAL CONSIDERATIONS

Extralegal considerations are those matters that are outside the specific legal issues in a case that might influence the governor's decision making. Research (Bright, 1994; Dodge, 1990; Foley and Powell, 1987) informs us that in the over fifteen thousand homicides committed each year, who gets the death penalty is related to considerations that have little to do with the presenting facts of the case. Factors such as the county in which the crime occurs, whether it is an election year, the victim's race, and whether the accused can afford to hire a competent attorney are key in determining who actually gets the *death penalty* in our society. Likewise, it may be that who gets *clemency* is due more to extralegal factors than to the legal issues related to the case. For example, the significant role of the media in winning a prisoner's release from death row is well known (Mello, 1997b; Radelet, Bedau, and Putnam, 1992).

Some of the Missouri clemency petitions try to influence the governor's clemency decision by offering reasons based on extralegal factors (see table 7.2), but all to no avail. In sixteen cases (32 percent), the argument was made that the death row prisoner was rehabilitated; one was a born-again Christian. In three cases (6 percent), the international community was mentioned in the petition as trying to influence the governor through the persuasion of the global human rights standards and treaties that endorse the abolition of the death penalty. Media attention is mentioned in nine (18 percent) of the cases. In five of the cases (10 percent), the victims' families did not want the execution to proceed. It does not appear that these extralegal factors mentioned in the clemency petitions made any impact in terms of winning clemency from the governor.

The only factor that distinguishes the two commutations from all the other clemency applications appears to be the role of personality.

The only "successful" clemency petitions were ones that had the benefit of significant personal influence. In the case of Bobby Shaw, there are no distinguishing features of his case other than the timing of the quantity and quality of material that inundated the governor's office on Mr. Shaw's behalf, endorsed by his postconviction attorney.

TABLE 7.2
Extralegal Factors

Extralegal Factor	Frequency	Cases
Born-again Christian	1	George Mercer
International community	4	A. J. Bannister, James Chambers, Frederick Lashley, Bobby Shaw
Victim's family	5	Ralph Davis, Frederick Lashley, David Leisure, Donald Reese, Jeff Sloan
Vietnam veteran	7	William Ted Boliek, Maurice Byrd, Leonard Laws, Sam McDonald, Darrell Mease, Donald Reese, Gary Roll
Competency to be executed	5	James Hampton, David Leisure, Richard Oxford, Bobby Shaw, Gerald Smith
Media attention	9	A. J. Bannister, William Ted Boliek, George Harris, Bruce Kilgore, George Mercer, Reginald Powell, Bobby Shaw, Gerald Smith, Glen Sweet
Constructive prisoner	16	A. J. Bannister, Walter Blair, William Ted Boliek, Ralph Davis, Milton Griffin El, Ricky Grubbs, Bruce Kilgore, Frederick Lashley, Leonard Laws, David Leisure, Kelvin Malone, Sam McDonald, George Mercer, Reginald Powell, Doyle Williams, Jessie Wise

At various critical stages of the clemency case, individuals made their unique contributions to advocate for Mr. Shaw. Mr. Shaw's attorney had the unique experience of personally meeting with the governor, but only because the victim's family had managed such an audience. Fairness required that Mr. Shaw's attorney be given the same opportunity. In addition, Bobby Shaw was the subject of a *Time* magazine article (Willwerth, 1993)—national coverage that brought to Missouri's attention the significance of the case. Such attention spurred an unusual number of Missourians to write the governor. What was at least as important in Mr. Shaw's case, however, was the combination of the Board of Probation and Parole's positive recommendation and the relative inexperience of the governor to death penalty clemency considerations.

The commutation of Darrell Mease appears to be the direct result of the governor's "awesome" face-to-face encounter with the pope. Although a cynical political observer might suggest that in responding to the pope, the governor was looking to win some Catholic votes, the spontaneity of his decision should be trusted as genuine. The governor reportedly went to St. Louis anticipating the pope's request and was preparing an opposite response.

CONCLUSIONS

If we thought that submitting a better, more complete, or full account-ing of the case and issues, or of the prisoner's social background and rehabilitation would make a difference in the clemency decision, we have been mistaken. Completeness *should* make a difference if we are looking to the governor to prevent miscarriages of justice, as does the U.S. Supreme Court. But the astonishing decline in the use of execu-tive clemency in death penalty cases means that clemency exists only in theory. There were no distinguishing features of the "successful" appeals in the Missouri clemency petitions that could serve to instruct future petitioners.

The considerations that did not move the governor to intervene to halt executions are serious and troubling. That these issues were not addressed by the courts before reaching the governor casts serious questions on the courts' commitment to fairness and justice. The peti-tions taken as a whole create a composite of recurring problems, sug-gesting systemic doubts about the nature of the justice system. Unfortunately, when the focus of the petitions is on the individual merits of each case, we are diverted from these fundamental questions. What we see in the petitions is a picture of an individual who is blamed for his own predicament by the attorney general and whose predicament is blamed on certain other individuals by the authors of the clemency petitions. But this study has suggested that rather than unique individual defects, there are patterns of problems inherent to capital litigation which, if not addressed, will be repeated in the future. Abramowitz and Paget (1964: 188) suggested that "executive clemency is a force by which the shortcomings of the criminal law are dramatized and a springboard for innovation in the criminal justice process." The governor who sees every complaint is particularly well situated to take the lead in updating and improving the delivery of criminal justice in the state.

It is quite remarkable that such dissimilar governors (two Democrats and one Republican) acted in very much the same way with respect to death penalty clemency petitions. The Republican John Ashcroft and the Democrat Roger Wilson granted no commutations, whereas the Democrat Mel Carnahan granted just two commutations while authorizing thirty-eight executions. With respect to death penalty clemency considerations, there is no substantive difference in policy between the governors in Missouri.[13]

In the political environment of apparently strong public support for the death penalty, it is extremely difficult to contradict the public's perception even when that perception is grounded in lack of information. The governor, however, misses an opportunity to educate the public when announcing his clemency decision. The "boilerplate" statement after each negative clemency decision maintains the public's ignorance, as well as its acquiescence, by not offering any discussion of the issues in the case.

The burden placed on the governor by the U.S. Supreme Court in the *Herrera* decision to be *the* fail safe for the justice system is too big of a burden. Ideally, the governor is a check on the judiciary, but in reality the governor is an elected official who may have plans for higher elective office. As such, he would find it difficult to take an unpopular stance. If the governor recognized the serious problems presented in capital cases by commuting death sentences (or even by granting a reprieve for further investigation and evaluation of the prisoner's claims), the governor would be challenging the entire administration of justice of both the state and federal courts. When votes are also at stake, this is an unrealistic expectation. Indeed, voter behavior can be inferred from the public response to the governor's decisions in death penalty clemency cases. The public reaction to denials of clemency petitions is a nonreaction, while an uproar of objection responds after each commutation.

Perhaps what is at stake in admitting error with the death penalty system is the suspicion that the whole justice system is broken. The U.S. Supreme Court justices worried about such consequences if they were to recognize the racism in Georgia's system of capital punishment:

> McCleskey's claim, taken to its logical conclusion, throws into serious question the principles that underlie our entire criminal justice system.

> . . . [I]f we accepted McCleskey's claim that racial bias has impermissibly tainted the capital sentencing decision, we could soon be faced with similar claims as to other types of penalty—*McCleskey v. Georgia* (1987: 315–16).

If the Supreme Court justices with their jobs secure through lifetime appointment are unwilling to recognize problems with the death penalty, why should the governor be expected to so provoke his own power base? During the 2000 campaign, former governor and then-senator John Ashcroft (2000) framed his reluctance to overturn a death sentence in terms of support for victims and for maintaining the legal system:

> Such an outcome would be unjust and would demonstrate a disrespect for our legal system and an utter lack of compassion for victims of crime, both living and dead. Capital punishment is society's ultimate consequence for those whose deeds so shatter the rules by which we live as to destabilize that system of rules itself.

Unfortunately, those on death row are not likely to influence many votes, and unless the governor intends to be the hero of the outcast and the marginal, the authority to grant clemency in death penalty cases will likely be unused. A governor who believes that votes will be lost by appearing to be against the death penalty will act as if that relationship were true. Governors will act as a fail safe only for their own political life, not for the life of a death row prisoner.

CHAPTER EIGHT

THE CLEMENCY ALTERNATIVE
Justice Denied

Unjust death verdicts are not a freak act of nature, but grow out of weakness in the court system. There are common characteristics in wrongful murder cases: public pressure for conviction, little physical evidence, and unreliable confessions given under police pressure. As the Illinois Supreme Court's Chief Justice stated, "Our faith in our criminal justice system . . . should not be viewed as an endorsement of the status quo."

Someday this case will repose in the Missouri State Archives for those who follow us to study. . . . How will those who follow us judge your decision?

> FROM THE CLEMENCY PETITION
> *for Bruce Kilgore,* CP#59,
> executed June 16, 1999[1]

BROKEN PROMISES

Examining fifty clemency petitions in Missouri death penalty cases shows that many broken promises are scattered throughout the criminal justice system. We have seen examples of these broken promises at each step in the litigation process, problems presented to the governor as problems for review and remedy. In the beginning of the homicide investigation, police often focus too quickly on one suspect to the exclusion of others, mishandle the suspect, coerce confessions, and even give false testimony at trial to resolve a crime of murder. Prosecutors, who are responsible for deciding to charge the accused with a capital crime, can push the acceptable limits of their job, particularly if the goal of winning a conviction overwhelms their concomitant responsibility to protect the rights of the accused. Withholding exculpatory evidence and taking advantage of inexperienced trial attorneys by excessive "over-the-line" arguments to the jury are some of the ways prosecutors can invalidate the fairness of the adversary system. In contrast to the well-supported prosecutors, too often defense attorneys have been inexperienced and poorly paid, and defendants have lost their lives because of their attorneys' mistakes. The clemency petitions suggest that judges at all levels of the judiciary are vulnerable to political pressures and may be as eager as the police and prosecutors to reach the finality of the death penalty sentence. Court trends reduce the traditional constitutional protections to considerations of form over substance, erecting procedural barriers to eliminate review of the merits of the death penalty cases. These problems cause us to question the reliability and arbitrariness of the death penalty judicial proceedings.

Although their voices have been discounted by media and prosecutors, death row prisoners, through these clemency petitions, raise significant doubts about the moral correctness in proceeding with executions, as well as raise significant uncertainties about the legal system itself. Despite the common perception that criminals have more rights than do crime victims, we have seen charges that basic rights are trampled in the determination to reach a conviction. Rather than being released because an aggressive defense discovers a legal loophole, the death row prisoner is more likely to be executed because of a legal technicality that tripped up the defense or postconviction attorney. Many believe that the death penalty is reserved for those who commit only the worst crimes. But we have seen that prosecutors often make deals with codefendants for testimony against the condemned, resulting in disproportionate sentences and unreliable results. Additionally, prosecutors have obtained death penalty sentences in cases that are not the most heinous crimes (e.g., barroom brawls or after withdrawal of plea agreements for a lesser offense). Another public misperception is that the condemned has had "his day in court," a perception that assumes that the trial was fair, that the jury had complete information, and that all of the appeals have been heard on their merits. However, we have seen that in virtually all cases, the jury does not have all the evidence, mostly because the defense lawyer does an inept job. Due to lack of experience and training coupled with essentially no resources to investigate, the defense attorney loses the trial and then loses the direct appeal opportunity to have a full and fair hearing. Whether it is discovered through investigation or by chance (such as when evidence is "found" or witnesses come forward much later), new information that is relevant is not able to be tested or considered (either by a jury or by the courts) because of procedural barriers created by the courts. The death penalty system does not take into account that reliable information takes time to emerge.

Reading Supreme Court decisions leads Steiker and Steiker (1995) to conclude that contrary to popular impression, "super due process" does not exist. For example, the Supreme Court ruled in *Murray v. Giar-rantano* (1989) that, as in ordinary criminal cases, there is no constitutional guarantee of legal assistance beyond the first appeal in death penalty cases. To expect a prisoner—usually someone with limited education, locked inside prison with limited use of a legal library and with no ability to investigate his case—to handle the legal intricacies of his own appeals within a brief amount of time, particularly under the pressure of his life held in the balance, seems unreasonable. This ruling (and others) only make sense if the Court gives a higher priority to reaching finality in the implementation of the death sentence rather than to careful review. Austin Sarat highlights an example of the Supreme Court's intent to facilitate executions:

> The much publicized execution of Robert Alton Harris is a telling reminder of the pressure on law to compromise its highest values and aspirations in order to turn death sentences into state killings. . . . Ultimately, the Supreme Court ordered that "no further stays shall be entered . . . except upon order of this court" (1999b: 6).

In the Harris case mentioned here, the Supreme Court ordered that no lower court could decide to grant a stay in the execution, even if it wanted to do so. Period. We see in this intervention that as a result of the desire for finality, appellants do not have full access to the courts' reviews. It is not too big of a leap to conclude that those who are most vulnerable in society, those with no resources, can be denied real justice when their lives are at stake. Thus, through the deception of following legal procedures, we are left "winking" at the arbitrariness and the lack of reliability in the legal process. It may be legal to proceed with the execution, but we cannot be sure it is the right action to take.

The courts have long been the repository of the rule of law, protecting those whose fundamental rights may have been violated. Certainly a wrongful conviction would fit the need for such protection. But the criminal justice system is reluctant to recognize mistakes and instead reinforces errors that originate at the trial stage of death penalty cases. Legal presumptions devised by the courts furnish judges (and all of us) with the blinders needed to reinforce the status quo. Courts have evolved into an institution that sets up so many procedural barriers to access substantive review that their ability or will (or both) to fashion remedies when injustice has occurred is defined to be outside of their power. The courts are no longer able or willing to be responsive to legal fairness, preferring to hide their heads in the sand, under a cloak of legal correctness. Consequently, the death penalty cases affirmed by the appellate courts are riddled with fundamental errors.

If the Missouri clemency petitions are given any credence, then it is apparent that these legal procedures no longer guarantee reliable outcomes. The Supreme Court essentially said as much in *Herrera* when it recognized the fallibility of the criminal justice system. It logically follows from *Herrera* that errors should be anticipated, rather than presumed they do not exist.

When the clemency petition reaches the governor's desk, the death row prisoner is out of legal options. The fact that the chief executive has virtually no limits on what is taken into account when considering the clemency request gives the appearance that the governor will overrule the judiciary when serious questions are raised. Although evidentiary rules of law do not restrict the governor's gaze, on the other hand, the governor has no formal or explicit standards to guide the clemency decision. Each clemency petition submitted by an attorney is written to distinguish the specific case from others the governor has considered previously. Obviously this approach is an attempt to elicit a different response than other clemency requests have received from the governor. Clemency petitions submitted by attorneys for the condemned are centered in the source of the *particular* problems faced by the *specific* condemned prisoner. But the reality is that the issues presented in the petitions are neither unique nor rare.

These death penalty clemency petitions ground the plea for mercy to the governor in legal or constitutional justifications (or both). The postconviction lawyers have investigated all the potential legal issues that might prove persuasive to the governor. Their claims are typically focused on attributing a lesser degree of responsibility to the condemned for his predicament. Rather than blaming personality or character flaws of the person on death row for his predicament, most of these clemency claims impute the pending execution to failures of individuals in the legal system. The concluding statement on behalf of Walter Blair is such an example of a lawyer's summation:

> Mr. Blair's case presents a situation where a person is facing society's ultimate penalty, and where the evidence supporting the conviction and sentence for this capital crime is certainly far from overwhelming. [Judge Heaney pointed out that Mr. Blair likely was innocent of that charge.] Where the destruction of a human life is involved, there should be abso-

lutely no doubt of guilt. In Mr. Blair's case, there is substantial doubt, both as to his guilt and the moral propriety and fairness of the death sentence imposed against him. Governor Carnahan, in his discretion, should therefore reaffirm the principles of equal justice and the value that this state places upon human life and permit Mr. Blair to live out the rest of his days in prison.

In most cases, juries and appellate courts sort out the innocent and an acceptable level of justice occurs which is normally consistent with, or at least does not seriously offend, contemporary standards of public policy and fair law enforcement. However, that does not always happen and did not happen in Mr. Blair's case. In this case, questionable evidence and clear racial prejudice were not found sufficient by the judiciary to grant Mr. Blair any relief from his conviction and death sentence. In particular, Mr. Blair's racial discrimination claims received a deaf ear from the courts due to his failure to meet technical and overtly rigid procedural rules effected by the courts. These compelling claims should not receive a deaf ear from Governor Carnahan. The Missouri Constitution and state law reflect the people's and legislature's recognition that there will be cases where it can be fairly concluded, as a matter of policy and fundamental fairness that the judicial system has not produced a reliable result and that there will be cases where circumstances have developed that would make the ultimate punishment of death an inappropriate exercise of the state's power. This case presents both of those compelling reasons for sparing Mr. Blair's life.[2]

Because the focus of the clemency petition is just one case, we lose sight of the systemic and organizational issues that are being presented. As in Mr. Blair's final petition, each clemency petition seeks to distinguish the condemned from the other death penalty prisoners to explain why this petitioner should be granted clemency when the others were not. By individualizing the cases, the fundamental flaws in the system are masked. In this book, we have seen the systemic flaws accumulate and have recognized the patterns of problems with the death penalty.

REFORMS: "TINKERING WITH THE MACHINERY OF JUSTICE"

These are not occasional errors, exceptions to the rule. Unfortunately, they are pervasive and systemic problems in the death penalty legal process that has evolved in the United States. The fairness of the adversary system depends on relatively equal opponents. Such is not the situation in death penalty cases when typically defense lawyers are inexperienced and fail to investigate or when prosecutors withhold evidence. When the goal is to win, the prosecution is willing to take advantage of the vulnerabilities of the defense in the noble cause of conviction. The fairness of the process depends on relatively neutral fact finders. Such is not the situation when police need an arrest to close the case and to satisfy an angry and fearful public, or when judges perceive the need for death penalty sentences in order to advance their career. Executions exact a high price from the legal system by perverting what is acceptable legal practice to satisfy the public's appetite for vengeance. "Capital punishment can only come to be regarded as normal state behavior by reimagining fundamental principles of fairness in criminal justice" (Zimring, 1999: 137).

As detestable as errors are for the condemned, errors do not serve the crime victims' families either. Given that the confidence in the reliability of the trial system is low, punishing the wrong person unnecessarily increases the costs of the administration of justice. When the real killer remains at large, public safety is not improved by executing another, nor is "closure" provided to the crime victim's family.

If we believed that the system could be fixed, there are numerous ways by which reforms can improve on the present death penalty system. What is needed in death penalty litigation is to bring practice into line with the ideals of fundamental fairness and thereby return integrity to the administration of justice. The following suggestions will require political will and courage to adopt and implement. Growing out of our experience with Missouri clemency petitions, we identify four interrelated domains that are particularly critical areas to address.

Effective Assistance of Counsel

Despite the general impression that defense attorneys raise vigorous defenses and can sabotage any criminal trial with errors justifying automatic reversal of convictions (Pizzi, 1999), we have seen that the quality of defense for death penalty cases is extremely low. Raising attorney qualifications to handle death penalty cases is essential. The American Bar Association has had criteria for effective assistance of counsel in death penalty cases for many years. These standards should be adopted and observed in all states and in all stages of the death penalty litigation. When life is at stake, the defense must be the best available. Because death penalty is a demanding specialty within criminal law, lawyers appointed to these cases should have "a certain level of experience, with a record of training, with a proven level of minimum competence in the skills required of the specialty, and with access to the legal knowledge peculiar to the specialty" (Bilionis and Rosen, 1997: 1,362). It is very likely that when effective defense counsel are appointed, other participants in the litigation process will be challenged to do their work constitutionally and thereby reduce some of the serious problems.

"The inmate's right to post-conviction remedies is meaningless without representation by counsel. Petitioning and preparing require a specialized knowledge of the procedural and substantive rules of capital litigation" (McGill, 1990: 226). Having a qualified attorney for the postconviction stage is also critical because some state procedures do not allow some claims for review until the postconviction stage (*Murray v. Giarrantano*, 1989, Justice Stevens, dissenting).[3] Death penalty litigation is among the most difficult and time-consuming kinds of litigation. Anthony Mello summarized a 1986 survey conducted by the American Bar Association that reported the estimated number of hours spent on a single case by private attorneys in just the postconviction stages ranged from 4,116 to 65 (Mello, 1997b: 158). Since "a typical lawyer in private practice devotes about 1,600 hours per year to active law practice" (Mello, 1997b: note 113), it is clear that one death penalty case could easily overwhelm a lawyer's other work. Unfortunately, opposition for providing adequate defense is formidable because of the costs.

Funding

If a state has the death penalty, then providing adequate state funding to ensure effective defense should rise to the level of a constitutional requirement. Unless the resources support the effective assistance of counsel and all that support entails, the death penalty will continue to be imposed in an arbitrary fashion (Bilionis and Rosen, 1997). Interestingly, where paying for death penalty prosecutions is a local matter, some municipalities decide that it is a luxury that cannot be afforded given the competing public safety needs of police and fire protection (Dieter, 1992).

Critical to providing competent defense representation is adequate state funding. The horror stories of what happens when spending caps are imposed or extreme underpayment occurs abound (Bright, 1994; Acker and Lanier, 1999). More than a symbolic gesture toward fairness in the adversary process, defense resources commensurate with the prosecutor's office is a minimum requirement to ensure equal protection of the laws. Even without considering available dollars, the imbalance in resources is evident simply by observing the differential in team members. The prosecution side always has the state highway patrol, the sheriff's department, and crime labs working with them, supporting their efforts to convict. The defense side has to hire others to do their investigation.

Adequate funding also includes financial support for investigators and experts, as well as the maintenance of a low case load such that adequate time is available to do a thorough job. The standards suggested by the ABA's guidelines should become model legislation for states to implement.

Due Process

How do we address the due process issues that are systemic flaws in the legal system generally? Certain reforms of the judicial and legal institutions might minimize the political influences.

One reform to possibly reduce the political influence on judges would give judges longer terms, so that they might feel greater independence from the controversies that typically surround death penalty cases (Uelmen, 1997: 1150). More trial decisions between elections could provide insulation from the public's focus on the death penalty. Another option intended to reduce political pressures is to move the trial of the capital case to a jurisdiction other than that where the crime occurred.

Second, beyond these general efforts to reduce the political influences on judicial behavior, several procedural changes have been suggested by various observers that are specific to the management of death penalty cases:

1. Do not allow the judge to impose the death sentence if the jury is dead-locked on sentencing;

2. Never permit a guilty plea without the counsel of a defense attorney;
3. Require two eyewitnesses, particularly when using jailhouse informants;
4. Videotape trials;
5. Do not permit the trial attorney to handle the direct appeal;
6. Broaden the scope for proportionality review by selecting a wider category of death-eligible cases for comparison; and
7. Restore habeas corpus.

Third, certain changes in the legal culture could occur:

1. Document all police leads;
2. Videotape all interrogations, confessions, and lineups;
3. Have one police investigation file that is used by both defense and prosecution;
4. Require the judge to read the case file before trial and summarize the case for the jury;
5. Require judges, prosecutors, defense counsel, and police to have annual continuing education training in death penalty law and procedure; and
6. Require appellate judges to give written reasons for their decisions in death penalty cases.

The Governor's Decision-Making Process

Because the clemency process is fraught with political overtones, this ultimate petition process needs to be restructured if, indeed, miscarriages of justice are to be prevented. Despite the Eighth Circuit decision in *Otey v. Hopkins* (1993) concluding that the petitioner had no fundamental right to a clemency hearing, most options for improving the neutrality and fairness of the clemency system focus on the role of the Board of Probation and Parole (Korengold, Noteboom, and Gurwitch, 1996; Palacios, 1996; Acker and Lanier, 2000).

The first suggestion to improve the clemency system is for the Board of Probation and Parole to hold *public* hearings to determine its recommendation to the governor. Since the governor is the ultimate decision maker in this process, the governor's office could be the forum for the public hearing. This would have the benefit of giving the governor direct information without any filters. Opening the secret process to media and the public is one way to hold officials accountable in their decision making. We have seen that in Missouri, the investigation conducted by the Board of Probation and Parole was likened to a

Star Chamber proceeding, wherein "justice" was obstructed. Daniel Kobil (1998: 542) identifies seven elements of due process in clemency proceedings to ensure that unfair judgments are not made. Such a hearing would not need to retry the case, but only consider the strength and validity of new information.

1. An independent, thorough investigation of the circumstances surrounding the clemency application conducted by the clemency authority;
2. The right of the defendant to attend a hearing before an impartial decision maker, with a provision for recusal where it can be demonstrated that the decision maker is biased;
3. The right of the defendant to present evidence and witnesses, secured by some sort of subpoena power;
4. The right of the defendant to challenge evidence and confront witnesses through cross-examination;
5. The right of the defendant to be represented by counsel (including the appointment of counsel for indigent defendants) and an adequate opportunity to prepare for the hearing;
6. The right of the defendant to have the hearing transcribed by videotape or a court reporter; and
7. The right of the defendant to receive a written summary of the findings and the decision.

An alternative strategy proposed to depoliticize the clemency process is to establish a respected three-judge panel to decide clemency petitions. Victoria Palacios (1996) suggests that a decision panel be appointed by an appointing panel, such that the political ties to any result are very distant. Both panels would be made up of prestigious persons who would assure the public that the best interests of the public would be considered. The selection of the appointing panel could be made by a bipartisan group including the governor.

Whether or not a board is involved in the clemency process, the clemency consideration should be a meaningful review (Lim, 1994). If the governor remains as the final decision maker in death penalty clemency applications, the governor must meet personally with the attorneys and publicly report an explanation for the clemency decision. This scheme has the advantage of restoring accountability for the pending execution and would educate the public about the administration of justice in the state.

THE INEVITABILITY OF CAPRICE
AND MISTAKE: POLITICS

In 1974, Charles Black could see the futility of attempting reform as he described the "inevitability of caprice and mistake" in the death penalty process. In 1994, Supreme Court Justice Blackmun argued that the death penalty is inherently contradictory and flawed (*Callins v. Collins*). After twenty years of trying to make it work constitutionally, Justice Blackmun declared that he would no longer "tinker with the death penalty process."

Most people are not aware of how the death penalty is actually administered. They do not need legal arguments or economic facts to form their opinion about it. Phoebe Ellsworth and Samuel Gross (1997: 95) report that "most people's attitudes toward capital punishment are basically emotional. The 'reasons' are determined by the attitude, not the reverse." Bill Bowers and Margaret Vandiver (1991a, b) confirm this observation that reasons come after opinions are formed. People process information through the filter of the worldview they already have. I have tried to convey information using the storytelling technique, hoping to evoke an emotional response to the clemency appeals.

In the movie *True Crime*, Clint Eastwood's character brings truth to power when he presents the governor with evidence to establish the innocence of the prisoner about to be executed. In reality, the "true crime" of the executive clemency process is that there is very little grace or mercy, nor is there any rational standard by which fundamental errors will be corrected. The sociopolitical climate in this country has made the executive clemency process basically useless as a remedy for inequity and injustice. No one takes responsibility for ensuring that justice will prevail as a form of decision making is technically followed. The reality of clemency as a fail safe, preventing miscarriages of justice, is a legal fiction. Perpetuation of this myth threatens our social fabric, generating cynicism and disrespect for the rules by which we want to live.

We find ourselves in a culture that *rushes to conviction*, which is fed by a media frenzy of emotion and drama, by the exploitation of victims, and by the need to measure career success through high-profile convictions. This rush to conviction reflects a desire for certainty when the world seems to be changing faster than we are able to handle, and a desire for winning no matter what the cost to our integrity. The courts now reflect this desire for certainty in reaching the finality of sentence no matter what values of fundamental fairness have to be denied.

> Punitive responses are liberating because they are so simple. We yearn to believe that seemingly intractable social and personal problems are actually responsive to direct and forceful action (Scheingold, 1984: 226).

In this sense, the death penalty is well embedded in our cultural fabric. The death penalty is the ultimate symbol for simplifying and focusing our uncertainties and frustrations within a framework of the well-accepted principle that "might makes right." The justification permeates all our interactions and convinces us that it is all right to use violence as a means if the end justifies it, if the goal is good enough. One of the problems with this notion of redemptive violence is that it "gives way to violence as an end in itself" (Wink, 1992: 25). When that happens, justice cannot survive.

Death penalty clemency petitions are a metaphor for the justice system. They represent our own petitions for the ideals of due process and fundamental fairness. We suspect that these concepts are merely illusory legal fictions, procedurally correct but empty of just results. We suspect that we are systematically executing *justice* as we execute people. We suspect that we are mentally incompetent, not understanding what is being done in our names. We are giving up our right to appeal by acquiescing to the limitations on the Great Writ of habeas corpus and thereby killing our democratic ideals of justice. To stay the execution machinery by commutation (or reprieve) is to save our own values and ideals from destruction.

APPENDIX 1

SELECTED MISSOURI REGULATIONS

MISSOURI CONSTITUTION

Article V, section 19. Terms of judges—Judges of the supreme court and of the court of appeals shall be selected for terms of twelve years, judges of the circuit courts for terms of six years, and associate circuit judges for terms of four years.

Article V, section 25(a). Nonpartisan selection of judges—courts subject to plan—appointments to fill vacancies.—Whenever a vacancy shall occur in the office of judge of any of the following courts of this state, to wit: The supreme court, the court of appeals, or in the office of circuit or associate circuit judge within the city of St. Louis and Jackson county, the governor shall fill such vacancy by appointing one of three persons possessing the qualifications for such office, who shall be nominated and whose names shall be submitted to the governor by a nonpartisan judicial commission established and organized as hereinafter provided. If the governor fails to appoint any of the nominees within sixty days after the list of nominees is submitted, the nonpartisan judicial commission making the nomination shall appoint one of the nominees to fill the vacancy.

MISSOURI REVISED STATUTES

Pardons by governor.

217.800.1. In all cases in which the governor is authorized by the constitution to grant pardons, he may grant the same, with such conditions and under such restrictions as he may think proper.
217.800.2. All applications for pardon, commutation of sentence or reprieve shall be referred to the board for investigation. The board shall investigate each such case and submit to the governor a report of its investigation, with all other information the board may have relating to the applicant together with any recommendations the board deems proper to make.
217.800.3. The department of corrections shall notify the central repository, as provided in section 43.500 to 43.530, R.S.Mo., of any action of the governor granting a pardon, commutation of sentence, or reprieve.

Mental disease or defect upon sentence to death.

552.060.1. No person condemned to death shall be executed if as a result of mental disease or defect he lacks capacity to understand the nature and purpose of the punishment about to be imposed upon him or matters in extenuation, arguments for executive clemency or reasons why the sentence should not be carried out.

552.060.2. If the director of the department of corrections has reasonable cause to believe that any inmate then in confinement in a correctional facility and sentenced to death has a mental disease or defect excluding fitness for execution, he shall immediately notify the governor who shall forthwith order a stay of execution of the sentence if there is not sufficient time between such notification and time of execution for a determination of the mental condition of such person to be made in accordance with the provisions of this section without such stay. The director shall also, as soon as reasonably possible, notify the director of the department of mental health and the prosecuting or circuit attorney of the county where the defendant was tried, the attorney general and the circuit court of the county where the correctional facility is located.

552.060.3. As soon as reasonably possible, after the notification prescribed in subsection 2 of this section, the circuit court of the county shall conduct an inquiry into the mental condition of the offender after first granting any of the parties entitled to notification an examination by a physician of their own choosing on proper application made within five days of such notification.

552.060.4. If the court, after such inquiry, certifies to the governor and to the director that the prisoner does not have a mental disease or defect of the type referred to in subsection 1 of this section, the governor shall fix a new date for the execution, if a stay of execution had previously been made, and shall issue a warrant for the new execution date to the chief administrative officer of the correctional facility, who shall then proceed with the execution as ordered. If the court, after such inquiry, certifies to the governor and to the director that the prisoner has a mental disease or defect of the type referred to in subsection 1 of this section, the offender shall not be executed but shall be held in the correctional facility subject to transfer to a mental hospital and further proceedings under section 552.050 if the provisions of section 552.050 are applicable. If any offender who has not been executed because of any certification by the director as herein provided is thereafter certified by the director as free of a mental disease or defect of the type referred to in subsection 1 of this section, the governor shall fix a new date for the execution and shall issue a warrant for the new execution date to the chief administrative officer of the correctional facility, who shall then take charge and custody of the offender and proceed with the execution as ordered in the warrant.

552.060.5. Nothing in this chapter shall be construed to limit the governor or any court in the exercise of any of their powers in any other manner under the law or Constitution of Missouri.

First degree murder, penalty.

565.020.1. A person commits the crime of murder in the first degree if he knowingly causes the death of another person after deliberation upon the matter.

565.020.2. Murder in the first degree is a class A felony, and the punishment shall be either death or imprisonment for life without eligibility for probation or parole, or release except by act of the governor, except that, if a person has not reached his sixteenth birthday at the time of the commission of the crime, the punishment shall be imprisonment for life without eligibility for probation or parole, or release except by act of the governor.

Trial Procedure, first degree murder.

565.030.4. If the trier at the first stage of a trial where the death penalty was not waived finds the defendant guilty of murder in the first degree, a second stage of the trial shall proceed at which the only issue shall be the punishment to be assessed and declared. Evidence in aggravation and mitigation of punishment, including but not limited to evidence supporting any of the aggravating or mitigating circumstances listed in subsection 2 or 3 of section 565.032, may be presented subject to the rules of evidence at criminal trials. Such evidence may include, within the discretion of the court, evidence concerning the murder victim and the impact of the crime upon the family of the victim and others. Rebuttal and surrebuttal evidence may be presented. The state shall be the first to proceed. If the trier is a jury it shall be instructed on the law. The attorneys may then argue the issue of punishment to the jury, and the state shall have the right to open and close the argument. The trier shall assess and declare the punishment at life imprisonment without eligibility for probation, parole, or release except by act of the governor:

1. If the trier does not find beyond a reasonable doubt at least one of the statutory aggravating circumstances set out in subsection 2 of section 565.032; or
2. If the trier does not find that the evidence in aggravation of punishment, including but not limited to evidence supporting the statutory aggravating circumstances listed in subsection 2 of section 565.032, warrants imposing the death sentence; or
3. If the trier concludes that there is evidence in mitigation of punishment, including but not limited to evidence supporting the statutory mitigating circumstances listed in subsection 3 of section 565.032, which is sufficient to outweigh the evidence in aggravation of punishment found by the trier; or
4. If the trier decides under all of the circumstances not to assess and declare the punishment at death. If the trier is a jury it shall be so instructed. If the trier assesses and declares the punishment at death it shall, in its findings or verdict, set out in writing the aggravating circumstance or circumstances listed in subsection 2 of section 565.032 which it found beyond a reasonable doubt. If the trier is a jury it shall be instructed before the case is submitted that if it is unable to decide or agree upon the punishment the court shall assess and declare the punishment at life imprisonment without eligibility for probation, parole, or release except by act of the governor or death. The court shall follow the same procedure as set out in this section whenever it is required to determine punishment for murder in the first degree.

Evidence to be considered in assessing punishment in first degree murder cases for which death penalty is authorized.

565.032.1. In all cases of murder in the first degree for which the death penalty is authorized, the judge in a jury-waived trial shall consider, or he shall include in his instructions to the jury for it to consider:

1. Whether a statutory aggravating circumstance or circum-

stances enumerated in subsection 2 of this section is established by the evidence beyond a reasonable doubt; and

2. If a statutory aggravating circumstance or circumstances is proven beyond a reasonable doubt, whether the evidence as a whole justifies a sentence of death or a sentence of life imprisonment without eligibility for probation, parole, or release except by act of the governor. In determining the issues enumerated in subdivisions (1) and (2) of this subsection, the trier shall consider all evidence which it finds to be in aggravation or mitigation of punishment, including evidence received during the first stage of the trial and evidence supporting any of the statutory aggravating or mitigating circumstances set out in subsections 2 and 3 of this section. If the trier is a jury, it shall not be instructed upon any specific evidence which may be in aggravation or mitigation of punishment, but shall be instructed that each juror shall consider any evidence which he considers to be aggravating or mitigating.

565.032.2. Statutory aggravating circumstances for a murder in the first degree offense shall be limited to the following:

1. The offense was committed by a person with a prior record of conviction for murder in the first degree, or the offense was committed by a person who has one or more serious assaultive criminal convictions;

2. The murder in the first degree offense was committed while the offender was engaged in the commission or attempted commission of another unlawful homicide;

3. The offender by his act of murder in the first degree knowingly created a great risk of death to more than one person by means of a weapon or device which would normally be hazardous to the lives of more than one person;

4. The offender committed the offense of murder in the first degree for himself or another, for the purpose of receiving money or any other thing of monetary value from the victim of the murder or another;

5. The murder in the first degree was committed against a judicial officer, former judicial officer, prosecuting attorney or former prosecuting attorney, circuit attorney or former circuit attorney, assistant prosecuting attorney or former assistant prosecuting attorney, assistant circuit attorney or former assistant circuit attorney, peace officer or former peace officer, elected official or former elected official during or because of the exercise of his official duty;

6. The offender caused or directed another to commit murder in the first degree or committed murder in the first degree as an agent or employee of another person;

7. The murder in the first degree was outrageously or wantonly vile, horrible or inhuman in that it involved torture, or depravity of mind;

8. The murder in the first degree was committed against any peace officer, or fireman while engaged in the performance of his official duty;

9. The murder in the first degree was committed by a person in,

or who has escaped from, the lawful custody of a peace officer or place of lawful confinement;

10. The murder in the first degree was committed for the purpose of avoiding, interfering with, or preventing a lawful arrest or custody in a place of lawful confinement, of himself or another;

11. The murder in the first degree was committed while the defendant was engaged in the perpetration or was aiding or encouraging another person to perpetrate or attempt to perpetrate a felony of any degree of rape, sodomy, burglary, robbery, kidnapping, or any felony offense in chapter 195, R.S.Mo.;

12. The murdered individual was a witness or potential witness in any past or pending investigation or past or pending prosecution, and was killed as a result of his status as a witness or potential witness;

13. The murdered individual was an employee of an institution or facility of the department of corrections of this state or local correction agency and was killed in the course of performing his official duties, or the murdered individual was an inmate of such institution or facility;

14. The murdered individual was killed as a result of the hijacking of an airplane, train, ship, bus or other public conveyance;

15. The murder was committed for the purpose of concealing or attempting to conceal any felony offense defined in chapter 195, R.S.Mo.;

16. The murder was committed for the purpose of causing or attempting to cause a person to refrain from initiating or aiding in the prosecution of a felony offense defined in chapter 195, R.S.Mo.;

17. The murder was committed during the commission of a crime which is part of a pattern of criminal street gang activity as defined in section 578.421.

565.032.3. Statutory mitigating circumstances shall include the following:

1. The defendant has no significant history of prior criminal activity;

2. The murder in the first degree was committed while the defendant was under the influence of extreme mental or emotional disturbance;

3. The victim was a participant in the defendant's conduct or consented to the act;

4. The defendant was an accomplice in the murder in the first degree committed by another person and his participation was relatively minor;

5. The defendant acted under extreme duress or under the substantial domination of another person;

6. The capacity of the defendant to appreciate the criminality of his conduct or to conform his conduct to the requirements of law was substantially impaired;

7. The age of the defendant at the time of the crime.

Supreme court to review all death sentences, procedure—powers of court—assistant to court authorized, duties.

565.035.1. Whenever the death penalty is imposed in any case, and upon the judgment becoming final in the trial court, the sentence shall be reviewed on the record by the supreme court of Missouri. The circuit clerk of the court trying the case, within ten days after receiving the transcript, shall transmit the entire record and transcript to the supreme court together with a notice prepared by the circuit clerk and a report prepared by the trial judge. The notice shall set forth the title and docket number of the case, the name of the defendant and the name and address of his attorney, a narrative statement of the judgment, the offense, and the punishment prescribed. The report by the judge shall be in the form of a standard questionnaire prepared and supplied by the supreme court of Missouri.

565.035.2. The supreme court of Missouri shall consider the punishment as well as any errors enumerated by way of appeal.

565.035.3. With regard to the sentence, the supreme court shall determine:

1. Whether the sentence of death was imposed under the influence of passion, prejudice, or any other arbitrary factor; and
2. Whether the evidence supports the jury's or judge's finding of a statutory aggravating circumstance as enumerated in subsection 2 of section 565.032 and any other circumstance found;
3. Whether the sentence of death is excessive or disproportionate to the penalty imposed in similar cases, considering both the crime, the strength of the evidence and the defendant.

565.035.4. Both the defendant and the state shall have the right to submit briefs within the time provided by the supreme court, and to present oral argument to the supreme court.

565.035.5. The supreme court shall include in its decision a reference to those similar cases which it took into consideration. In addition to its authority regarding correction of errors, the supreme court, with regard to review of death sentences, shall be authorized to:

1. Affirm the sentence of death; or
2. Set the sentence aside and resentence the defendant to life imprisonment without eligibility for probation, parole, or release except by act of the governor; or
3. Set the sentence aside and remand the case for retrial of the punishment hearing. A new jury shall be selected or a jury may be waived by agreement of both parties and then the punishment trial shall proceed in accordance with this chapter, with the exception that the evidence of the guilty verdict shall be admissible in the new trial together with the official transcript of any testimony and evidence properly admitted in each stage of the original trial where relevant to determine punishment.

565.035.6. There shall be an assistant to the supreme court, who shall be an attorney appointed by the supreme court and who shall serve at the pleasure of the court. The court shall accumulate the records of all cases in which the sentence of death or life imprisonment without probation or parole was imposed after May 26, 1977, or such earlier date as the court may deem appropriate. The assistant shall provide the court with whatever extracted information the court desires with respect thereto, including but not limited to a synopsis or brief of the facts in the record concerning the crime and the defendant. The court shall be authorized to employ an appropriate staff, within the limits of appropriations made for that purpose, and such methods to compile such data as are deemed by the supreme court to be appropriate and relevant to the statutory questions concerning the validity of the sentence. The office of the assistant to the supreme court shall be attached to the office of the clerk of the supreme court for administrative purposes.

565.035.7. In addition to the mandatory sentence review, there shall be a right of direct appeal of the conviction to the supreme court of Missouri. This right of appeal may be waived by the defendant. If an appeal is taken, the appeal and the sentence review shall be consolidated for consideration. The court shall render its decision on legal errors enumerated, the factual substantiation of the verdict, and the validity of the sentence.

MISSOURI SUPREME COURT RULES

Rule 27.26 Felonies—sentence unlawful—motion to vacate or correct form and scope of motion—notice to prosecuting attorney—appointment of counsel—hearing—order—effect of order—appeal.

A prisoner in custody under sentence and claiming a right to be released on the ground that such sentence was imposed in violation of the Constitution and laws of this state or the United States, or that the court imposing such sentence was without jurisdiction to do so, or that such sentence was in excess of the maximum sentence authorized by law or is otherwise subject to collateral attack, may file a motion at any time in the court which imposed such sentence to vacate, set aside, or correct the same. . . . (repealed February 11, 1987, effective January 1, 1988)

Rule 29.15 Conviction after trial correction.

a. Nature of Remedy—Rules of Civil Procedure Apply. A person convicted of a felony after trial claiming that the conviction or sentence imposed violates the constitution and laws of this state or the constitution of the United States, including claims of ineffective assistance of trial and appellate counsel, that the court imposing the sentence was without jurisdiction to do so, or that the sentence imposed was in excess of the maximum sentence authorized by law may seek relief in the sentencing court pursuant to the provisions of this Rule 29.15. This Rule 29.15 provides the exclusive procedure by which such person may seek relief in the sentencing court for the claims enumerated. The procedure to be followed for motions filed pursuant to this Rule 29.15 is governed by the rules of civil procedure insofar as applicable.

The following section (b) became effective July 1, 2000 and former section (b) below as repealed that date.

b. Form of motion—Cost Deposit Not Required—Time to File—Failure to File, Effect of. A person seeking relief pursuant to this Rule 29.15 shall file a motion to vacate, set aside or correct the judgment or sentence substantially in the form of Criminal Procedure Form No. 40.

No cost deposit shall be required.

If an appeal of the judgment or sentence sought to be vacated, set aside or corrected was taken, the motion shall be filed within ninety days after the date the mandate of the appellate court is issued affirming such judgment or sentence. If no appeal of such judgment or sentence was taken, the motion shall be filed within ninety days of the date the person is delivered to the custody of the department of corrections.

If:
1.   An appeal of such judgment or sentence is taken;
2.   The appellate court remands the case resulting in entry of a new judgment or sentence; and
3.   An appeal of the new judgment or sentence is taken, the motion shall be filed within ninety days after the date the mandate of the appellate court is issued affirming the new judgment or sentence.

If no appeal of such new judgment or sentence is taken, the motion shall be filed within ninety days of the later of:
1.   The date the person is delivered to the custody of the department of corrections; or
2.   The date the new judgment or sentence was final for purposes of appeal.

Failure to file a motion within the time provided by this Rule 29.15 shall constitute a complete waiver of any right to proceed under this Rule 29.15 and a complete waiver of any claim that could be raised in a motion filed pursuant to this Rule 29.15.

c.   Clerk's duties.

d.   Contents of Motion. The motion to vacate shall include every claim known to the movant for vacating, setting aside, or correcting the judgment or sentence. The movant shall declare in the motion that the movant has listed all claims for relief known to the movant and acknowledging the movant's understanding that the movant waives any claim for relief known to the movant that is not listed in the motion.

e.   Pro Se Motion—Appointment of Counsel Amended Motion, Required When. When an indigent movant files a pro se motion, the court shall cause counsel to be appointed for the movant. Counsel shall ascertain whether sufficient facts supporting the claims are asserted in the motion and whether the movant has included all claims known to the movant as a basis for attacking the judgment and sentence. If the motion does not assert sufficient facts or include all claims known to the movant, counsel shall file an amended motion that sufficiently alleges the additional facts and claims. If counsel determines that no amended motion shall be filed, counsel shall file a statement setting out facts demonstrating what actions were taken to ensure that (1) all facts supporting the claims are asserted in the pro se motion and (2) all claims known to the movant are alleged in the pro se motion. The statement shall be presented to the movant prior to filing. The movant may file a reply to the statement not later than ten days after the statement is filed.

f.   Withdrawal of Counsel.

g.   Amended Motion Form, Time for Filing Response by Prosecutor.

h.   Hearing Not Required, When.

i.   Presence of Movant—Record of Hearing—Continuance of Hearing—Burden of Proof.

j.   Findings and Conclusions Judgment. The court shall issue findings of fact and conclusions of law on all issues presented, whether or not a hearing is held. If the court finds that the judgment was rendered without jurisdiction, that the sentence imposed was illegal, or that there was a denial or infringement of the rights given movant by the constitution of Missouri or the constitution of the United States as to render the judgment subject to collateral attack, the court shall vacate and set aside the judgment and shall discharge the movant or resentence the movant or order a new trial or correct the judgment and sentence as appropriate.

k. Appeal Standard of Appellate Review.

l. Successive Motions. The circuit court shall not entertain successive motions.

m. Schedule.

Rule 29.16 Conviction after trial—correction—death sentence—appointment of counsel.

a. When a motion is filed as provided in Rule 29.15 to set aside a sentence of death, the court shall find on the record whether the movant is indigent. If the movant is indigent, the court shall cause to be appointed two counsel to represent the movant. If movant seeks to reject the appointment of counsel, the court shall find on the record, after a hearing if necessary, whether the movant is able to competently decide whether to accept or reject the appointment and whether the movant rejected the offer with the understanding of its legal consequences. Unless the movant is so competent and understands the legal consequences, movant shall not be permitted to reject the appointment of counsel.

b. All counsel appointed as provided in this Rule 29.16 shall be members of The Missouri Bar or shall be admitted to practice in the particular case as provided in this Court's Rule 9. At least one of the counsel shall meet the following qualifications:

1. Have attended and successfully completed within two years immediately preceding the appointment at least twelve hours of training or educational programs on the post-conviction phase of a criminal case and federal and state aspects of cases in which the death penalty is sought; and

2. Have at least three years litigation experience in the field of criminal law; and

3. Have participated as counsel or co-counsel to final judgment in at least five post-conviction motions involving class A felonies in either state or federal trial courts; and

4. Have participated in either state or federal court as counsel or co-counsel to final judgment in at least:
   A. three felony jury trials; or
   B. five direct criminal appeals in felony cases.

Counsel shall certify to the state public defender in such form as the defender may require that counsel meets the qualifications of this Rule 29.16 prior to filing counsel's entry of appearance in the case.

c. Counsel appointed to represent the movant shall not have represented the movant at trial or on the direct appeal therefrom.

d. As to any counsel appointed as provided in this Rule 29.16, the state public defender shall provide counsel with reasonable compensation and shall provide reasonable and necessary litigation expenses.

e. This Rule 29.16 shall be applicable to all motions filed on or after July 1, 1997, as provided in Rule 29.15.

APPENDIX 2

INVENTORY OF CASES

Since 1977 and through 2000, the governors of Missouri have considered fifty clemency petitions.[1] Forty-five of the cases that went to the governors were denied, with the executions subsequently taking place. Two petitions (for Bobby Shaw and Darrell Mease) resulted in the commutation of the death sentence to a sentence of life without parole. The petition on behalf of Lloyd Schlup resulted in a stay, which permitted further advocacy and subsequent resolution of the case, which took him *off* death row. One petitioner (William Ted Boliek) was given a stay until a three-judge panel could rule on the issues; however, the governor never appointed the panel. During the time period of 1977–2000, thirty men (19 percent) and five women (100 percent) had their sentences reversed and remanded by the courts before reaching the governor's desk. (Six male prisoners had their death sentences reinstated.) Three others on death row were given stays when the director of the Department of Corrections said she had cause to believe that they had a mental disease or defect, excluding fitness for execution (Chuck Mathenia,[2] Roosevelt Pollard, and Steve Parkus). The stays are issued in order to hold a hearing on competency. The courts ruled Mr. Mathenia and Mr. Pollard incompetent and hence not eligible for execution until their mental conditions improve. Mr. Parkus's case is pending. These competency cases are not included in this research because there were no actual clemency petitions that needed action by the governor.

The fifty clemency cases are listed in chronological order by execution date.

January 6, 1989	**George "Tiny" Mercer** George Mercer was convicted of the murder of Karen Keeton of Kansas City in 1978. Mr. Mercer maintained his innocence of the killing. Questions were raised about the application of the two aggravating factors to the facts of the case. A codefendant was given a life sentence, while Mr. Mercer was given the death penalty.
January 18, 1990	**Gerald Smith** Gerald Smith received the death sentence for the 1980 murder of Karen Roberts in St. Louis. In a sworn affidavit in 1988, Timothy Smith, brother of Gerald, identified another brother, Eugene, as the person who actually killed Ms. Roberts. Timothy's story was supported independently by other individuals and was more in line with the physical evidence of the case. Over the years, Gerald, who had a history of psychological disorders and suicide attempts, told two different stories of the murder. One was consistent with Timothy's, while the other was used by Gerald when he apparently wanted to

end his life. He is considered a "volunteer" because he did not want his appeals to continue.

May 11, 1990   **Winford Stokes**
Winford Stokes was convicted of the stabbing murder of Pamela Benda of University City in 1978. He was also charged with the murder of an elderly woman in 1977. As part of a plea agreement, Mr. Stokes was to plead guilty to second degree murder in both cases in exchange for fifty-year sentences to run concurrently. An incorrect statement about him in the local paper resulted in his refusal to accept the plea agreement, and he was subsequently convicted of capital murder and given the death sentence. Mr. Stokes was African-American, the victim was a Caucasian female, and Mr. Stokes was convicted by an all-Caucasian jury. The judge also refused to allow the jury to consider that as recently as three weeks prior to the murder, the victim had sought police protection from her boyfriend because of death threats and repeatedly inflicted physical violence.

In a dissenting opinion, Judge Seiler wrote: "I am unable to agree with permitting the prosecution to get by with not serving defense counsel until the morning of the trial with notice of aggravating circumstances. For the state to seek to take a man's life is a serious matter and we should insist that the state proceed in a fair and orderly fashion. The state knows that it must make known in advance of trial the evidence in aggravation proposed to be introduced. This necessarily means timely notice, and notice on the morning of trial is not timely. The matter of aggravating circumstances is no trifling matter. Without aggravating circumstances, no death penalty is possible. The defendant is entitled to know what is claimed in this regard. Defense counsel needs time to appraise the state's claim and to prepare to meet it. This cannot be done when notice is not given until the morning of the trial. A remark by the prosecutor a month earlier that he intends to seek the death penalty is no substitute" (*State v. Stokes,* 638 S.W.2d 726).

May 17, 1990   **Leonard Laws**
Leonard Laws was given the death sentence for the 1980 murders of Charles and Lottie Williams of Glenco. The undisputed evidence from trial transcript was that Mr. Laws provided the lookout and was outside the building while two others actually committed the murders. One of the other codefendants received a fifteen-year sentence in exchange for testimony. The other codefendant was executed in 1990. Mr. Laws is considered a "volunteer" because he did not want his appeals to continue.

August 31, 1990   **George Gilmore**
George Gilmore was sentenced to death for the 1979–80

murders of four elderly people: Mary Luella Watters, Woodrow Elliott, and Clarence and Lottie Williams. Mr. Gilmore grew up in a very deprived and abusive home in which both parents were alcoholic. While in school Mr. Gilmore attended a program for mentally retarded students who were educable. Records show he had a Benet IQ score of 65 (mental health experts consider a valid IQ score of 75 or less to be one of the indicators of mental retardation). Mr. Gilmore also suffered two significant head injuries in 1973 and 1980.

| August 23, 1991 | **Maurice O. Byrd** |

Maurice Byrd was executed for the murders of James Wood, Carolyn Turner, Edna Ince, and Judy Cazaco in Pope's Cafeteria in Des Peres in 1980. Four years after Mr. Byrd's trial, an unbiased eyewitness came forward identifying two other African-American men as individuals she encountered coming out of the mall near the cafeteria early on the morning of the murders. (The witness said she waited to come forward for fear of retaliation by the real killers.) She recalled one of the men was carrying a large bag. The witness had recognized Mr. Byrd as someone she had previously seen working in the mall and knew he was not one of the two men she saw at the mall that morning.

The prosecution had no eyewitnesses, but relied on pretrial statements (later recanted) made by Mr. Byrd's wife that he told her he had killed three people in Missouri. The prosecution relied on the self-interested testimony of jail cell mates who were in a position to gain advantage in their own cases by testifying against Mr. Byrd. This case also had serious issues of racial bias in that Mr. Byrd was an African-American and the victims in the case were Caucasians. He was tried and convicted by an all-Caucasian jury after the state prosecution used its peremptory strikes to exclude the African-American veniremen.

| October 21, 1992 | **Ricky Lee Grubbs** |

Ricky Lee Grubbs was convicted of killing Jerry Thornton in 1984. Psychological testing throughout his childhood found Mr. Grubbs had IQ scores in the low 70s. He received failing grades all his life and was placed in special education classes for two years. A psychiatric evaluation indicated Mr. Grubbs had low mental function and was not able to think through the consequences of his actions. Also, his intoxication at the time of the crime diminished his conscious control, which, combined with his low mental function, rendered Mr. Grubbs incapable of forming the necessary intent to deliberate.

| January 27, 1993 | **Martsay Bolder** |

Early in 1979, Theron King was assigned as Mr. Bolder's

cell mate in prison. Mr. King was twenty years older than Mr. Bolder, and he used his age and experience to taunt and harass Mr. Bolder. Eventually the harassment became too much for Mr. Bolder. In March of that year, Mr. Bolder stabbed Theron King. Evidence obtained much after the trial indicated that Mr. King died of an infection caused by hospital staff six weeks after the stabbing, when they removed fluid from Mr. King's chest by passing a hypodermic needle through the location of his abdominal wound. Mr. Bolder requested that the governor convene a hearing to determine whether using the wound area for this procedure constituted malpractice.

June 9, 1993   **Bobby Shaw**
While in prison serving a life sentence for killing his sister's common-law husband, Mr. Shaw killed Walter Farrow, a corrections officer. Mr. Shaw's mental condition prevented him from being fully responsible for his crimes. Mr. Shaw did not receive a fair trial because the jury and judge who imposed the death sentence were misinformed about Mr. Shaw's mental disabilities. Procedural technicalities prevented the courts from correcting the injustice that occurred. His death sentence was commuted to life without parole by Governor Carnahan.

July 21, 1993   **Walter Blair**
Walter Blair, an African-American, was convicted of the contract murder of Kathy Jo Allen, a Caucasian, in 1979. The case against Mr. Blair relied primarily upon the testimony of Ernest Jones, a police informant. Mr. Jones testified that Mr. Blair had told him, before and after the murder, of the plot to kill Ms. Allen. However, Mr. Jones's credibility was suspect because he received immunity for any part he played in the murder. Ironically, police officers arrested Mr. Jones the day after the shooting when they learned he and his brother had pawned a ring stolen from the victim's boyfriend during the kidnapping. Officers also realized Mr. Jones had stolen the murder weapon in a burglary of his next-door neighbor's home. Furthermore, the victim's boyfriend identified Mr. Jones in a police lineup as the person who had kidnapped Ms. Allen at gunpoint before she was murdered. Two other witnesses observed a man matching Mr. Jones's description leaving the scene of the murder just after they heard shots fired. Eventually, six more witnesses came forward in the months before Mr. Blair's execution, four of them reporting that Mr. Jones boasted he killed Kathy Jo Allen and helped frame Mr. Blair. Another admitted he dropped Mr. Jones off at the victim's apartment just before the kidnapping and murder. Mr. Jones's girlfriend also stated in an affidavit that she

and Mr. Jones had lied about Mr. Blair's involvement in the killing. Mr. Blair was convicted by an all-Caucasian jury in a trial in which the prosecutor, in his closing statements, called the victim "the lovely white woman" and Mr. Blair "the black man with the gun."

July 28, 1993

Frederick Lashley
Frederick Lashley was just seventeen years old when he was convicted of the stabbing death of his disabled cousin and foster mother, Janie Tracy, on April 9, 1981. Mr. Lashley came from a physically abusive home. He began drinking heavily at the age of ten and began abusing drugs at age eleven. Mr. Lashley was not known to be violent toward the victim or any other family member. On the day of the murder he tried PCP (phencyclide) for the first time. PCP is known to induce psychotic behavior and can cause its user to be dangerous. The family of Ms. Tracy did not want the execution to take place.

October 6, 1993

Frank Guinan
Frank Guinan was given the death sentence for murdering fellow inmate John McBroom at the prison in Jefferson City in 1982. Psychological testing in 1990 and 1991 found that Mr. Guinan did not have the ability to "deliberate" at the time of the homicide. Testing concluded he had "mild to moderate" brain damage that prevented him from thinking "logically or clearly in any kind of stressful situation. . . . [He can] act, but can't think." Mr. Guinan had a history of attempted suicide and had taken extensive psychotropic medications in prison. Mr. Guinan's trial attorney offered no mitigating evidence during the penalty phase of his trial. The jury also never had the opportunity to consider evidence from four eyewitnesses who saw the stabbing of Mr. McBroom and would have testified that another inmate wielded the knife. Moreover, at least one of these eyewitnesses had sworn that he was intimidated by prison officials into not testifying to what he actually saw. Other witnesses not called at the trial would testify that it was common knowledge among inmates and corrections officials at the Missouri State Penitentiary that Richard Zeitvogel, rather than Mr. Guinan, had killed Mr. McBroom.

November 19, 1993
March 22, 1999

Lloyd Schlup
Mr. Schlup was convicted of a murder that happened in prison. The prosecution withheld information about the state's key witnesses, two Department of Corrections officers: one's criminal record and the demotion of the other. Not a single prisoner, black or white, said that Mr. Schlup participated in the crime. Even a prison video demonstrated that Mr. Schlup was in another part of the

prison at the time of the crime. There were nearly twenty eyewitnesses to the crime who could have testified that Mr. Schlup was not there if the trial attorney had done an adequate job. Many inconsistent statements of the corrections officers call into question the truth of their testimony. There was direct evidence that Rocky Jordan was guilty of this crime, as well as Mr. Schlup's own statement of his innocence given on the day of the murder. The issue of ineffective counsel was raised. Mr. Schlup's death sentence was stayed by Governor Carnahan to allow the U.S. Supreme Court to rule on Mr. Schlup's case. The Supreme Court ordered an evidentiary hearing, which resulted in the judge ordering the death sentence vacated. A plea agreement was made on March 22, 1999 when the prosecutor filed to retry the case.

May 3, 1995

Emmitt Foster

Codefendant Michael Phillips received a life sentence plus two thirty-year sentences for the 1983 killing of Travis Walker and the related assault of DeAnn Keys in North St. Louis. Emmitt Foster was sentenced to death, although there was evidence to support his claim of innocence. The prosecution withheld exculpatory evidence of the investigation report, and there was no physical evidence to link Mr. Foster to the scene of the crime. The only eyewitness (Ms. Keys) sustained four gunshot wounds to the back of the head prior to the identification of her assailants. From all evidence it was clear that she was shot in an area of the apartment that would have precluded her from seeing the second assailant.

This evidence would have presented reasonable doubt as to the guilt of Mr. Foster, but was not heard by the jury. Ineffective assistance of counsel resulted in Mr. Foster receiving a death sentence for the murder.

June 21, 1995

Larry Griffin

Larry Griffin was sentenced to death for the June 26, 1980, drive-by shooting of Quintin Moss, a known drug dealer. The alleged motive for the crime was revenge for Mr. Moss killing Mr. Griffin's brother several months earlier. The prosecution's only direct evidence of Mr. Griffin's guilt was presented through the eyewitness testimony of Robert Fitzgerald, a career criminal and federally protected witness, whose car allegedly had broken down on the corner shortly before the crime occurred.

Thirteen years later in a federal prison, Mr. Fitzgerald admitted committing perjury when he positively identified Mr. Griffin in court as the person he saw shoot Moss. Mr. Fitzgerald also testified that the police suggested to him that he pick out Mr. Griffin's photo before he did so. Also in 1993, another witness came forward with testimony supporting Mr. Griffin's innocence. Kerry Caldwell was a hit man for a drug gang that operated in St. Louis in the 1980s. In 1990 he also joined the federal witness protection program and became a prosecution witness in another case. He subsequently testified before a federal judge that he was the lookout man when three men—other than Mr. Griffin—killed Mr. Moss.

July 26, 1995   **Robert Anthony Murray**
Both Tony Murray and his older brother, William, were involved in the robbery that took place in the apartment prior to the murders of Jeffrey Jackson and Craig Stewart in 1985. Conflicting court testimony of the two women victims who escaped made it difficult to determine who actually did the shooting. However, there were many other witnesses who could have testified that William was the shooter. Yet, William received a life sentence while Tony received a death sentence. William later confessed to being the killer. Ineffective assistance of counsel resulted in Tony's execution.

November 15, 1995   **Robert Sidebottom**
Robert Sidebottom was convicted of killing his seventy-four-year-old grandmother, Mae Sidebottom. The cutoff of federal funds resulted in the abrupt closing of the Capital Punishment Resource Center, which had provided legal counsel to Mr. Sidebottom for six years. No legal counsel was available to file a habeas corpus petition in federal court.

November 29, 1995   **Anthony J. LaRette**
Anthony LaRette was given the death sentence for the murder of Mary Fleming in 1980. Records show that no less than eight institutions over thirty years diagnosed and treated Mr. LaRette for temporal lobe epilepsy. This condition resulted in seizures that caused him to go into a rage, foam at the mouth, involuntarily urinate, rip off his clothes, and black out. Upon waking, Mr. LaRette would have no memory of his actions. At various times in his life, these seizures occurred one to three times a week, some lasting as long as forty minutes. At least one doctor reported that his assaults on women were probably committed during these blackout periods. It was difficult to find medication to treat Mr. LaRette because of other medical conditions he had. None of this information was presented to the jury.

December 6, 1995   **Robert O'Neal**
Robert O'Neal was convicted of killing fellow inmate Arthur Dade in the Missouri State Penitentiary in 1984. The prosecution failed to disclose that one of its lead witnesses, Officer Maylee, had a prior criminal record. Disclosure of that information certainly would have

substantially reduced, if not destroyed, Officer Maylee's credibility at trial.

February 21, 1996   **Jeffrey Paul Sloan**
Jeffrey Sloan admitted to killing his father, his mother, and his brothers in December 1985. The jury never heard significant mitigating factors including substantial physical and emotional abuse that was perpetrated upon Jeff by his father. Neighbors, although alarmed by the abuse, declined to alert authorities. Psychiatric evaluations indicated significant cognitive deficiencies that were the result of a learning disability or profound head trauma (or both). Psychological testing endorsed a possible diagnosis of paranoid schizophrenia and clear evidence of disordered thinking. Mr. Sloan's attorney was disbarred shortly after Jeff's trial, having been convicted of laundering drug money.

April 10, 1996   **Doyle Williams**
Kerry Brummett drowned, while handcuffed, in 1981 in the Missouri River in Clay County after running from Doyle Williams and John Morgan. Both Mr. Williams and Mr. Morgan had earlier assaulted Mr. Brummett and had weapons that they could have used to shoot the victim had they wished. Mr. Morgan testified that neither he nor Mr. Williams forced the victim into the water or pushed him under. After the victim ran into the river, Mr. Williams dove into the water to look for him. Mr. Williams received the death penalty; Mr. Morgan received a lesser sentence.

July 31, 1996   **Emmett Nave**
Mr. Nave was fifty-five years old in 1996 and of African and Native American descent. Emmett was sentenced to die for killing his landlady in 1983 in Jefferson City during a drunken rampage. His court-appointed attorney, Julian Ossman, represented four other death-sentenced defendants in Missouri. His attorney asked only three questions when interviewing potential jury members, presented no evidence to show that Emmett's mental capacity was diminished because of chronic alcoholism, and gave a closing argument that took only a half-page for the court reporter to transcribe.

In 1990 federal district court judge Clyde Cahill granted Emmett a writ of habeas corpus and reversed his death sentence on ten grounds of ineffective assistance of counsel. However, the Eighth Circuit Court of Appeals reversed the decision, finding seven of the ten claims of ineffective assistance of counsel to be procedurally barred (because one of his state appellate attorneys made a mistake in not raising these claims on appeal) and the other three claims to be without merit. Emmett's death sentence was reinstated.

August 7, 1996   **Thomas Battle**
Always asserting his innocence of the murder of Birdie Johnson in 1980, Thomas Battle admitted to intending to commit burglary when he entered her house with two accomplices. But Mr. Battle insisted he fled when the victim woke and made a noise. Much substantial and credible evidence of innocence was not presented to the jury because Mr. Battle's attorney had never tried a capital case. Two witnesses implicated Elroy Preston, a man who had committed other murders and who had confessed to murdering Ms. Johnson. The evidence was never considered by appellate courts because of procedural barriers.

August 21, 1996   **Richard Oxford**
Richard Oxford was convicted for the double murder of Harold and Melba Wampler, a rural Jasper County couple, in 1986. According to psychiatric evaluations, Mr. Oxford demonstrated behavioral and intellectual abnormalities beginning at an early age and increasing in severity as he got older. At ten years of age, he was sniffing airplane glue and was found "blue" from the use. He was referred for psychiatric treatment at eleven years of age and from that time on, he was institutionalized in juvenile treatment centers or incarcerated for the majority of the time.

December 11, 1996   **Richard Zeitvogel**
Richard Zeitvogel was sentenced to death for the killing of fellow inmate Gary Dew in a Jefferson City prison in 1983. Mr. Zeitvogel was a witness to an attempted murder in the basement of the prison chapel. He helped prison officials solve the crime by identifying Mr. Dew as one of the attackers. Mr. Dew's attorney, Julian Ossman, told Mr. Dew who identified him. While awaiting sentencing, despite Mr. Dew's threats of retaliation against Mr. Zeitvogel for "snitching" on him, Mr. Dew and Mr. Zeitvogel were placed in the same cell. After Mr. Dew's death when Mr. Zeitvogel was charged with capital murder, Julian Ossman, the same attorney who represented Mr. Dew, was appointed to represent Mr. Zeitvogel. Mr. Ossman failed to adequately present evidence of self-defense to the jury or evidence that the chapel incident led to Mr. Dew's death.

January 29, 1997   **Eric Schneider**
Eric Schneider was one of three men convicted in the robbery and killings of Richard Schwendemann and Ronald Thompson in their home in 1985. One of the codefendants who participated in the stabbings was sentenced to three consecutive life sentences. Another defendant, who cooperated with police in the investigation, was sentenced to thirty years in prison.

August 6, 1997   **Ralph Feltrop**
Ralph Feltrop maintained that he killed his live-in girl-friend, Barbara Ann Roam, in self-defense in 1987. The victim's known propensity for physically attacking her boyfriends, and Mr. Feltrop's passive personality and unusual psychological background, all suggested he did act in self-defense. Mr. Feltrop's attorney failed to present any of this information to the jury.

August 13, 1997   **Donald Reese**
Mr. Reese was found guilty of killing Chris Griffith and James Watson at a rifle range in 1988. His conviction and sentence were based on a coerced inculpatory statement that was written by a sheriff for Mr. Reese to sign. Substantial information that should have been presented at trial was that Mr. Reese was clinically depressed and probably suicidal at the time of the involuntary statement. In addition, there were no fingerprints or other unique physical evidence connecting him to the crimes. Mr. Reese received inadequate representation by counsel at trial. The procedural restrictions placed upon the federal courts prevented meaningful review of his constitutional claims.

August 20, 1997   **Andrew Six**
Andrew Six and his uncle, Donald Petary, were convicted of the killing of twelve-year-old Kathy Allen in northern Missouri in 1987. The jury that found Mr. Six guilty of first degree murder was unable to agree that he be sentenced to death. The decision whether Mr. Six should live or be put to death was made by the trial judge, who had urged the bankrupt county to go ahead with the capital trial. Judge Webber imposed the death sentence just an hour and a half after the jury announced their impasse.

August 27, 1997   **William Ted Boliek**
The victim, Jody Harless, was killed on a rural road in southern Missouri. Three people were present when she died. The four had left Kansas City earlier that day because three of them had robbed a reputed motorcycle gang member and drug dealer only a few days before. They feared the police and retribution by the motorcycle gang. All were under the influence of drugs, alcohol, and lack of sleep at the time Jody died. Mr. Boliek says he pulled the trigger in an attempt to scare her and wounded her, but not fatally. He claims he did not fire the fatal shotgun wound to the face. His lawyer did not discover his long history of substantial and well-documented mental disorders. Compounding the lawyer issue was the prosecutor's misconduct in introducing highly prejudicial inadmissible evidence of a tattoo of a shotgun on Mr. Boliek's shoulder. The governor

granted Mr. Boliek a stay, but never appointed a board of inquiry. His codefendant pleaded guilty to second degree murder.

September 24, 1997   Samuel L. McDonald
Samuel McDonald was convicted of killing Robert Jordan, an off-duty St. Louis police officer, in 1981 in the course of a robbery. Through the failure of his trial counsel, the jurors did not know that psychiatric evaluations revealed that Mr. McDonald had a full complement of symptoms related to post-traumatic stress disorder (PTSD), including frequent flashbacks of memories from his tour of duty as a machine gunner during the Vietnam War. Mr. McDonald recalled being traumatized by many war experiences, including one documented night battle in which more than 75 percent of the soldiers in his company were killed. He spent five terrifying days stuck behind enemy lines, unsure whether he'd be captured or killed. This disorder caused Mr. McDonald to have a "diminished capacity to deliberate and choose his behavior."

October 22, 1997   Alan J. Bannister
A. J. Bannister never denied killing Darrell Ruestman in 1982. However, he consistently maintained that the shooting was the result of a struggle between the two men and not the deliberate contract killing proposed by the prosecution. Mr. Bannister's court-appointed attorney conducted little or no investigation into the facts of the case. In addition, his counsel presented no defense during either the guilt or penalty phases of trial.

February 25, 1998   Reginald Powell
Reginald Powell was barely eighteen years old when he killed Freddie Miller and Lee Miller in St. Louis after they apparently had attacked him. Mr. Powell, who had a history of drug and alcohol abuse, had been found to have an IQ of 65 and had been previously placed in a public school special education program. Testing also indicated that Mr. Powell was severely impaired by an auditory selective attention disorder.

Mr. Powell's trial was hampered by the fact that his inexperienced trial attorney had an affair with him and did not represent his interests effectively. A competent lawyer would have recommended accepting the state's offer to plead guilty in return for a life sentence. Mr. Powell's attorney was devastated by his conviction. By not informing her client of his fundamental right to testify, Mr. Powell's attorney adversely affected the fairness of the trial. Even without hearing from Mr. Powell, the jury could not agree on a death sentence, so it was the trial judge alone who made the sentencing decision.

March 25, 1998   **Milton Griffin El**
Milton Griffin El was convicted of the killings of Loretta Trotter and Jerome Redden in 1986 during an apartment robbery that involved five men. The jury that convicted Griffin El sentenced him to life imprisonment for the murder of Ms. Trotter, but could not decide on the penalty for the murder of Mr. Redden. The trial judge sentenced him to death for the murder of Mr. Redden. The codefendant, who was identified by all involved as the instigator of the crime and who also participated in the stabbing, received a life sentence.

April 22, 1998   **Glennon Paul Sweet**
Glen Sweet was convicted of killing highway patrol trooper Russell Harper in 1987 outside of Springfield. Serious questions remain concerning the police investigation practices used in the case. Mr. Sweet's trial attorney failed to develop a variety of leads to create reasonable doubt in the jurors.

January 13, 1999   **Kelvin Malone**
Kelvin Malone was convicted of the 1981 fatal shooting of William Parr, a St. Louis cabdriver. Mr. Malone's trial lawyer did not seriously work on his case until about two weeks prior to the jury trial. He presented no evidence during the trial's guilt phase. Some of his mistakes include: not calling material witnesses from the scene who would have cast doubt on the prosecution's case; a total failure to prepare and address the sudden and unfair in-court identification of Mr. Malone as being a man near Mr. Parr's cab; overlooking the inconclusiveness of ballistic reports that allegedly connected Mr. Malone with Mr. Parr's death; and the omission of presenting true mitigating evidence during Mr. Malone's penalty phase. Mr. Malone passed a polygraph indicating he truthfully stated he did not kill the victim.

February 24, 1999   **James Rodden**
James Rodden was convicted of the 1983 murders of his roommate, Joe Bob Arnold, and Lynn Cherry Trunnell, a woman he had just met in a tavern. In most cases involving multiple crimes that occurred in the same episode, the prosecution joins all of the crimes together for one trial because the proof of each crime is based upon the same evidence. In this case, the prosecution severed the two murders for two separate trials. The arbitrary nature of the death penalty is shown in that both juries, which heard the same evidence, convicted Mr. Rodden of capital murder. Yet one jury recommended life without parole and the other recommended death. The only differences between the two trials were that Mr. Rodden only testified about self-defense in the trial in which he received the life without parole sentence, and the

defense attorney did not call any mitigating witnesses in the second trial.

March 10, 1999   **Roy Roberts**
Roy Roberts was sentenced to death for allegedly holding a prison guard, Thomas Jackson, while two other prisoners stabbed him to death during a riot in 1983 at the Moberly Training Center for Men. Serious questions remain whether Mr. Roberts had any part in the killing. A Department of Corrections (DOC) investigation of the riot, which included interviews of many guards and prisoners, did not mention Mr. Roberts. Soon after the stabbing, guards confiscated their bloody clothes from Mr. Driscoll and Mr. Carr. No blood was found on Mr. Roberts's clothes. A few weeks after the DOC report, one guard, Mr. Halley, recalled seeing Mr. Roberts holding Mr. Jackson during the riot. Mr. Roberts was convicted primarily on the testimony of Mr. Halley and two other guards, one of whom had to be hypnotized before he could recall seeing Mr. Roberts holding the guard. Several prisoners and the guard he admittedly fought during the riot corroborated his testimony. A few days before being executed, Mr. Roberts also passed a polygraph test in which he maintained his innocence.

April 14, 1999   **Roy Ramsey**
Mr. Ramsey received the death sentence, while his brother Billy got a twenty-five-year sentence in exchange for testifying against Roy in the robbery/murders of Garnett and Betty Ledford in Grandview in 1988. The prosecutor made inflammatory closing statements, calling Roy "Rambo" fourteen times. Billy, who is the likely killer, was eligible for parole in 2000.

April 28, 1999   **Ralph Davis**
Ralph Davis received a death sentence for the 1985 murder of his wife, Susan, whose body was never found. Mr. Davis was initially charged with second degree murder, a noncapital offense under Missouri law for which the maximum punishment is life with eligibility for parole after fifteen years. Mr. Davis's court-appointed attorney knew that the prosecutor intended to upgrade the charge to first degree murder and seek the death penalty if the case was not disposed of as scheduled. Knowing this fact, and without consulting Mr. Davis, he nevertheless sought a continuance. Ironically, at the hearing, Mr. Davis opposed a continuance.

May 26, 1999   **Jessie Lee Wise**
Jessie Lee Wise was given the death sentence for the 1988 murder of Geraldine McDonald. At the same time he was representing Mr. Wise, the lead attorney was running for prosecutor. Mr. Wise felt his lawyer was disregarding his input and suggestions. The trial lawyers filed

a motion to have Mr. Wise declared incompetent to stand trial without his permission. As a result, Mr. Wise requested to act as his own attorney at trial and was permitted to do so. Then the judge refused to permit Mr. Wise to present available evidence suggesting another theory of the homicide.

Only after his trial did the prosecutor's office "inadvertently discover" videotapes of key evidence. Mr. Wise did accept help from other lawyers at the penalty phase, but the judge would not give counsel even one day to prepare for the penalty hearing. The federal courts violated the Antiterrorism and Effective Death Penalty Act of 1996 requiring them to appoint at least one attorney with three years of felony appeal experience to represent him in his habeas corpus appeal. The federal courts retroactively applied the statute to limit the issues he could appeal.

June 16, 1999   **Bruce Kilgore**
Both Bruce Kilgore and his codefendant, Willie Luckett, were convicted in separate trials of the stabbing death of Marilyn Wilkins in 1986. Only Mr. Luckett had motive to kill the victim. On the day before the murder, Mr. Luckett's employers fired him because the victim reported that he was stealing food from the restaurant where they worked together. The guilt phase jury instructions identified Mr. Luckett as the person who stabbed the victim. During the penalty phase, the state's theory changed when Mr. Luckett's girlfriend shocked everyone in the courtroom and declared for the first time that Mr. Kilgore admitted stabbing the victim. Previously, Mr. Luckett's girlfriend had given statements to the police and other authorities, but it was only when she testified before Mr. Kilgore's jury that she stated Mr. Kilgore told her he had killed the victim. Just prior to her testimony, Mr. Luckett's girlfriend received probation for her role in the victim's death. Only Mr. Kilgore received the death penalty despite his credible claim that it was Mr. Luckett who actually killed the victim.

June 30, 1999   **Robert Walls**
There were two other codefendants in this case who were also convicted for the 1985 murder of Fred Harmon in his home in St. Louis. Like Robert Walls, Terry Wilson and Tommy Thomas had also walked away from the halfway house, had prior records, and participated in the murder. Yet only Mr. Walls received the death sentence for the crime. Mr. Walls received ineffective assistance of counsel, and more important, the prosecutor withheld exculpatory evidence from the defense. The other defendants received life and life without parole sentences. Mr. Wilson had a parole hearing date in 2000.

September 1, 1999   **David Leisure**

There were two other codefendants convicted for the 1980 car bombing that killed James Michaels. Paul Leisure and Anthony Leisure, cousins of David, who planned the bombing, were also convicted in separate trials, yet neither received the death penalty. Instead, each was sentenced to life imprisonment without possibility of parole for fifty years. The federal presentence investigation report ranked the cousins as first and second in culpability. It ranked David third. Fred Prater, the admitted maker of the bomb, received no prison sentence in exchange for being a chief prosecutorial witness.

David Leisure was represented by a collections attorney who used a law student as his messenger to and from David and whose thinking he relied on for strategy.

February 10, 2000   **Darrell Mease**

Mr. Mease was convicted of one count of first degree murder and three counts of armed criminal action for the killing of Lloyd Lawrence, his wife, and their nineteen-year-old paraplegic grandson. On appeal Mr. Mease claimed the admission of photographs and a videotape of the victims, improper argument by the prosecutor, and ineffective assistance of counsel resulted in an unconstitutional sentence of death. His sentence was commuted by Governor Carnahan to life without parole after a personal petition by Pope John Paul II in St. Louis.

March 22, 2000   **James Hampton**

James Hampton had been incarcerated most of his life and had attempted suicide on more than one occasion. In 1992 Mr. Hampton killed Frances Keaton in rural Callaway County and fled to New Jersey. In the process of being arrested there for another homicide, Mr. Hampton attempted suicide by shooting himself in the head. Consequently, a significant portion of his left frontal lobe was removed. As a result, he suffered from seizures and memory loss. Evaluation by a neurologist revealed the frontal lobe injury affected his judgment and resulted in severe paranoia that rose to the level of delusion. Mr. Hampton refused to continue the appeals that were available to him and expressed a wish to be executed.

June 28, 2000   **Bert Hunter**

Bert Hunter was convicted of the 1988 murders of Mildred Hodges and her son Richard in Jefferson City. Although Mr. Hunter originally pled guilty and asked to be given a death sentence without assistance of counsel, he did so at a time when he was depressed to the point of being suicidal. While waiting for trial, he tried to kill himself and was placed on suicide watch. At the time of his plea, the court noted inconsistencies in his statements and the autopsy report but accepted the guilty plea because that was Mr. Hunter's "desire" and "wish." The court also questioned Mr. Hunter's mental competency and ordered an evaluation. Within a few months before he was sentenced, Mr. Hunter asked the court to set aside his guilty plea because it was made under duress. All the doctors who examined him concluded he was self-destructive at the time of his plea. The trial judge refused to set aside the guilty plea and instead sentenced him to death. As a result, Mr. Hunter was the first person executed in Missouri since 1976 who did not have a jury trial or the assistance of a lawyer. Mr. Hunter gave up his appeals and is considered a "volunteer."

August 30, 2000   **Gary Roll**
Gary Roll never denied his part in the killings in 1992 of Randy Scheper, an alleged drug dealer, his mother, Sherry, and brother, Curtis. His trial counsel conducted no pretrial investigation and urged his client to waive his right to be tried before a jury and plead guilty, with false assurances he would receive a life sentence. It was clear his attorney was not ready for trial when he did not ask questions on voir dire, did not make an opening statement, and did not cross-examine the state's first witness. Counsel did not seek any form of mental evaluation and failed to present evidence to the judge that showed that Mr. Roll's drug addiction stemmed from a botched oral surgery by military doctors in 1974. It was while under the influence of alcohol, marijuana, and LSD that Mr. Roll, who had no prior history of crime, committed the killings.

September 13, 2000 **George Harris**
George Harris was given a death sentence for killing Stanley Willoughby in the living room of a drug house in 1989. Due largely to the incompetence of his trial counsel, Mr. Harris's story that he lawfully acted in self-defense against a violent man who was physically threatening him was never effectively told or properly presented to a jury.

November 15, 2000 **James Chambers**
James Chambers was convicted of killing Jerry Oestricker on May 29, 1982, outside a lounge in Arnold after an argument in the bar. Both men had been drinking. The crime lacked the cool deliberation and premeditation needed for a capital sentence.

NOTES

PREFACE

1. The governors of Missouri have all been male.
2. In some circumstances, the attorney did not file a petition. In such instances, the petition was filed by a coalition of religious leaders in Missouri is used.

CHAPTER ONE: INTRODUCTION

1. Submitted by John Landwehr, attorney for applicants (Michele Coleman, Jefferson City, Missouri; Peter DeSimone, executive director of Missouri Association for Social Welfare; Bishop W. T. Handy Jr., Missouri Area United Methodist Church; Bishop William Jones, Episcopal Diocese of Missouri; Most Reverend John Leibrecht, bishop of the Catholic Diocese of Springfield–Cape Girardeau; Most Reverend John L. May, archbishop of the Catholic Diocese of St. Louis; Most Reverend Michael F. McAuliffe, bishop of the Catholic Diocese of Jefferson City; Elder Roy Schaefer, Reorganized Church of Latter Day Saints; Most Reverend John J. Sullivan, bishop of the Catholic Diocese of Kansas City–St. Joseph; Reverend James Tomlinson, Church of the Brethren; Right Reverend Arthur Vogel, bishop of the Episcopal Diocese of West Missouri; Dr. John L. Williams, Presbyterian Synods of Mid-America).
2. In 1998, Karla Faye Tucker was executed in Texas despite vigorous protest by Reverend Pat Robertson, leader of a major conservative evangelical religious group. "Any justice system that is worthy of the name must have room for mercy. Executing Tucker is more an act of vengeance than it is appropriate justice." (Robertson quoted in *Christianity Today*, 1998.) Her repentance and conversion to being a "born-again Christian" was a genuine spiritual change, but her "rehabilitation" could not stop her execution.
3. *State v. Duren*, 547 S.W.2d 476 (Mo. 1977) (en banc).
4. "Postconviction remedies provide relief for constitutional, jurisdictional, and fundamental errors. Under the Uniform Post-Conviction Procedure Act, 1982, an inmate may obtain relief for the following reasons: 1. either the conviction obtained or the sentence imposed was based on an unconstitutional statute; 2. the conviction obtained was based on conduct that is constitutionally protected; 3. the court lacked jurisdiction over the inmate or the subject matter; 4. the sentence was not authorized by law; 5. evidence not previously heard requires vacation of the conviction or the sentence in the interest of justice; 6. there is a significant change in substantive or procedural law that, in the interest of justice,

should be applied retrospectively; 7. the inmate's custody was unlawful" (McGill, 1990: 219).

5. Referring to the (1985–1993) Ashcroft administration in Bobby Shaw's clemency petition, 1993: 13.

CHAPTER TWO: THE POLICE INVESTIGATION

1. Submitted by D. Korey Johnson, attorney at law.
2. Only 13 percent of all murders in 1998 were perpetrated by persons classified as strangers (Sourcebook, 1999).
3. Marta H. Hilney and Charles Maas, attorneys for petitioner. See also *State v. Reese*, 798 S.W.2d 69 (Mo. banc 1990); *Reese v. Delo*, 94 F.3d 1177 (8th Cir. 1996).
4. Kent E. Gipson, counsel for applicant. See also *State v. Griffin*, 662 S.W.2d 854 (Mo. banc 1983); 469 U.S. 873 (1984); *Griffin v. State*, 748 S.W.2d 756 (Mo. App. 1988); *Griffin v. Delo*, 946 F.2d 1356 (8th Cir. 1991); *Griffin v. Delo*, 961 F.2d 793 (8th Cir. 1992); *Griffin v. Delo*, 33 F.3d 895 (8th Cir. 1994); *Griffin v. Delo*, 515 U.S. 1154 (1995).
5. Based upon Mr. Caldwell's testimony, several men are serving sentences of life without parole in the federal penitentiary. Recently, the St. Louis prosecutors have filed state capital murder charges against many of the Moorish Temple defendants and have indicated that they will seek the death penalty against each of them for drug-related murders committed during the 1980s. To attempt to obtain death sentences against these individuals, the prosecution intends to use Kerry Caldwell as a prosecution witness in their upcoming state court trials. If any of the Moorish Temple defendants are sentenced to death and later come before the federal courts for judicial review, will those very same courts overturn their death sentence because Mr. Caldwell lacks credibility?

CHAPTER THREE: THE PROSECUTOR'S MISCONDUCT

1. Kent Gipson, attorney for Walter J. Blair.
2. Cedric D. Brown, counsel for petitioner. See also *State v. Foster*, 700 S.W.2d 440 (Mo. banc 1985); *Foster v. State*, 748 S.W.2d 903 (Mo. App. 1988); *Foster v. Delo*, 11 F.3d 1451 (8th Cir. 1993).
3. A 27.26 hearing is an opportunity to present arguments that the felony sentence is unlawful and make an appointment of counsel request. This hearing was repealed effective January 1, 1988.
4. Michael J. Gorla and Timothy K. Kellett, attorneys for petitioner. See *State v. O'Neal*, 718 S.W.2d 498 (Mo. banc 1986).
5. Louis C. DeFeo, attorney for applicants (Joyce Armstrong, Eastern Missouri ACLU, St. Louis; Benedictine Sisters, Our Lady of Peace Community, Columbia, Missouri; Right Reverend John Buchanan, bishop of the Episcopal Diocese of West Missouri; Marjorie Byler, Amnesty International–USA, Midwest Region; Michele Coleman, Jefferson City, Missouri; Reverend Norm Dake, Church in Society Commission, Missouri-Kansas Synod, Evangelical Lutheran Church in America; Peter DeSimone, Mis-

souri Association for Social Welfare; Fellowship of Reconciliation, Columbia, Missouri; Bishop W. T. Handy Jr., Missouri Area United Methodist Church; the Right Reverend William A. Jones Jr., Episcopal Diocese of Missouri; Most Reverend John Leibrecht, bishop of the Catholic Diocese of Springfield–Cape Girardeau; Most Reverend John L. May, archbishop of the Catholic Diocese of St. Louis; Most Reverend Michael F. McAuliffe, bishop of the Catholic Diocese of Jefferson City; Bill Ramsey, American Friends Service Committee, St. Louis; Elder Roy Schaefer; Most Reverend John J. Sullivan, bishop of the Catholic Diocese of Kansas City–St. Joseph; Right Reverend Arthur Vogel, bishop of the Episcopal Diocese of West Missouri; Dr. John L. Williams, Presbyterian Synods of Mid-America). See *State v. Byrd*, 723 S.W.2d 37.

6. Scholars point out that there are more subtle forms of racism that are not considered in this discussion, having to do with the decision to charge the defendant with capital murder. Sorenson and Wallace (1993) have offered an analysis of all stages of litigation in Missouri death penalty cases and conclude that racial disparity shows up primarily in the prosecutor's decision to charge the defendant.

CHAPTER FOUR: THE DEFENSE ATTORNEY

1. Bruce Livingston and Gino Battisti, attorneys for appellant. See *Powell v. Bowersox*, 895 F. Supp. 1298, 1302 (E.D. Mo. 1995); *State v. Powell*, 798 S.W.2d 709 (Mo. banc 1990); *Powell v. Bowersox*, 112 F.3d 966 (8th Cir. 1997).

2. This issue of competency was the only factor that seemed to succeed with the governor for commutation or stay. William Ted Boliek received a stay for further hearings on competency, and in one case (Bobby Shaw), the death sentence was commuted. William Ted Boliek received a stay after filing a clemency petition in order to conduct competency hearings. Four persons on death row were given stays when the director of the Department of Corrections said she had cause to believe that they had a mental disease or defect, excluding fitness for execution (Chuck Mathenia, Elroy Preston, Marvin Jones, and Roosevelt Pollard). Steve Parkus is awaiting a competency hearing. They all remain on death row until their mental conditions change.

3. Elizabeth Unger and Cedric Brown, attorneys for counsel for petitioner. See *State v. Ralph Davis*, 814 S.W.2d 593 (Mo. banc 1991).

4. Michael Shipley, attorney for petitioner. See *Roll v. United States*, 548 F. Supp. 97 (E.D. Mo. 1982); *Roll v. Bowersox*, 177 F.3d 697 (1999).

5. Mark A. Thornhill and Gardiner B. Davis, attorneys for appellant. See *State v. Bolder*, 635 S.W.2d 673 (Mo. banc 1982), *cert. denied*, 459 U.S. 1137 (1983); *Bolder v. Armontrout*, 713 F. Supp. 1558 (W.D. Mo. 1989); *Bolder v. Armontrout*, 921 F.2d 1359 (8th Cir. 1990), *cert. denied*, 112 S. Ct. 154 (1991) (Lay, C. J., dissenting); *Bolder v. Armontrout*, 928 F.2d 806 (8th Cir. 1991) (Lay, C. J., specially dissenting from denial for petition of rehearing en banc with whom McMillian, J., concurs).

6. 713 F.2d at 1529.

7. 928 F.2d 806.

8. *State v. Bolder*, 635 S.W.2d 673, 691–92 (Mo. banc 1982), *cert. denied*, 459 U.S. 1137 (1983) (Seiler, J., dissenting, in which Bardget, J., concurs).

9. *Bolder v. Armontrout*, 713 F. Supp. 1558, 1567 (W.D. Mo. 1989); *Bolder v. Armontrout*, 921 F.2d 1359, 1370 (8th Cir. 1990), *cert. denied*, 112 S. Ct. 154 (1991) (Lay, C.J., dissenting); *Bolder v. Armontrout*, 928 F.2d 806 (8th Cir. 1991) (Lay, C.J., specially dissenting from denial for petition of rehearing en banc with whom McMillian, J., concurs).

10. Louis DeFeo Jr., attorney for applicants: Joyce Armstrong, Eastern Missouri ACLU; Benedictine Sisters, Our Lady of Peace Community; Right Reverend John Buchanan, as bishop of the Episcopal Diocese of West Missouri; Marjorie Byler, Amnesty International–USA, Midwest Region; Michele Coleman, Peter DeSimone, Missouri Association for Social Welfare; Fellowship of Reconciliation, Columbia, Missouri, chapter; Bishop W. T. Handy Jr., Missouri Area United Methodist Church; the Right Reverend William A. Jones Jr., Episcopal Diocese of Missouri; Most Reverend John Leibrecht, bishop of the Catholic Diocese of Springfield–Cape Girardeau; Most Reverend John L. May, archbishop of the Catholic Diocese of St. Louis; Most Reverend Michael F. McAuliffe, bishop of the Catholic Diocese of Jefferson City; Bill Ramsey, American Friends Service Committee, St. Louis; Elder Roy Schaefer, Reorganized Church of Latter Day Saints; Most Reverend John J. Sullivan, bishop of the Catholic Diocese of Kansas City–St. Joseph; Reverend James Tomlinson, Church of the Brethren; Dr. John L. Williams, Presbyterian Synods of Mid-America. See *State v. Laws*, 661 S.W.2d 526 (Mo. banc 1983).

11. See, for example, the research of Dr. David Niles, George Washington University, "Relationships between Combat Experiences, Post Traumatic Stress Disorder Symptoms and Alcohol Abuse among Active Duty Vietnam Veterans," *Dissertation Abstracts International* 49 7-B (1989): 2868.

12. This is clearly inconsistent with numerous U.S. Supreme Court cases going back to *Lockett v. Ohio*. Again, this is a testament to the current ineffectuality—despite judicial assertions to the contrary—of the clemency process.

13. Elena Franco, Susan Hunt, Sean O'Brien, attorneys for appellant. See *State v. Zeitvogel*, 707 S.W. 2d 365 (Mo. banc 1986).

14. Lew Kollias, John Tucci, and Antonio Manansala, attorneys for appellant. See *Malone v. State*, 747 S.W.2d 695 (Mo. App., E.D. 1988); *Malone v. State*, 798 S.W.2d 149 (Mo. banc 1990); *Malone v. Vasquez*, 138 F.3d 711 (8th Cir. 1998).

15. See David K. Colapinto, Stephen Cohn, and Michael Cohn, "Protecting the 'Accused' and the Public from Forensic Fraud: Misconduct in the FBI Crime Lab," *Guild Practitioner* 55 (winter 1998): 32–36.

16. *Sanders v. State*, 807 S.W.2d 493 (Mo. banc 1991).

17. *Johnson v. Mississippi*, 108 S. Ct. 1981 (1988).

18. Robert Sidebottom was executed without having a lawyer to handle his appeals; Jessie Wise, in part, acted as his own lawyer; Bert Hunter pled guilty without a trial and without a lawyer to counsel him; and Gary Roll waived his right to a jury in both the trial and sentencing.

19. See Moore, 1996 (note 32 and at 1634) for a list of horrors.

20. Adequate funding is the other crucial aspect of providing effective representation to death penalty defendants. It is very difficult to learn what the state will pay a qualified defense attorney to handle a capital trial. I have been told that Missouri offered one attorney just three thousand

dollars to take a case. A privately hired attorney would require one hundred thousand dollars up front just to begin work on a capital case.

CHAPTER FIVE: THE TRIAL JUDGE

1. Richard Sindel and Jerilyn Lipe, counsel for Ralph Feltrop.
2. The quality of the judiciary is a concern. Although merit plans, screening committees, and popular elections are designed to ensure a competent judiciary, it has often been charged that many judicial appointments are made to pay off political debts or to reward cronies and loyal friends. Also not uncommon are charges that those desiring to be nominated for judgeships are required to make significant political contributions (Senna and Siegel, 1998: 265).
3. Leo Griffard and Cheryl Rafert, counsel for Andrew Six. See also *U.S v. Six*, 857 F.2d 458 (8th Cir. 1988); *State v. Six*, 805 S.W.2d 159 (Mo. banc), *cert. denied*, 502 U.S. 871 (1991).

CHAPTER SIX: APPELLATE COURTS

1. Joseph P. Teasdale and John William Simon, attorneys for applicant. See *State v. Leisure*, 749 S.W.2d 366 (Mo. banc 1988) (direct appeal); *Leisure v. State*, 828 S.W.2d 872 (Mo. banc 1992) (Rule 29.15); *Leisure v. Bowersox*, 990 F. Supp. 769 (E.D. Mo. 1998); 119 S. Ct. 1939 (1999).
2. Until the recent change in the habeas corpus law, all the appeals available to death penalty prisoners are theoretically the same as the appeals for ordinary criminal defendants, with the exception that the first appeal is a direct mandatory appeal to the state supreme court
3. R.S.Mo. 565.014.3(3). The state supreme court must also determine (1) whether the sentence of death was "imposed under the influence of passion, prejudice, or any other arbitrary factor, and (2) whether the evidence supports the aggravating circumstance(s) found." (R.S.Mo. 565.014.3(1–2).
4. While a court of appeals judge, Warren Burger believed that "[d]efense counsel generally are clogging the system by an excess of zeal" (Scheingold, 1984: 151).
5. In Frederick Lashley's case, the clemency petition claimed that "the Missouri Supreme Court has failed to follow Missouri law. It refused to consider similar cases in reviewing petitioner's appeal" (1993: 23).
6. Clearly, reasonable persons will disagree, but dissenting opinions in appellate reviews would indicate that the governor has a serious matter to decide. Such dissent could also serve to bolster the commutation decision, should the governor so choose. An excerpt gives a flavor of the tone of disagreement:

> I am startled by the State's argument that defendant was required to disclose the location of the body, lest he be labeled "cynical" and "remorseless" and thus condemned to death. This is an incredible theory, fraught with danger. Common sense teaches that to require the defendant to locate a body during the penalty phase is to trample the right of defendant to maintain his inno-

cence. There is diminished use for appeals, post-conviction proceedings, or even habeas corpus if the defendant must somehow admit his guilt in pointing to the body. This concept bootstraps the defendant into an untenable position and it offends the constitution. Blackmar, J., dissenting from Missouri Supreme Court's affirmation of conviction and sentence for Ralph Davis (814 S.W.2d 593, Mo. banc 1991).

7. Kent Gipson and George Winger, attorneys for applicant. See also *State v. Chambers*, 714 S.W.2d 527 (Mo. banc 1986); *State v. Chambers*, 671 S.W.2d 781 (Mo. banc 1984); *Chambers v. Armontrout*, 907 F.2d 825 (8th Cir. en banc 1990), *cert. denied*, 498 U.S. 950 (1990); *State v. Chambers*, 891 S.W.2d 93 (Mo. banc 1994); *Chambers v. Bowersox*, 157 F.3d 560 (8th Cir. 1998).

8. 714 S.W.2d at 534.

9. *Biondi v. State*, 699 F.2d 1062.

10. *State v. McCoy*, 971 S.W.2d 861.

11. *State v. Hill*, 866 S.W.2d 160.

12. R.S.Mo. 565.035.3 (1984).

13. *Chambers v. Bowersox*, 157 F.3d at 570.

14. *State v. Chambers*, 714 S.W.2d at 534.

15. Douglas Laird, attorney for defendant. See also *Sloan v. Delo*, 54 F.3d at 1371 (8th Cir. 1995).

16. R.S.Mo. 565.030.4 (1986).

17. 54 F.3d at 1385. See *Stringer v. Black*, 503 U.S. 22 (1992).

18. *State v. Bolder*, 65 S.W.2d 673 (Mo. 1982); *State v. Amrine*, 741 S.W.2d 665 (Mo. 1987); *State v. Murray*, 744 S.W.2d 762 (Mo. 1988).

19. See *State v. Petary*, 790 S.W.2d 243, 245 (Mo. 1990); *State v. Mease*, 842 S.W.2d 98, 112–13 (Mo. 1992); *State v. Whitfield*, 837 S.W.2d 503, 514 (Mo. 1992); *State v. Debler*, 856 S.W.2d 641, 646 (Mo. 1993); *State v. Ramsey*, 864 S.W.2d 320 (1993).

20. Gerald A. Sims Jr. and Kent E. Gipson, attorneys for Milton Griffin El. See also *State v. Griffin*, 756 S.W.2d 475 (Mo. banc); *Griffin v. State*, 794 S.W.2d 659 (Mo. banc 1990).

21. Milton changed his name to Milton Griffin El after being incarcerated for this offense.

22. *Griffin v. State*, 794 S.W.2d 659, 666 (Mo. banc 1990).

23. See *Martin v. Bissonette*, 118 F.3d 871 (1st Cir. 1997); *United States v. Perez*, 1197 WL 691075 (2d Cir. November 7, 1997); *United States v. Skandier*, 125 F.3d 178 (3d Cir. 1997); *Green v. Johnson*, 116 F.3d 1115 (5th Cir. 1997); *Arredondo v. United States*, 120 F.3d 275 (6th Cir. 1997); *Young Soo Koo v. McBride*, 124 F.3d 869 (7th Cir. 1997); *Naddi v. Hill*, 106 F.3d 275 (9th Cir. 1997); *United States v. Kunzman*, 125 F.3d 1363 (10th Cir. 1997); *Hardwick v. Singletary*, 122 F.3d 935, modified on rehearing en banc, 126 F.3d 1312 (11th Cir. 1997).

24. *Muniz v. Johnson*, 114 F.3d 43 (5th Cir. 1997); *Lyons v. Ohio Adult Parole Authority*, 105 F.3d 1063 (6th Cir. 1997); *Porter v. Gramley*, 112 F.3d 1308 (7th Cir. 1997); *United States v. Asrar*, 108 F.3d 217 (9th Cir. 1997); *Hunter v. United States*, 101 F.3d 1565 (11th Cir. 1996) (en banc).

25. Since Milton Griffin El's case, the U.S. Supreme Court has decided that the retroactive application of the AEDPA is constitutional in *Slack v. McDaniel*, 120 S. Ct. 1595 (2000).

26. It is ironic that this law would be applied retroactively when other court

decisions (*Teague v. Lane*, 489 U.S. 288 [1989]) have not been, to the detriment of several death row prisoners.

27. *Gregg v. Georgia*, 428 U.S. 153 (1976); *Woodson v. North Carolina*, 428 U.S. 280 at 306 (1976). See Korengold, Noteboom, and Gurwitch, 1996; Gross, 1996.
28. See Larry Griffin's petition at 40.
29. 28 U.S.C. sec. 2254d; *Marshall v. Lonberger*, 459 U.S. 422 (1983); *Sumner v. Mata*, 449 U.S. 539 (1981).
30. *Rose v. Lundy*, 455 U.S. 509 (1982).
31. *Smith v. Murray*, 477 U.S. 527 (1986).
32. *Teague v. Lane*, 489 U.S. 288 (1989).
33. Uelmen (1997) recognizes that the rates of affirming death sentences are increasing over time. This is happening in Missouri as well. Since reinstatement, only 45 of the 162 Missouri death penalty sentences were reversed (28 percent), and six (17 percent) of those reversals were ultimately reinstated. Of those executed, only one had his original sentence reversed.

CHAPTER SEVEN: GOVERNORS' DECISIONS: FAIL SAFE OR FICTION?

1. Bruce D. Livingston and Leonard Frankel, attorneys for the petitioner.
2. Three states (Idaho, Missouri, Nebraska) during the years with data available had no executions but did have commutations. Tennessee was the only state with more commutations than executions for the study period (1960–1962). With information taken mostly from the study by Abramowitz and Paget, Acker and Lanier (2000: 212–15) report commutation rates in capital cases in fifteen states before 1972, which range from 36 executions to 1 commutation in Arizona between 1930 and 1963 to 358 executions to 235 commutations in North Carolina between 1903 and 1963 (for a low ratio of 3 to 2). Vandiver (1993) reports that in Florida between 1924 and 1966, Florida granted clemency to 59 (23.1 percent) while executing 196 (76.9 percent).
3. While governor, John Ashcroft "explained that he would not impose his opinion without information that the justice system has failed to operate" (Korengold, Noteboom, and Gurwitch, 1996: 366).
4. This action so angered African-American voters and others that it probably cost him the election. Because his portrayal of Judge White as "soft on crime" was unreasonable, particularly when compared with other judges on the Missouri bench that Mr. Ashcroft had appointed when he was governor, the death penalty was less of an issue than the senator's alleged racism.
5. The current practice is for the governor's legal counsel to schedule a private meeting with the lawyers for the condemned. Sometimes those lawyers bring along other lawyers who had worked on earlier stages of the case. Pointing toward the reality of the political considerations of the death penalty, one legal adviser suggested to the lawyer for the prisoner that if he can make the governor look good, then the commutation might happen!

6. James P. Tierney, Jonathan R. Haden, Brian C. Fries, David T. M. Powell, attorneys for the condemned (see first case study in chapter 6).
7. In summary, the major issues are: 62 percent raise a claim of innocence, 72 percent have new information to be presented, 75 percent claim poor defense counsel, 43 percent claim prosecutorial misconduct, and 59 percent claim the appellate courts erred in their interpretation of the law or in applying procedures; 45 percent of the clemency petitions indicated dissent by appellate judges with some decision; and 57 percent of death row prisoners had a psychological problem that would mitigate their first degree conviction.
8. While Governor Carnahan was out of the country, then–Lieutenant Governor Roger Wilson permitted two executions to proceed.
9. Governor Ashcroft gave Bobby Shaw a stay, then Governor Carnahan commuted his sentence to life without parole.
10. Gerald Smith, Richard Oxford, David Leisure, James Hampton (Smith and Hampton were "volunteers"). Overall, thirteen clemency petitions (26 percent) requested a stay and appointment of a board of inquiry.
11. Sean O'Brien is unique among criminal defense attorneys. When he was lead attorney on a capital case, he was successful 100 percent of the time in death penalty clemency petitions. Petitioners have their best chance of winning a stay if they have Sean O'Brien as their attorney or a one in three chance of succeeding if the claim is mental incompetency.
12. The board of inquiry was never appointed, thereby leaving the prisoner in a correctional limbo.
13. It has been suggested that Governor Carnahan's office encouraged the director of the Department of Corrections to request competency hearings when appropriate, which served to remove several death row prisoners from the danger of execution. Such a policy would be an intervention endorsed by statute, which distinguishes the Carnahan administration from other Missouri governors. However, it does not impact how the governor deals with those actually in need of clemency.

CHAPTER EIGHT: THE CLEMENCY ALTERNATIVE: JUSTICE DENIED

1. Burton Shostak, John Tucci, Antonio Manansala, attorneys for Bruce Kilgore.
2. Kent Gipson, attorney for Walter Blair. See also *State v. Blair*, 638 S.W.2d 739 (Mo. 1982); *Blair v. Armontrout*, 643 F. Supp. 785 (W.D. Mo. 1986); *Blair v. Armontrout*, 916 F.2d 1310 (8th Cir. 1990); *Blair v. Armontrout*, 976 F.2d 1130 (8th Cir. 1992).
3. An additional consideration deals with how to appoint the counsel. When the state takes the low bidder, the likely result will be shortcuts and ineffective work. This practice should be avoided at all costs. Competitive and reasonable costs are necessary to support effective defense work.

APPENDIX 2: INVENTORY OF CASES

1. This appendix draws heavily from a report published in January 2001, "Miscarriages of Justice," written with Stephana Landwehr, Rita Linhardt, Margaret Phillips, and Jeff Stack.

2. On May 25, 1993, the Missouri Supreme Court issued a death warrant and set an execution date for June 4, 1993, just ten days later. On June 2, Governor Carnahan issued a sixty-day stay of execution to give time for a review of his application for clemency. When the Missouri Supreme Court rescheduled the execution for August 18, the director of the Department of Corrections set a competency hearing necessitating an open-ended stay by the governor. The governor did not have to make a decision on the clemency issues.

GLOSSARY

Primary source is *Black's Law Dictionary* (1979).

Accessorial Liability   Criminal responsibility of one who acts with another before, during, or after the perpetration of a crime.

Aggravating Circumstances   Generally, any circumstance that is part of the commission of a crime which adds to its injurious consequences, but which is above and beyond the essential elements of the crime itself. The Missouri death penalty statute identifies seventeen aggravating circumstances, of which at least one must be found beyond a reasonable doubt before the jury can consider the death penalty.

Appellant   The one who is making the appeal.

Arraignment   Procedure whereby the accused is brought before the court to plead to the criminal charge in the indictment. The charge is read and the plea is taken.

Bifurcated Trial   If guilt is determined in a capital death case (guilt phase), then the appropriate penalty is decided, usually by the same jury, after another trial (penalty phase). This permits defendants who do not wish to testify about their guilt or innocence to be able to say why they should not be killed.

Certificate of Appealability   Replaces the old certificate of probable cause. This is a document that permits the appellant to proceed with the appeal of habeas corpus. The certificate of appealability identifies the specific issues on which the appellant may proceed.

Certiorari   A *writ of certiorari* is an order issued by an appellate court to a lower court when the higher court has discretion on whether to hear an appeal. If the writ is denied, the court refuses to hear the appeal and, in effect, the judgment below stands unchanged. If the writ is granted, then it has the effect of ordering the lower court to produce a certified record of a particular case so that the higher court may inspect the proceedings to ascertain whether there were any irregularities.

Court-Appointed Attorney   In cases where the defendant is not able to afford hiring a private attorney, the state is required to appoint an attorney to handle the defense. Although the U.S. Supreme Court has ruled that the right to an appointed attorney is only for the trial and the first appeal, Missouri now provides legal assistance for all appeals. This was not always the case, however. Additionally, the qualifications for eligibility to be appointed counsel do not require specific experience with death penalty appeals. Also, the fees for services remain below those of the private bar.

Custodial Interrogations   Questioning initiated by police officers after person has been taken into custody or otherwise deprived of freedom in any significant way; custody can occur without formality of arrest and in areas other than in police station.

Directed Verdict In a case in which the party with the burden of proof has failed to present a prima facie case for jury consideration, the trial judge may order the entry of a verdict without allowing the jury to consider it, because, as a matter of law, there can be only one such verdict.

Discovery The pretrial devices that can be used by one party to obtain facts and information about the case from the other party in order to assist the party's preparation for trial.

En Banc Refers to a session where the entire membership of the court will participate in the decision rather than the regular quorum.

Exculpatory Evidence Evidence that tends to justify, excuse, or clear the defendant from alleged guilt.

Exhausted To use up, deplete, wholly expend.

Habeas Corpus The primary function of the writ of habeas corpus is to release from unlawful imprisonment. The role of the writ is not to determine the prisoner's guilt or innocence, but whether the prisoner is restrained of his liberty by due process. A criminal defendant can petition for a writ of habeas only after having been convicted and having exhausted the state appellate remedies.

Habeas Corpus Ad Testificandum The writ, meaning "you have the body to testify," used to bring up a prisoner detained in a jail or prison to give evidence before the court.

Harmless Error Error that is not sufficient in nature or effect to warrant reversal, modification, or retrial.

Inculpatory In the law of evidence, going or tending to establish guilt.

Indigent Poor or poor person.

Information A written accusation made by a public prosecutor, without the intervention of a grand jury indictment.

Jurisprudence The philosophy of law.

Mental Capacity or Competence The ability to understand the nature and consequences of the act in which a person is engaged.

Miranda Rule Prior to any questioning initiated by police officers after a person is taken into custody, the person must be warned that: (1) he has a right to remain silent; (2) any statement he makes may be used as evidence against him; (3) he has a right to the presence of an attorney; (4) if he cannot afford an attorney, one will be appointed for him prior to any questioning if he so desires. Unless and until these warnings or a waiver of these rights are demonstrated at the trial, no evidence obtained in the questioning may be used against the accused.

Mitigating Circumstances Evidence that can be considered as extenuating or reducing the degree of moral culpability.

Movant One who makes the motion before a court.

Nolle Prosequi   A formal entry on the record by the prosecutor declaring that the case will not be prosecuted further.

Penal Interest   Relating to a penalty or punishment.

Peremptory Challenge   The right to challenge a juror without giving a reason for the challenge. In most jurisdictions each party has a specified number of such challenges and after using all of them is required to give a reason for any other challenges (this challenge is known as *challenge for cause*).

Plain Error   Those errors which are obvious, which affect the substantial rights of the accused, and which, if uncorrected, would be an affront to the integrity and reputation of judicial proceedings. Like fatal error, fundamental error, harmful error, reversible error, substantial error: such only as may reasonably be held to have worked substantial injury or prejudice to complaining party. Such errors generally give the party a right to new trial, as contrasted with "harmless" errors, which do not.

Plurality   An opinion of an appellate court in which more justices join than in any concurring opinion (though not a majority of the court) is a plurality opinion as distinguished from a majority opinion in which a larger number of the justices on the panel join than not.

Postconviction Relief Proceedings   Hearings and appeals following a defendant's conviction and sentence of death and direct appeal.

Presumption   Assumption lending probability toward belief.

Procedural Bar   Prevents the court from considering evidence that is not presented in the first appeal. Since the case of *Coleman v. Thompson* (1991), even where the failure to present evidence in the first state postconviction hearing is clearly due to incompetent appointed counsel, the prisoner is forever bound by the lawyer's mistakes.

Procedural Default   When a party fails to submit an appeal in a timely or proper (according to the rules of the court) fashion or fails to appeal an issue, that party is in default and a judgment by default may be entered by the court. In other words, when the appellant does not follow the formal steps in a judicial proceeding, the ability to correct the error(s) can be denied by the court.

Recusal   When a judge is disqualified (or disqualifies himself or herself) from hearing a lawsuit because of interest or prejudice.

Retribution   Something given or demanded in payment. It is punishment based on the theory which is based on the fact that every crime demands payment in the form of punishment.

Retroactivity   When a court decision creates a new rule, the question is whether the rule will also apply to cases that occurred before the rule was decided. The court's practice seems to be that unless specifically mentioned in the new rule, the application of the new rule to past cases will not apply.

Scintilla   A trace of evidence.

Sequestration   To separate or isolate jurors from contact with the public during the course of a sensational trial.

Subpoena   A command to appear at a certain time and place to give testimony upon a certain matter.

Successor Habeas Proceedings   Once a prisoner has filed a petition for a writ of habeas corpus, any additional habeas petitions are called "successor." The intent of the AEDPA was to eliminate successor habeas petitions.

Suppression Hearing   A pretrial proceeding in criminal cases in which a defendant seeks to prevent the introduction of evidence alleged to have been seized illegally.

Venireperson   Prospective juror, a member of a pool of jurors.

Verification   Confirmation of correctness by signature or oath of actual person.

Voir Dire   The preliminary examination that the court and lawyers may make of potential jurors, where competency, interest, and bias are questioned.

Waive   To abandon, throw away, renounce, repudiate, or surrender a claim, a privilege, a right, or the opportunity to take advantage of some defect, irregularity, or wrong voluntarily.

Writ   An order issued from a court requiring the performance of a specified act.

BIBLIOGRAPHY

Abramowitz, Elkan, and David Paget. 1964. "Executive Clemency in Capital Cases." *New York University Law Review* 39: 136–92.

Acker, James, and Charles Lanier. 1999. "Ready for the Defense? Legislative Provisions Governing the Appointment of Counsel in Capital Cases." *Criminal Law Bulletin* 35: 429–77.

———. 2000. "May God—or the Governor—Have Mercy: Executive Clemency and Executions in Modern Death-Penalty Systems." *Criminal Law Bulletin* 36: 200–237.

Acker, James, Robert Bohm, and Charles Lanier, eds. 1998. *America's Experiment with Capital Punishment*. Durham, N.C.: Carolina Academic Press.

Alter, Jonathan. 2000. "The Death Penalty on Trial." *Newsweek*, 12 June, 24–34.

American Bar Association. 1980. *Standards for Criminal Justice*. Boston, Mass.: Little, Brown.

———. 1989. *American Bar Association Guidelines for the Appointment and Performance of Counsel in Death Penalty Cases*. Washington, D.C.

American Bar Association and the Bureau of National Affairs. 1997. *ABA/BNA Lawyers' Manual on Professional Conduct*. Washington, D.C.

Ammons, Linda. 1994. "Discretionary Justice: A Legal and Policy Analysis of a Governor's Use of the Clemency Power in the Cases of Incarcerated Battered Women." *Journal of Law and Policy* 3: 1–79.

Amsterdam, Anthony. 1999. "Selling a Quick Fix for Boot Hill: The Myth of Justice Delayed in Death Cases." In *The Killing State*, edited by Austin Sarat. New York: Oxford University Press, 148–83.

Antiterrorism and Effective Death Penalty Act of 1996. Public Law 104-132 (S. 735); April 24, 1996. 110 Stat. 1214.

Argersinger v. Hamlin. 407 U.S. 25 (1972).

Armstrong, Ken, and Steve Mills. 2000. "Gatekeeper Court Keeps Gates Shut: Justices Prove Reluctant to Nullify Cases." *Chicago Tribune*, 12 June, news section 1.

Ashcroft, John. 2000. "It Is the People's Collective Self-Defense." *St. Louis Post-Dispatch*, 18 May.

Batson v. Kentucky. 106 S. Ct. 1712 (1986).

Becker, Christine. 1995. "Clemency for Killers? Pardoning Battered Women Who Strike Back." *Loyola of Los Angeles Law Review* 29: 297–342.

Bedau, Hugo. 1990. "The Decline of Executive Clemency in Capital Cases." *N.Y.U. Review of Law and Social Change* 18: 255–72.

———. 1993. "A Retributive Theory of the Pardoning Power?" *University of Richmond Law Review* 27: 185–200.

———, ed. 1997. *The Death Penalty in America: Current Controversies*. New York: Oxford University Press.

Belli, Melvin M. 1975. "The Story of Pardons." *Case and Comment* 80: 28–38.

Biddle v. Perovich, 274 U.S. 480 (1927).

Bilionis, Louis, and Richard Rosen. 1997. "Lawyers, Arbitrariness, and the Eighth Amendment." *Texas Law Review* 75: 1,301–71.

Black, Charles L. 1974. *Capital Punishment: The Inevitability of Caprice and Mistake*. New York: W. W. Norton.

Blackstone, William. 1974. *Commentaries on the Laws of England*. Chicago: University of Chicago Press.

Blaustein, Susan. 1997. "Habeas Corpus Has Been Undermined by the Supreme Court." In *The Death Penalty*, edited by P. Winters. San Diego: Greenhaven Press.

Blumberg, Abraham. 1979. *Criminal Justice: Issues and Ironies*. 2d ed. New York: New Viewpoints.

Bohm, Robert M. 1999. *Deathquest: An Introduction to the Theory and Practice of Capital Punishment in the United States*. Cincinnati, Ohio: Anderson Publishing.

Bowers, William, and Margaret Vandiver. 1991a. "New Yorkers Want an Alternative to the Death Penalty." Cited in *Public Opinion, Crime, and Criminal Justice*, by Julian Roberts and Loretta Stalans. Boulder, Colo.: Westview Press, 2000.

———. 1991b. "Nebraskans Want an Alternative to the Death Penalty." Cited in *Public Opinion, Crime, and Criminal Justice*, by Julian Roberts and Loretta Stalans. Boulder, Colo.: Westview Press, 2000.

Bowers, William, and G. Pierce. 1980. "Deterrence or Brutalization: What Is the Effect of Executions?" *Crime and Delinquency* 26: 453–84.

Brady v. Maryland, 373 U.S. 83 (1963).

Bright, Stephen. 1994. "Counsel for the Poor: The Death Sentence Not for the Worst Crime, But for the Worst Lawyer." *Yale Law Journal* 103: 1,935.

———. 1996. "The Death Penalty as the Answer to Crime: Costly, Counterproductive, and Corrupting." *Santa Clara Law Review* 36: 1,069–96.

———. 1998. "The Politics of Capital Punishment: The Sacrifice of Fairness for Executions." In *America's Experiment with Capital Punishment*, edited by James Acker, Robert Bohm, and Charles Lanier. Durham, N.C.: Carolina Academic Press.

———. 2000. "Elected Judges and the Death Penalty in Texas: Why Full Habeas Corpus Review by Independent Federal Judges Is Indispensable to Protecting Constitutional Rights." *Texas Law Review* 78: 1,805–37.

Bright, Stephen, and Patrick Keenan. 1995. "Judges and the Politics of Death: Deciding between the Bill of Rights and the Next Election in Capital Cases." *Boston University Law Review* 75: 759–835.

Brown, Edmund (Pat), with Dick Adler. 1989. *Public Justice, Private Mercy: A Governor's Education on Death Row*. New York: Weidenfeld and Nicolson.

Burnett, Cathleen. 1994. "Does the Death Penalty Deter Prison Homicide: A Case Study Approach." Paper presented at the annual meeting of the American Society of Criminology, Miami, Florida, November.

———. 1996. "A Different Kind of Death." *Christian Social Action* 9: 25–27.

———. 1998a. "Frivolous Claims by the Attorney General." *Social Justice* 25: 184–204.

———. 1998b. "The Oldest Woman on Death Row: Faye Copeland." Paper presented at the annual meeting of the American Society of Criminology, Washington, D.C., November.

———. 2000. "Petitions for Life: Executive Clemency in Missouri Death Penalty Cases." *Richmond Journal of Law and the Public Interest* 5: 1–28.

———. "Witnessing the Execution: Protocols of State-Sponsored Homicides." *Humanity and Society* (forthcoming).

Burnett, Cathleen, Stephana Landwehr, Rita Linhardt, Margaret Phillips, and Jeff Stack. 2001. "Miscarriages of Justice: Review of Missouri's Clemency Applications Supports a Moratorium on Executions." Report presented at a press conference, 16 January, in the Missouri state capitol.

Caldwell v. Mississippi, 472 U.S. 320 (1985).

Callins v. Collins, 510 U.S. 1141 (1994).

Carnahan, Mel. 2000. "Complete Confidence in Guilt of Those Executed." *St. Louis Post-Dispatch*, 12 May.

Casper, Juliet. 1995. "Postconviction Remedies." *Journal of Criminal Law and Criminology* 85: 838–939.

Center of Social Sciences and Public Policy Research (CSSPPR). 1999. *Telephone Survey of Missouri Residents' Opinions on the Death Penalty*. Springfield, Mo.: Southwest Missouri State University.

Christianity Today. 1998. "The Lesson of Karla Faye Tucker." 6 April, 15.

Cochran, J. K., M. B. Chamblin, and M. Seth. 1994. "Deterrence or Brutalization? An Impact Assessment of Oklahoma's Return to Capital Punishment." *Criminology* 32: 107–34.

Colapinto, David K., Stephen Cohn, and Michael Cohn. 1998. "Protecting the 'Accused' and the Public from Forensic Fraud: Misconduct in the FBI Crime Lab." *Guild Practitioner* 55: 32–36.

Coleman v. Thompson, 111 S. Ct. 2546 (1991).

Cook, Kimberly. 1998. *Divided Passions*. Boston: Northeastern University Press.

Cooper, Lee. 1997. Personal correspondence from president of the American Bar Association, 21 April.

Coyle, Marcia, Fred Strasser, and Marianne Lavelle. 1990. "Fatal Defense." *National Law Journal* 12 (June 11): 30.

Crank, John P., and Michael A. Caldero. 2000. *Police Ethics: The Corruption of Noble Cause*. Cincinnati, Ohio: Anderson Publishing.

Dantzker, Mark. 2000. *Understanding Today's Police*. 2d ed. Upper Saddle River, N.J.: Prentice-Hall.

Death Penalty Information Center (DPIC). 2001. "Facts about Clemency." www.deathpenaltyinfo.org/clemency.html.

Dieter, Richard. 1992. *Millions Misspent: What Politicians Don't Say about the High Costs of the Death Penalty*. Washington, D.C.: Death Penalty Information Center.

Dodge, Lowell. 1990. *Death Penalty Sentencing: Research Indicates Pattern of Racial Disparities*. Washington, D.C.: General Accounting Office.

Dzialo, Michael. 1986. "Death Row Today: A Ten-Year Wait to Die." New York: Amnesty International.

Ellsworth, Phoebe, and Samuel Gross. 1997. "Hardening of the Attitudes: Americans' Views on the Death Penalty." In *The Death Penalty in America: Current Controversies*, edited by Hugo Bedau. New York: Oxford University Press.

Engle v. Isaac, 456 U.S. 107 (1982).

Equal Justice USA. 2000. *Moratorium News!* Summer/Fall. Hyattsville, Md.: Quixote Center.

Espy, Watt, and J. O. Smykla. 1994. *Executions in the United States, 1608–1987: The Espy File* (codebook). Tuscaloosa, Ala.: J. O. Smykla (producer). Ann

Arbor, Mich.: Inter-University Consortium for Political and Social Research (distributor).

FBI. 2001. *Uniform Crime Reports*. Bureau of Justice Statistics, Washington, D.C.: U.S. Government Printing Office.

Finer, J. J. 1973. "Ineffective Assistance of Counsel." *Cornell Law Review* 58: 1,077–1,120.

Foley, Linda. 1987. "Florida After the Furman Decision: The Effect of Extralegal Factors on the Processing of Capital Offense Cases." *Behavioral Sciences and the Law* 5: 16–22.

Furman v. Georgia, 92 S. Ct. 2726 (1972).

Galliher, John F., Gregory Ray, and Brent Cook. 1992. "Abolition and Reinstatement of Capital Punishment During the Progressive Era and Early Twentieth Century." *Journal of Criminal Law and Criminology* 83: 538–76.

Green v. United States, 365 U.S. 301 (1961).

Gregg v. Georgia, 428 U.S. 153 (1976).

Gross, Samuel R. 1996. "The Risks of Death: Why Erroneous Convictions Are Common in Capital Cases." *Buffalo Law Review* 44: 469–500.

Hall, Donna. 1986. "Deterrent or Delusion?" *The Defender* (July/August): 25–30.

Hancock, Barry, and Paul Sharp, eds. 2000. *Criminal Justice in America*. Upper Saddle River, N.J.: Prentice-Hall.

Haney, Craig. 1998. "Mitigation and the Study of Lives: On the Roots of Violent Criminality and the Nature of Capital Justice." In *America's Experiment with Capital Punishment*, edited by James Acker, Robert Bohm, and Charles Lanier. Durham, N.C.: Carolina Academic Press.

Hanks, Gardner. 1997. *Against the Death Penalty: Christian and Secular Arguments Against Capital Punishment*. Scottsdale, Pa.: Herald Press.

Harris v. Nelson, 394 U.S. 286 (1969).

Harris, Leslie A. "Resolution of the House of Delegates, February 1997." American Bar Association Section of Individual Rights and Responsibilities: Section of Litigation.

Healy, Patrick. 1977. *National Prosecution Standards*. Chicago, Ill.: National District Attorneys Association.

Herrera v. Collins, 113 S. Ct. 853 (1993).

Holcomb, Jefferson. 2000. "The Use of Executive Clemency in Ohio." Ph.D. diss., Florida State University, School of Criminology and Criminal Justice.

Holten, Gary, and Lawson Lamar. 1991. *The Criminal Courts: Structures, Personnel, and Processes*. New York: McGraw Hill.

Huff, Ron, Arye Rattner, and Edward Sagarin. 2000. "Guilty Until Proved Innocent: Wrongful Conviction and Public Policy." In *Criminal Justice in America*, edited by B. Hancock and P. Sharp. Upper Saddle River, N.J.: Prentice-Hall, 218–29.

Janoff, Gerald. 1995. "State v. Jones: Louisiana Capital Juries Must Not Be Informed of the Governor's Clemency Power." *Tulane Law Review* 69: 861–76.

Johnson, Julius, ed. 1999–2000. *Official Manual State of Missouri*. Jefferson City, Mo.

Kane, Gregory. 2000. "Another Death Penalty Supporter Seeks Moratorium on Executions." *The Kansas City Star*, 18 July.

Katzenbach, Nicholas deB. 1967. *The Challenge of Crime in a Free Society*. Washington, D.C.: U.S. Government Printing Office.

Klasmeier, Coleen. 1995. "Towards a New Understanding of Capital Clemency and Procedural Due Process." *Boston University Law Review* 75: 1,507–39.

Klein, Richard. 1986. "The Emperor *Gideon* Has No Clothes: The Empty Promise of the Constitutional Right to Effective Assistance of Counsel." *Hastings Constitutional Law Quarterly* 13: 625–93.

Kobil, Daniel T. 1991. "The Quality of Mercy Strained: Wresting the Pardoning Power from the King." *Texas Law Review* 69: 569–641.

———. 1993. "Due Process in Death Penalty Commutation: Life, Liberty, and the Pursuit of Clemency." *University of Richmond Law Review* 27: 201–26.

———. 1998. "The Evolving Role of Clemency in Capital Cases." In *America's Experiment with Capital Punishment*, edited by James Acker, Robert Bohm, and Charles Lanier. Durham, N.C.: Carolina Academic Press.

Korengold, Michael, Todd Noteboom, and Sara Gurwitch. 1996. "And Justice for Few: The Collapse of the Capital Clemency System in the United States." *Hamline Law Review* 20: 349–70.

Krause, Joan. 1994. "Of Merciful Justice and Justified Mercy: Commuting the Sentences of Battered Women Who Kill." *Florida Law Review* 46: 699–773.

Latzer, Barry. 1998. *Death Penalty Cases: Leading Supreme Court Cases on Capital Punishment*. Boston: Butterworth-Heinemann.

Lazarus, Edward. 1998. *Closed Chambers*. New York: Times Books.

LeCesne, Blaine. 1997. "Tipping the Scales toward Death: Instructing Capital Jurors on the Possibility of Executive Clemency." *University of Cincinnati Law Review* 65: 1,051–91.

Ledewitz, Bruce, and Scott Staples. 1993. "The Role of Executive Clemency in Modern Death Penalty Cases." *University of Richmond Law Review* 27: 227–40.

Lee v. Kemna, 213 F.3d 1037 (2000).

Liebman, Ellen. 1985. "Appellate Review of Death Sentences: A Critique of Proportionality Review." *U.C. Davis Law Review* 18: 1,433–80.

Liebman, James, Jeffrey Fagan, and Valerie West. 2000. *A Broken System: Error Rates in Capital Cases, 1973–1995*. New York: Columbia University.

Liebman, James, Jeffrey Fagan, Valerie West, and Jonathan Lloyd. 2000. "Capital Attrition: Error Rates in Capital Cases, 1973–1995." *Texas Law Review* 78: 1,839–65.

Lifton, Robert Jay, and Greg Mitchell. 2000. *Who Owns Death? Capital Punishment, the American Conscience, and the End of Executions*. New York: HarperCollins.

Lim, Daniel. 1994. "State Due Process Guarantees for Meaningful Death Penalty Clemency Proceedings." *Columbia Journal of Law and Social Problems* 28: 47–82.

Lindh v. Murphy, 117 S. Ct. 2079 (1997).

Lockett v. Ohio, 438 U.S. 586 (1978).

Loftus, Elizabeth. 1979. *Eyewitness Testimony*. Cambridge, Mass.: Harvard University.

MacFarlane, Walter. 1993. "The Clemency Process in Virginia." *University of Richmond Law Review* 27: 241–80.

Mapp v. Ohio, 367 U.S. 643 (1961).

Margolis, Emanuel. 1994. "Habeas Corpus: The No-Longer Great Writ." *Dickinson Law Review* 98: 557–629.

Marquart, J. W., and J. R. Sorensen. 1989. "A National Study of the Furman-Commuted Inmates: Assessing the Threat to Society from Capital Offenders." *Loyola of Los Angeles Law Review* 23: 5–28.

Marshall, Thurgood. 1986. "Remarks on the Death Penalty Made at the Judicial Conference of the Second Circuit." *Columbia Law Review* 86: 1–10.

Maryland v. Brady, 373 U.S. 83 (1967).

McFarland, Sam G. 1983. "Is Capital Punishment a Short-Term Deterrent to Homicide: A Study of the Effects of Four Recent American Executions." *Journal of Criminal Law and Criminology* 74: 1,014.

McFarland v. Scott, 512 U.S. 1256 (1994).

McGill, Alice. 1990. "Murray v. Giarrantano: Right to Counsel in Postconviction Proceedings in Death Penalty Cases." *Hastings Constitutional Law Quarterly* 18: 211–36.

McKoy v. North Carolina, 494 U.S. 433 (1990).

McMann v. Richardson, 397 U.S. 759 (1970).

Mello, Michael. 1997a. "Outlaw Executive: 'Crazy Joe,' the Hypnotized Witness, and the Mirage of Clemency in Florida." *Journal of Contemporary Law* 23: 1–177.

———. 1997b. *Dead Wrong*. Madison, Wis.: University of Wisconsin Press.

Mercer v. Armontrout, 864 F.2d 1429 (8th Cir. 1988).

Merlo, Alida, and Peter Benekos. 2000. *What's Wrong with the Criminal Justice System: Ideology, Politics, and the Media*. Cincinnati: Anderson Publishing.

Meserve, Robert. 1998. *Annotated Model Rules of Professional Conduct*. 4th ed. Chicago, Ill.: Center for Professional Responsibility, American Bar Association.

Millin, Russ. 2000. Statement read at press conference in Kansas City, Mo., 13 February.

Mills, Steve, Ken Armstrong, and Douglas Holt. 2000. "Flawed Trials Lead to Death Chamber: Bush Confident in System Rife with Problems." *Chicago Tribune*, 11 June, news section 1.

Mills v. Maryland, 486 U.S. 367 (1988).

Miranda v. Arizona, 384 U.S. 436 (1966).

Moore, Kathleen. 1993. "Pardon for Good and Sufficient Reasons." *University of Richmond Law Review* 27: 281–88.

Moore, Michael D. 1996. "Tinkering with the Machinery of Death: An Examination and Analysis of State Indigent Defense Systems and Their Application to Death-Eligible Defendants." *William and Mary Law Review* 37: 1,617–71.

Murder Victims' Families for Reconciliation. 2161 Massachusetts Avenue, Cambridge, Massachusetts 02140.

Murray v. Giarrantano, 109 S. Ct. 2765 (1989).

Myers, Larry. 1997. "An Appeal for Clemency: The Case of Harold Lamont Otey." In *The Death Penalty in America*, edited by Hugo Bedau. New York: Oxford University Press.

Note. 1981. "A Matter of Life and Death: Due Process Protection in Capital Clemency Proceedings." *Yale Law Journal* 90: 889–911.

O'Brien, Sean. 1990. "Addressing the Needs of Attorneys for the Damned." *UMKC Law Review* 59: 517–21.

———. 2000. "Law Professors Call for Moratorium." Statement read at press conference on 21 April, UMKC School of Law, Kansas City, Missouri.

Ogletree, Benjamin Robert. 1998. "The Antiterrorism and Effective Death Penalty Act of 1996, Chapter 154: The Key to the Courthouse Door or Slaughterhouse Justice?" *Catholic University Law Review* 47: 603–73.

Ohio Adult Parole Authority v. Woodard, 523 U.S. 272 (1998).

Otey v. Hopkins, 5 F.3d 1125 (1993).

Packer, Herbert. 1968. "Two Models of the Criminal Process." In *The Limits of the Criminal Sanction,* by Herbert Packer. Stanford, Calif.: Stanford University Press.

Paduano, Anthony, and Clive Stafford Smith. 1991. "The Unconscionability of Sub-Minimum Wages Paid Appointed Counsel in Capital Cases." *Rutgers Law Review* 43: 281–353.

Palacios, Victoria. 1996. "Faith in Fantasy: The Supreme Court's Reliance on Commutation to Ensure Justice in Death Penalty Cases." *Vanderbilt Law Review* 49: 311–72.

Peterson, Ruth, and William Bailey. 1998. "Is Capital Punishment an Effective Deterrent for Murder? An Examination of Social Science Research." In *America's Experiment with Capital Punishment,* edited by James Acker, Robert Bohm, and Charles Lanier. Durham, N.C.: Carolina Academic Press.

Pietrkowski, Henry. 1993. "The Diffusion of Due Process in Capital Cases of Actual Innocence after *Herrera.*" *Chicago Kent Law Review* 70: 1,391–1,442.

Pizzi, William. 1999. *Trials Without Truth: Why Our System of Criminal Trials Has Become an Expensive Failure and What We Need to Do to Rebuild It.* New York: New York University Press.

Powell v. Alabama, 287 U.S. 35 (1932).

Prejean, Helen, C.S.J. 1993. *Dead Man Walking.* New York: Vintage Books.

Pulley v. Harris, 104 S. Ct. 871 (1984).

Radelet, Michael, Hugo Bedau, and Constance Putnam. 1992. *In Spite of Innocence: Erroneous Convictions in Capital Cases.* Boston: Northeastern University Press.

Radelet, Michael, and Barbara Zsembik. 1993. "Executive Clemency in Post-*Furman* Capital Cases." *University of Richmond Law Review* 27: 289–314.

Rankin, Joseph. 1979. "Changing Attitudes Toward Capital Punishment." *Social Forces* 58: 194–211.

Redlich, Norman (compiler). 1984. *Standards of Professional Conduct for Lawyers and Judges.* Boston: Little, Brown.

Ringold, Solie. 1966. "The Dynamics of Executive Clemency." *American Bar Association Journal* 52: 240–43.

Rivkind, Nina, and Steven Shatz. 2001. *Cases and Materials on the Death Penalty.* St. Paul, Minn.: West Group.

Roberts, Julian, and Loretta Stalans. 2000. *Public Opinion, Crime, and Criminal Justice.* Boulder, Colo.: Westview Press.

Rothman, Meah Dell. 1976. "The Pardoning Power." *Columbia Journal of Law and Social Problems* 12: 149–220.

Sandys, Marla. 1998. "Stacking the Deck for Guilt and Death: The Failure of Death Qualification to Ensure Impartiality." In *America's Experiment with Capital Punishment,* edited by James Acker, Robert Bohm, and Charles Lanier. Durham, N.C.: Carolina Academic Press.

Sarat, Austin, ed. 1999a. *The Killing State.* New York: Oxford University Press.

———. 1999b. "Capital Punishment as a Legal, Political, and Cultural Fact: An Introduction." In *The Killing State,* edited by Austin Sarat. New York: Oxford University Press.

Scheck, Barry, Peter Newfeld, and Jim Dwyer. 2000. *Actual Innocence.* New York: Doubleday.

Scheingold, Stuart. 1984. *The Politics of Law and Order.* New York: Longman.

Schlup v. Delo, 115 S. Ct. 851 (1995).

Schmall, Lorraine. 1996. "Forgiving Guin Garcia: Women, the Death Penalty, and Commutation." *Wisconsin Women's Law Journal* 11: 283–326.

Schmalleger, Frank. 2001. *Criminal Justice: A Brief Introduction*. Upper Saddle River, N.J.: Prentice-Hall.

Schumacher, Daryl. 1997. "Intruders at the Death House: Limiting Third-Party Intervention in Executive Clemency." *John Marshall Law Review* 30: 567–92.

Senna, Joseph, and Larry Siegel. 1998. *Essentials of Criminal Justice*. Belmont, Calif.: West/Wadsworth Publishing.

Shelly, Barbara. 1997. "A Distinction State Could Do Without." *Kansas City Star*, 18 July.

Silverman, Stephen. 1995. "There Is Nothing Certain Like Death in Texas: State Executive Clemency Boards Turn a Deaf Ear to Death Row Inmates' Last Appeals." *Arizona Law Review* 37: 375–98.

Sorensen, Jonathan, and Donald Wallace. 1993. "Capital Punishment in Missouri: Examining the Issue of Racial Disparity." Paper presented at the annual meeting of the American Society of Criminology, Phoenix.

Sorensen, Jonathan, R. Wrinkle, V. Brewer, and J. Marquart. 1999."Capital Punishment and Deterrence: Examining the Effect of Executions on Murder in Texas." *Crime and Delinquency* 45: 481–93.

Sourcebook of Criminal Justice Statistics. 1999. Table 3.139: Murders and Non-Negligent Manslaughter Known to Police. Washington, D.C.: Bureau of Justice Statistics, 298–99.

Stafford, Samuel. 1977. *Clemency: Legal Authority, Procedure, and Structure*. Williamsburg, Va.: National Center for State Courts.

State v. Dale Patterson, 618 S.W.2d 665 (Mo. banc 1981).

State v. Preston, 673 S.W.2d 1 (Mo. 1984).

State v. Reuscher, 827 S.W.2d 710 (Mo. banc 1992).

State v. Sandles, 740 S.W.2d 169 (Mo. banc 1987).

Steiker, Carol, and Jordan Steiker. 1995. "Sober Second Thoughts: Reflections on Two Decades of Constitutional Regulation of Capital Punishment." *Harvard Law Review* 109: 355–438.

Strach, Phillip John. 1999. "Ohio Adult Parole Authority v. Woodard: Breathing New 'Life' into an Old Fourteenth Amendment Controversy." *North Carolina Law Review* 77: 891–929.

Strickland v. Washington, 466 U.S. 668 (1984).

Sudnow, David. 1965. "Normal Crimes: Sociological Features of the Penal Code in a Public Defender Office." *Social Problems* 12 (3): 255–76.

Suni, Ellen. 1982. "Recent Developments in Missouri Criminal Law: Homicide." *UMKC Law Review* 50: 440–90.

———. 1986. "Recent Developments in Missouri: The Death Penalty." *UMKC Law Review* 54: 553–89.

———. 1990. "Capital Punishment in Missouri: Recent Developments in the Interpretation and Administration of the Death Penalty." *UMKC Law Review* 59: 523–80.

Taylor, Stuart. 1994. "He Didn't Do It." *American Lawyer* (December): 69–78.

Thompson v. Calderon, 151 F.3d 918 at 937 (1998).

Thomson, E. 1997. "Deterrence Versus Brutalization: The Case of Arizona." *Homicide Studies* 1: 110–28.

———. 1999. "Effects of an Execution on Homicides in California." *Homicide Studies* 3: 129–50.

Tiedeman v. Benson, 122 F.3d 518 (8th Cir. 1997).

Uelmen, Gerald. 1997. "Crocodiles in the Bathtub: Maintaining the Independence of State Supreme Courts in an Era of Judicial Politicization." *Notre Dame Law Review* 72: 1,133–53.

U.S. v. Bagley, 473 U.S. 667 (1985).

Vandiver, Margaret. 1993. "The Quality of Mercy: Race and Clemency in Florida Death Penalty Cases, 1924–1966." *University of Richmond Law Review* 27: 315–44.

Vick, Douglas. 1995. "Poorhouse Justice: Underfunded Indigent Defense Services and Arbitrary Death Sentences." *Buffalo Law Review* 43: 329–460.

Wallace, Donald, and Jonathan Sorensen. 1994. "Missouri Proportionality Review: An Assessment of a State Supreme Court's Procedures in Capital Cases." *Notre Dame Journal of Law, Ethics, and Public Policy* 8: 281–315.

Whitmore v. Gaines, 24 F.3d 1032 (8th Cir. 1994).

Willwerth, James. 1993. "The Voices Told Him to Kill." *Time*, 7 June, 46–49.

Wink, Walter. 1992. *Engaging the Powers: Discernment and Resistance in a World of Domination*. Minneapolis: Fortress Press.

Yackle, Larry. 1996. "A Primer on the New Habeas Corpus Statute." *Buffalo Law Review* 44: 381–449.

Young v. Hayes, 218 F.3d 850 (8th Cir. 2000).

Zimring, Franklin. 1999. "The Executioner's Dissonant Song: On Capital Punishment and American Legal Values." In *The Killing State*, edited by Austin Sarat. New York: Oxford University Press.

INDEX

Tables are indicated by an italicized t following the page number.